HAMPTONS BABYLON

Life Among the Super-Rich on America's Riviera

PETER FEARON

A Birch Lane Press Book
Published by Carol Publishing Group

A Birch Lane Press Book
Published by Carol Publishing Group
Birch Lane Press is a registered trademark of Carol Communications, Inc.

Editorial, sales and distribution, rights and permissions inquiries should be addressed to Carol Publishing Group, 120 Enterprise Avenue, Secaucus, N.J. 07094.

In Canada: Canadian Manda Group, One Atlantic Avenue, Suite 105, Toronto, Ontario M6K 3E7

Carol Publishing Group books may be purchased in bulk at special discounts for sales promotion, fund-raising, or educational purposes. Special editions can be created to specifications. For details, contact Special Sales Department, Carol Publishing Group, 120 Enterprise Avenue, Secaucus, N.J. 07094.

Manufactured in the United States of America
10 9 8 7 6 5 4 3 2

Library of Congress Cataloging-in-Publication Data

Fearon, Peter, 1951–
    Hamptons Babylon : life among the super-rich on America's Riviera
/ by Peter Fearon.
        p.   cm.—("A Birch Lane Press book.")
    ISBN 1–55972–470–6
    1. Hamptons (N.Y.)—Social life and customs.   2. Millionaires—New
York (State)—Hamptons—Social life and customs.   3. Celebrities—
New York (State)—Hamptons—Social life and customs.   4. Hamptons
(N.Y.)—History.   I. Title.   II. Series.
F127.S9F42   1998
974.7'25—dc21
                                                                98–4817
                                                                    CIP

To my darling wife Marcy,
whom I love passionately...and forever

The author is pleased to acknowledge the contribution of Ken Chandler, editor of the *New York Post*, to the preparation of this volume.

Contents

HAMPTONS BABYLON

PROLOGUE

Just Another Weekend in the Hamptons

IT IS JUST ANOTHER summer weekend in the Hamptons.

At the twenty-two-acre old-money estate in Southampton of Revlon vice-chairman Howard Gittis and his wife Lynette, some 240 guests are walking the buzz-cut lawns of the spacious palm gardens, where trophy trees have been strategically planted to look as if they have been put in place by the hand of God. The guests are armed with martinis and mimosas and are munching on canapés and asparagus salad. The food hasn't just been catered. It's been designed by food stylist Rick Ellis, who created the food for the movie *The Age of Innocence*.

A huge sapphire-and-white tent is billowing gently by the glistening Tiffany-blue pool, and ponies are giving rides to linen-clad children. Seven uniformed valet parkers have been gunning dozens of Mercedeses, Porsches, and BMWs into parking spaces for an hour. The party is a sea of Chanel, Wang, Armani, and Versace, with white-jacketed waiters fawning over the surgically augmented second wives of some of Wall Street's most voracious predators.

Rising above the undulating chatter of the usual Hamptons afternoon benefit garden party is the din made by the other party animals—scores of coiffured dogs. The canine guests, the guests of honor, have a separate buffet: dog biscuits arrayed in wicker baskets and water in porcelain bowls.

Financier Ron Perelman is chatting with Gittis, his aide-de-camp in the Revlon empire. Writer Carl Bernstein, a ubiquitous Hamptons figure, is strolling with movie producer Martin Bregman. Ralph Lauren, tanned and diminutive, is gossiping with the hostess about his plans for an upcoming charity fashion show. The garden party, in the grounds of the eleven-bedroom Gittis mansion, shrouded from view by a Berlin Wall of high hedges, is a crossroads for the Southampton Old Guard and the Hamptons nouveau-billionaire elite, with a sprinkling of socially acceptable celebrities as part of the floor show. But the dogs are the real floor show.

Howard and Lynette Gittis have reached the pinnacle of prestige in the Hamptons. They are 1997 cochairs of the Southampton Hospital annual benefit gala. This is a "preparty" party—about six weeks pre— and one of eight planned for the period leading up to the big bash. Mrs. Gittis is determined to raise about $1.6 million—more money than her Old Guard rivals ever did—and she's equally determined to let them know it by arranging for a *New York Times* reporter and photographer to cover her parties as if they were Mideast summits.

Ralph Lauren has promised a celebrity-packed fund-raising fashion show, Ron Perelman will throw an exclusive cocktail party at his sixty-acre East Hampton spread, and oilman David Koch is staging a checkbooks-out dinner party. But they will be hard put to upstage the galloping Gittises. At this party the guests are expected to pay a thousand dollars each to have their dogs sit for portraits by photographer Valerie Shaff. The portraits will appear in a glossy journal handed out to guests on the night of the main benefit so everyone will know who gave and who didn't.

Among the first in line is Cornelia Bregman, whose dog, Lilly, is a fashionable breed: a King Charles spaniel. Lilly is wearing a green bow with a bone pattern on her right ear to mark the occasion.

"Please! Please!" Cornelia Bregman tells the *New York Times* reporter. "Lilly is not just a King Charles spaniel. She's a Blenheim Cavalier King Charles spaniel—a champion Blenheim. You know, like Winston Churchill had."

The Gittis home is unusually suited to the entertaining of dogs. The Gittis decorator, Thomas Jayne, who is mingling with the blueblood guests, explains to anyone who asks that the black-and-white checkerboard marble throughout the mansion's first-floor halls was chosen to match Max and Scooter, the family's springer spaniels.

It is just another summer weekend in the Hamptons.

The Hamptons Hobos are on the prowl. The Hobos—Ho's for short, for reasons that will become obvious—are an all-girl gang of New York City twenty-somethings. Their official membership roll peaked at seventeen and, one summer when everyone seemed to have boyfriends, dipped as low as nine. They come to the Hamptons most weekends during the summer without places to stay, often without transportation, and armed only with cell phones and an uncanny knack of discovering the locations of the best parties. The name of the game is finding a place to stay for a night or the whole weekend, which usually entails seeking some stranger with a bed to share. The search begins almost as soon as the group leaves Manhattan, usually in pairs.

"We stay in touch with these," says Jennifer, flicking open a pancake-flat phone. She's a strikingly proportioned twenty-six-year-old editorial assistant with a New York business publication and the grande dame of the group. "Whoever gets a line on a party tells the others, but we try not to all go to the same ones. It crowds the field."

The Hamptons Hobos go back to 1993, when Jennifer paid a large proportion of her annual salary for a summer share in Quogue, an unfashionable distance from the beach. Summer romances came so thick and fast that she found she had slept only a few nights at the house. "I got to thinking," she explains. "What do I need a rental for?" The following year, she and three friends started coming to the Hamptons in the expectation of instant romance—or at least sex—and a place to stay.

"Usually it's 'like at first sight.' I know if it's going to work out. I've only had a couple of weird experiences," she says. "Once I went back to this gorgeous guy's even more gorgeous house, but it turned out he had a roommate and I was sleeping with both of them. It was just too...too everything. Another time I struck right out and I snuck out onto somebody's beach with a blanket. One time I slept in someone's car. But those times are rare."

Several times throughout the weekend, the Hamptons Hobos check on each other. After Labor Day, they hold a dinner at a Manhattan restaurant to close the season and trade stories. This weekend promises good hunting. "I've found a great-sounding party on Further Lane—that's Raider's Row—Wall Street East." She flips open her phone again to spread the word.

It's just another summer weekend in the Hamptons.

At the Bridgehampton Polo Club at Two Trees some four thousand people are gathered, but relatively few of them are watching the polo. Most of them appear to be involved in a less arcane spectator sport:

watching each other. The real polo fans are among those who have gathered for tailgate parties off the rear of Range Rovers, Hummers, and Mercedes station wagons on the far side of a vast, fairway-quality field leased from real estate magnate and polophile David Walentas for a bargain-basement $100,000 per six-week season.

On the other side, beneath a tent behind a white picket fence, are the people whom the *East Hampton Star* sometimes refers to as the Usual Suspects: the instantly recognizable Hamptons names and faces. Calvin Klein, a patron, is there, and so is Kelly Klein, but they're not together because—well, they're no longer together. Cindy Crawford has come with playboy boyfriend Rande Gerber and his niece Chase. There's Carol Alt, Christie Brinkley, Billy Baldwin and Chynna Phillips, Bianca Jagger, Jerry Seinfeld's startlingly endowed ex-girlfriend Shoshanna Lonstein, anchor Matt Lauer, Donna Karan's daughter Gabby, Randy Quaid, Liz Hurley, and dozens of other famous names.

Victoria's Secret model Stephanie Seymour is an ever-present figure. She's married to the man who founded Bridgehampton Polo, magazine owner Peter Brant, who is also America's best amateur player. Brant and the other serious patrons and players hope to graft polo onto the Hamptons scene as more than simply a social event. They have won significant sponsorship from the likes of Mercedes Benz.

The teams are formidable because they include professional polo players from Argentina, which is to polo what Brazil is to soccer and Colombia is to coffee. The pros get a six-figure salary, all expenses, and a free summer rental in the Hamptons. However, most of the "Tent People" are so involved in their own spectacle that the chukker in progress, between Peter Brant's White Birch, ranked fourth in the world, and Revlon, owned by Bear Stearns partner Mickey Tarnopol, ranked sixth, seems almost an afterthought.

In addition to the celebrity sideshow, Bridgehampton Polo usually has a sponsor's promotion or a charitable benefit going on. One weekend it was a silent auction of celebrity jeans, and a heartening array of stars donated their worn clothing—Michael Jackson, Sharon Stone, Whoopi Goldberg, Madonna, Magic Johnson, Tyra Banks. Celebs were in there buying too.

"Look," shouted one guest, "for the right amount of money you too can get into Christy Turlington's jeans. That has to be worth the trip." Today the sideshow is Tommy Lee Jones. He's been trying to keep a low profile with a hot and heavy new girlfriend, but this is a paparazzi-patrolled event. Suddenly there's a shout—"Get out of my face!"—as

Jones confronts a photographer who has ventured too near. There is such a scene that now everyone knows Jones is there, and more paparazzi are loading up. On the field a goal is scored—but who's watching?

It's just another summer weekend in the Hamptons.

The streets of East Hampton are as clogged with traffic as the West Side Highway at five in the afternoon—only the drivers are less patient. There are no parking spaces, and the vehicles are oozing aimlessly like blood through a diseased liver. At Nick & Toni's restaurant on North Main Street in East Hampton, a couple is trying to bluff their way to a table. Hamptons restaurants are even more pretentious and exclusionary than those in Manhattan, although Nick & Toni's has something of a family atmosphere—if you're family. And as in Manhattan, they are also bleachers from which to spy celebrities.

It's a good night for stars. Matthew Broderick and Sarah Jessica Parker are in Noelle's Country Market in Bridgehampton. Close by are Kim Basinger and Alec Baldwin, and a few tables from them is Caroline Kennedy Schlossberg. But Nick & Toni's, popular despite having no valet parking, is the place for celebrities. This night Robert De Niro, Steven Spielberg, writer Robert Benton, and art dealer Larry Gagosian all drop by, De Niro smirking as he dips hot, thick Tuscan bread in a saucer of Monini olive oil. Most of the people who will wait as long as it takes for a table know that Nick & Toni's is owned by Toni Ross, daughter of Time Warner mogul Steve Ross, and her husband, Jeff Salaway. Other than naming the restaurant, he hasn't used the name Nick since he was at college. A bluffer who wants to be seated with his girlfriend never gets a table. "Nick's a friend of mine. He said I could have a table any time," he says. There's a guffaw from staff and customers alike as the remark spreads down the line. "Why is that funny?" says the bluffer, embarrassed and indignant.

It's just another weekend in the Hamptons.

On the Hampton Jitney, the luxury bus that takes New Yorkers on the long, tedious journey from the Upper East Side of Manhattan through the Long Island suburbs to the Hamptons, some of the passengers are irritated and upset. There are those with reservations who are angry at the have-nots who managed to jump the line, get seats ahead of them, and crowd the bus. There are those who don't like pets who are angry at those who have theirs with them. And there are the passengers who have pets who are angry about having to pay an extra ten dollars for them, even though they are carrying them in boxes on their knees. Then there are the passengers who aren't talking on cell phones who are irritated by the ones who are. The Jitney's attractive hostess, who distributes muffins, drinks, and magazines and collects fares, is trying to keep everyone smiling, but Jitney passengers are notorious for kvetching.

There were so many complaints about the cell phone users that the company restricted their use. Then there were complaints about the restrictions. The passengers even complained about the reading lights. The bus manufacturers had received not one single complaint from any bus line about the strength of the reading lights, but there were so many from the Hampton Jitney that extra-strong lights were installed. The happiest passengers are the executives who sent their assistants on board ahead of them to grab the window seats. There's a steady ambient chatter from them, as almost all are ignoring the windows and are busy talking on their cell phones.

The Hampton Jitney carries numerous celebrities. Monica Seles, Lauren Bacall, Rod Steiger, Roy Scheider, and Julie Andrews have all been spotted in its plush seats. Today, most passengers don't notice the celebrity in their midst. Close to the rear, in sweats instead of his trademark white suit and red tie, is *Bonfire of the Vanities* author Tom Wolfe. As the Hampton Jitney pulls off the traffic-snarled highway to try to work the back roads, there is a cheer of encouragement from the weary passengers.

It's just another weekend in the Hamptons.

Long Island is shaped like a gigantic beached whale 120 miles long, most of it less than twenty miles wide. The head, the New York City boroughs of Brooklyn and Queens, is at the western end, almost crashing against the island of Manhattan. The mouth, with the lower jaw formed by a narrow peninsula, seems to be investigating a tasty morsel in the shape of Staten Island. Its enormous body stretches east out into the Atlantic Ocean, the tail forked either side of the Great Peconic Bay. It is a comparatively new addition to the Atlantic coastline, just a few thousand years old, and was carved out by the leading edge of an enormous glacier that dug out Long Island Sound.

The glacier retreated, leaving an island with broad stretches of flatland dotted with lakes, gullies, and enormous boulders called erratics. It also left a spectacular, meandering coastline of deep, rocky inlets and wide, pristine beaches. The narrow southern fork of Long Island's tail stretches from Shinnecock Bay to the easternmost tip of the island, Montauk Point, marked by a lighthouse ordered built by George

Washington in 1792. Between those two points is one of the most naturally beautiful places on earth, a forty-mile stretch of countryside and coastline featuring warm, sandy beaches caressed by the ocean, rolling dunes, and broad meadows, dotted with towns, villages, and hamlets.

These communities—from west to east—are Southampton, Water Mill, Bridgehampton, Sag Harbor, Sagaponack, Wainscott, Springs, East Hampton, Amagansett, and Montauk. Collectively they are known to outsiders as the Hamptons, although few who spend a significant part of the year there use that name. Over the years, the definition of the Hamptons has broadened to include Hampton Bays, Quogue, and Westhampton Beach, and some have even used the word "Hamptons" to define the whole East End of Long Island.

Every spring 120,000 New Yorkers migrate to the Hamptons for as long as they can: a weekend or two, or, for those who can afford it, the whole season. From Memorial Day to Labor Day—and, for an increasing number of Hamptons lovers, from Easter to Thanksgiving—the Hamptons blossoms into the richest, most opulent, and most glamorous resort on earth, a summer paradise for movie stars, models, Hollywood producers, New York writers and artists, rock stars, Wall Street tycoons, European princesses, old-money socialites, and anyone else who can afford the price of admission to the world's biggest, most lavish party.

It is like nowhere else on the planet. Only in the Hamptons will a visitor glimpse Barbra Streisand waiting for takeout with Donna Karan, Christie Brinkley exercising her favorite horse, Alec Baldwin playing softball cheered on by Kim Basinger, Martha Stewart grocery shopping, Calvin Klein taking a stroll, Kurt Vonnegut chatting with E. L. Doctorow, or Billy Joel cruising for a parking space, all within a few miles on a single balmy afternoon.

More than simply a fashionable destination for celebrities, it is one of the most dense concentrations of wealth, and therefore power, anywhere in the world. The old Soviet Union's military machine acknowledged the Hamptons' uniqueness in this regard. In the seventies the Soviets became concerned that, should nuclear Armageddon come on a summer weekend, some of America's wealthiest power brokers might be aware of it only as an especially marvelous sunset—and, theoretically at any rate, survive the destruction of New York City by conveniently being in their dachas in the Hamptons. So they acknowledged the village of East Hampton as a separate primary nuclear target, fixing as ground zero the old Hook Windmill, built in 1806 by Nathaniel Dominy and one of the finest examples of windmill architecture in the United States.

But the heart of Hamptons life is neither the superrich nor the superstars. In 1990 the gossip writer James Revson, who covered the Hamptons social and celebrity scene, claimed Hamptons dwellers form a network of interconnected cliques whose members socialize almost exclusively with each other. According to Revson, whose life and career were tragically cut short by AIDS, those cliques are similar to the sets and gangs that develop in high schools, and their members have cooler-than-thou attitudes that are about as mature.

They are primarily composed not of famous faces but of famous names. The Literary Rat Pack includes John Irving, E. L. Doctorow, Betty Friedan, Kurt Vonnegut, Joseph Heller, Peter Matthiessen, Gail Sheehy, George Plimpton, Nora Ephron, and Nick Pileggi. They use Bobby Van's restaurant in Bridgehampton, once a watering hole of Truman Capote, as a clubhouse. The Art Mob, according to Revson, is led by artists Larry Rivers, Julian Schnabel, Robert Dash, Ross Bleckner, Eric Fischl, and April Gornik and includes poets Kenneth Koch and John Ashberry and critic John Gruen. Then there is the Further Lane Gang, living on exclusive Further Lane in East Hampton. It includes James Brady, Kathleen Turner, Ron Delsener, Edgar Bronfman Jr., and Billy Joel. Leading members of the horsey set, whose annual highlight is the Hamptons Classic equestrian event, include Kelly Klein, Ralph Lauren, Stephanie Powers, Michael Cimino, and, surprisingly, Tom Wolfe, who is said to prefer their company over that of his fellow scribes.

And it would be wrong to think of the Hamptons as a white social preserve like Newport or Palm Beach. From the forties on, African Americans who could afford to have made their summer home in the Hamptons. Three developments in Sag Harbor are largely African-American enclaves. Prominent African Americans who have made second homes on the East End over the years include William Henry Hastie, the first African-American federal judge, Sugar Ray Robinson, Eartha Kitt, Lena Horne, Lionel Hampton, Dorothy Dandridge, and Congressman Adam Clayton Powell Jr.

One of the first Europeans to gaze at the beaches of the Hamptons was probably the Florentine explorer Giovanni da Verrazano, who described Long Island and Manhattan in 1524 but failed to claim the territories. At that time Long Island already had a contented population of Indians, with the Montauket and Shinnecock tribes occupying the East End.

These tribes lived an easy life compared to the Plains Indians. The land was fertile; the beaches and shallow waters abounded in shellfish. Indians made wampum for trade from whelk shells. But this easy life made them passive, and they were vulnerable prey when Europeans came.

While the western end of Long Island was colonized by the Dutch, the East End was colonized from New England. In 1633, just thirteen years after the *Mayflower* arrived at Plymouth Rock, colonists in Massachusetts sent a ship to explore the Connecticut coast and returned with news that Indians on Long Island were friendly, produced vast quantities of wampum, and were open to trade. For the colonists, this was like the discovery of oil or gold centuries later, because wampum, highly prized jewelry made from shells, could be traded among Indians of most tribes for furs and was central to the colonial economy.

Eager to stop the Dutch from expanding east from Brooklyn and securing the new-found source of wealth, several families from Lynn, Massachusetts, relocated to Long Island. They landed at Conscience Point on Peconic Bay in 1640 and founded Southampton.

A year later the Hamptons had its first sex scandal. A pioneer settler named George Wood was accused of fathering the illegitimate child of a Shinnecock Indian girl who was little more than a child herself. He was heavily fined.

These first Hamptonites were followed by others drawn by reports of fertile land, a long and temperate growing season, and friendly tribes. East Hampton was settled in 1648, then Wainscott, Springs, Bridgehampton, Shelter Island, Sagaponack, and Amagansett. The new villages retained their founders' distinctive New England architecture and culture, qualities still discernible today. Even after the British took full control of New York, the East End of Long Island remained a quintessentially New England colony, trading only with Connecticut and Massachusetts and sending suspected witches to be tried in Connecticut.

When the new colonists arrived, there was already one small and slightly eccentric European community nearby. In 1639, Lion Gardiner, a military engineer who built a fort at Saybrook, Connecticut, had been granted thirty-five hundred acres of land on what is now Gardiner's Island. He created his own Eden for himself and his family and retainers. He further expanded his personal domain when he was rewarded with large stretches of land for rescuing a local Indian chief's daughter who had been raped by marauding Pequot tribesmen. Gardiner's Island remains in the family despite a bitter feud over access to the island in the

1980s. It is the only land grant of its kind in the United States that is still in the possession of the descendants of original family.

The Indians may have been friendly to the colonists—teaching them about agriculture, how to butcher a beached whale, where to find the best lobsters, oysters, crabs, and clams, and how to trawl for fish from the beaches—but contact with Europeans was fatal for the indigenous people. Smallpox, alcoholism, and other diseases of European origin virtually wiped them out in only two generations.

The East End was occupied by the British for seven years during the Revolutionary War, following Washington's defeat in the Battle of Long Island in 1776. The first attempt at a British landing at Montauk had been prevented by a handful of Minutemen from Sag Harbor, a thriving port established in 1730. The same Minutemen marched under a stars-and-stripes flag later used as the basis for the flag of Betsy Ross.

Many families simply fled to Connecticut, but those who remained behind experienced a brutal occupation of plunder, repression, and confiscation. After the defeat of the British, the refugees returned, and the Hamptons remained an agricultural backwater while Sag Harbor prospered as a premier whaling port. Distance and poor roads kept the eastern communities of the island remote from New York, but as early as the mid-nineteenth century the Hamptons had its first spark of glamour. Julia Gardiner, a beautiful twenty-four-year-old descendant of Lion Gardiner, married John Tyler, the fifty-four-year-old tenth president of the United States, and the Gardiner estate became a summer White House.

The complex processes that turned a remote collection of farming communities into a summer colony of glamour, wealth, and power also began in the mid-nineteenth century, not with the First Family but with painters. The Hamptons' unique natural beauty was first discovered by artists.

PART ONE

Artists and Writers

Introduction

HENRY FERGUSON AND GILBERT BURLING began exploring the East End of Long Island and particularly the Hamptons in the 1860s. They and other landscape painters found there not only an area of unparalleled natural beauty but a phenomenally intense light, which seems to be generated by the reflections of the Atlantic, the bays, and Long Island Sound across the narrow peninsulas. Artists were also attracted by the unique variety of landscapes and the fact that pristine countryside and dramatic seascapes existed side by side.

In 1877 the artist Winslow Homer and a dozen New York friends founded the Tile Club, which met in Greenwich Village to while away the winter evenings in gossip, banter, and decorating Spanish tiles. Its members included some of the greatest artistic talents of the day: William Merritt Chase, Thomas Moran, Childe Hassam, J. Alden Weir, Edwin Austin Abbey, Augustus Saint-Gaudens, and the architect Stanford White. *Scribner's* magazine commissioned the Tile Club members to produce and illustrate a series of articles on Long Island villages.

The following spring they began traveling through Long Island by train looking for landscape and seascape subjects, as well as to escape the unhealthy New York climate. They became enchanted by the South Fork and made trips to East Hampton each year for the next decade. It was this group of artists whose praise in *Scribner's* first popularized the Hamptons as a summer resort. White recommended the Hamptons to his wealthy friends and picked up numerous commissions for shingled summer homes. Moran, who was socially prominent in addition to being a successful artist, became the first artist to establish a permanent Hamptons home and helped found East Hampton's exclusive Maidstone Club.

15

Chase, who sported a monocle and boutonniere and kept a white wolfhound and a servant in a robe and fez constantly in attendance, established a fashionable summer art school, the Shinnecock Summer School of Art, in the Hamptons. Over a thousand pupils, most of them women, painted under his direction in outdoor classes. Numerous rival schools flourished.

A subsequent generation of artists, known as the Ashcan Group for their commonplace subject matter, rediscovered the Hamptons in 1912. In the thirties European refugees established another colony, including Max Ernst, Fernand Léger, Salvador Dalí, André Breton and Marcel Duchamp. They were encouraged and financed by Gerald and Sara Murphy, the wealthy friends of Hemingway and Fitzgerald who are credited with popularizing the French Riviera in the twenties. After World War II, Willem de Kooning, James Brooks, Alfonso Ossorio, Roy Lichtenstein, Larry Rivers, and James Rosenquist all made their homes and studios in the Hamptons and also helped redefine American art.

The presence of an artists' colony attracted writers, and writers ultimately came to outnumber them. Truman Capote, Arthur Miller, John Steinbeck, and many other major writers all came to the Hamptons. But the Hamptons' most famous artist, the man who launched a canvas revolution from a shack, had neither money nor social connections. He was not inspired by the legendary light and never tried to capture the Hamptons' landcapes or seascapes. His name was Jackson Pollock.

CHAPTER 1

Jackson Pollock: Wayward Genius

On November 3, 1945, Jackson Pollock, then little known outside a small circle of artists and critics, and his new bride, Lee Krasner, set out for the Hamptons. A storm was descending, and it was almost dark by noon, when their journey began. By the time they reached their destination, the tiny community of Springs, the storm was at its height. The Pollocks were unable to find the key to their new home and had to rouse a neighbor to help them break in.

Their new home was an unlikely place for the birth of a revolution in American art. It was a two-story farmhouse on Fireplace Road with a wide porch and bay windows, built in 1902. There was a barn, which was to become his studio, several outbuildings, and a little under five acres of open fields. There was no bathroom and no hot water in the kitchen, and the only heat in the house came from a wood-burning kitchen stove. These were primitive living conditions for what was to be one of the worst winters in the Hamptons for ten years.

Artists had been coming to the Hamptons for generations. During the war years, surrealist painters who had escaped from Germany and France lived out their exile in the Hamptons. Robert Motherwell and Willem de Kooning had also built studios there. But that was East Hampton. Artists were part of the summer scene. Springs was another world.

Most of the 370 inhabitants of Springs were descended from a handful of settlers who had founded the community in the 1640s. They had existed in a historical backwater, still speaking a form of Elizabethan English after three centuries of near isolation. They called themselves "Bonackers" after Accabonac Harbor. Bonacker, sometimes written bonaker, is applied indiscriminately to all born-and-bred blue collar Hamptonites, but strictly speaking refers only to those who make their living from the land and sea. Springs was Bonacker heartland. The local economy was as simple as it had been in the seventeenth century: clams and scallops from the bay and potatoes from the fields. Jackson Pollock would have seemed an eccentric figure in any community, but to his new neighbors in Springs he appeared both a maniac and an intruder.

Pollock was thirty-three when he moved to Springs with Lee Krasner. He had been a struggling artist in New York for years, sometimes shoplifting for food or, more often, art supplies. For most of his years of obscurity he had a reputation as a belligerent drunk, a poor draftsman, a not very talented painter, and an artist little interested in art theories. He worked as a "squeegee man" churning out silkscreen prints in a Manhattan print shop and as an elevator operator and frame maker at the Museum of Non-Objective Painting, later renamed the Guggenheim.

Young artists employed at the museum had to submit their own work once a month for appraisal. Pollock's was routinely torn to pieces, figuratively and sometimes literally. Even so, fired by drink, he would tell his fellow artists and museum workers of the artists whose work hung on its walls: "Arp? I could do an Arp! Klee? I could do a Klee easy!"

Later many would claim credit for discovering Pollock. The real credit, however, goes to the painter Piet Mondrian. Pollock's break came in 1943 when he submitted some work for inclusion in a show of young artists organized by the wealthy collector and gallery owner Peggy Guggenheim. She had owned galleries in Paris and London; during World War II, she brought her significant collection to New York and opened a new gallery called Art of This Century. Her assistant, Howard Putzel, admired Pollock's submission, but Peggy Guggenheim dismissed it as trash.

Mondrian was one of the jurors. His clean, carefully constructed works could not have been more unlike Pollock's frantic canvases. But Mondrian badly wanted a protégé of his own included in the show, and to deflect attention from his scheming, he focused on Pollock's work, telling Guggenheim how much he admired it. He was trying to prove he was completely impartial so that when his own protégé's work came up, no one would suspect him of bias. In truth, he probably detested Pollock's muddy painting, but once he had told Peggy Guggenheim how much he liked it, suddenly Guggenheim liked it too.

That was the beginning of a long and tempestuous association between Pollock and Guggenheim, who supported him with a monthly stipend for years. She ultimately dumped him onto another gallery owner and collector, Betty Parsons, shortly before he became famous and his paintings started to sell. Guggenheim gave Pollock a number of one-man shows and energetically pushed his work on collectors—who remained, however, uninterested.

She also asked Pollock to paint a large mural for her apartment. After months of inactivity, his vast canvas was still untouched, and he was scheduled to show the painting in less than twenty-four hours. Pollock began painting frantically, trying to capture, he said later, a stampede he had seen in a dream. When he was finished, and with the paint barely dry, he rolled up the canvas, took it to Guggenheim's, and found it was almost a foot too long. He proceeded to get roaring drunk while two other artists put up the canvas after cutting off the extra foot. At a reception for critics and collectors, Pollock staggered through the throng and urinated in the marble fireplace.

Pollock's paintings at that time were characterized by broad, energetic lines and great swirls of color, giving a disturbing sense of frenetic action and energy. Even avant garde critics found them impenetrable; early reviewers said Pollock was undisciplined and his paintings mud.

However, Pollock's career was to be saved by the art critic Clement Greenberg. Greenberg was a bizarre and complex man who loved to shock and had a sadistic streak that numerous girlfriends discovered to their cost. He was a contrarian, always seeking opportunities to take the opposite of the prevailing view. He had become an art critic primarily because there was a glut of literary critics. His credentials were meager. He had completed a summer school art course and audited a few lectures elsewhere. He got a job as art critic with the magazine *The Nation*. The art market at the time was booming. Although the conceit remained that Paris was the center of the art world, the reality was that the driving forces, the money, the collectors, the patrons, and a number of the artists were now in New York rather than Paris.

A few months before his move to Springs, Pollock was given a one-man show by Guggenheim. As usual, his canvases remained blank until panic set in; then there was a flurry of activity. The show was given a lukewarm reception. Some critics were even cooler in their views, describing his work as "baked macaroni" and "an explosion in a shingle mill." Another said Pollock "does not seem to be especially talented."

However, Greenberg, whose great talent was giving an intellectual underpinning to what was otherwise impenetrable, wrote: "Pollock's one-man show establishes him...as the strongest painter of his generation and perhaps the greatest one to appear since Miró. He is not afraid to look ugly. All profoundly original art looks ugly at first." Those words were the beginning of the Pollock legend. Greenberg continued his critical support even in the face of Pollock's drunken scorn.

Pollock, Krasner, and some friends spent that summer in a beachfront shack at Louse Point in the Hamptons. Krasner organized the trip because she knew that Pollock's drinking, depression, and violence were accentuated by the overpowering heat of the city in summer, and she was desperate to get him out into the country. A few weeks earlier he had alarmed her by almost murdering a fellow painter, Philip Guston. They had an argument over representational versus nonrepresentational art that ended in a vicious fistfight that left both of them bloodied and exhausted.

To everyone's surprise, Pollock so enjoyed that summer that when they returned to New York in September, they almost immediately made plans to move to the Hamptons full-time. They found the Springs farmhouse and persuaded Peggy Guggenheim to lend them the money to buy it.

At first, there was little to do but keep warm. The farmhouse and just about every building needed work, and for months Pollock painted little. When the spring came, he hauled the barn up on a concrete platform and turned it into his studio.

Pollock managed to cement relations with his new neighbors because he impressed them with his prodigious drinking binges at the local bar Jungle Pete's or, less often, the Elm Tree Inn in Amagansett. No one, they reasoned, who could drink for three straight days, punch his hand through a window for no particular reason, urinate in the street, sleep in the gutter for twelve hours, then come back to Jungle Pete's for more could be all bad. The local police soon knew Jackson Pollock better than his fellow artists in New York City did. Entries like "Found Jackson Pollock drunk on side of the road. Took him home" appeared in the police blotter on numerous occasions. Sometimes, however, when he was unruly as well as drunk, Pollock was not taken home but made to spend the night in a cell.

Pollock also befriended the owner of the local general store, Dan Miller, and persuaded him to accept some paintings in lieu of money. Miller became Pollock's therapist, in effect, advising him on every aspect of his life—art, family, drinking, marriage, and sex.

Lee Krasner could do little to keep Pollock away from his new Bonacker friends, but she was able to control his old New York friends' access to him. Those who she feared encouraged his drinking binges she banished from Springs, sometimes at the door of the farmhouse after the long journey from the city. Often Pollock had no idea Krasner had sent friends away. Other times she was more blatant. When she heard that Robert Motherwell's wife had taken Pollock for a spin in her sports car, she convinced herself Maria Motherwell was plotting an affair. She refused to allow Pollock to see either of them again, and Pollock was sent out to tell Robert Motherwell. "Lee's forbidden me ever to see you," he said one day when Motherwell called.

The only guests Krasner willingly allowed beyond the porch were those who could help Pollock's career or who were her allies. Among them was Clement Greenberg, who lectured Pollock on eliminating any vestige of representational forms in his paintings. It was against this background that Pollock developed the technique that created his legend and changed the course of Western art. Because he was working on large canvases that no easel could hold, he was forced to place them flat on the floor. In the freezing cold in the unheated barn early in 1947, Pollock began to fling and drip paint, waving a paint-coated stick or brush high above the canvas, creating shapes and images in the air, then watching them drop and destroy themselves on the canvas.

Precisely how and why that technique occurred to Pollock has been a source of speculation for decades. When Pollock became a celebrity, many other artists claimed that they had been producing drip paintings for years. It is true that as far back as the 1870s Whistler had used a drip technique in some of his paintings. Surrealists and Dadaists had used similar techniques to create random images. Max Ernst had waved a leaky bucket over canvas, and others had squeezed thick wads of paint from tubes directly onto the canvas. But Pollock took the flamboyant technique several steps further, refusing any contact between artist and canvas—"working," in Lee Krasner's words, "in the air above the painting."

Pollock's Bonacker friends were convinced he had discovered the technique while in a drunken rage in his studio, and he did often work when he was both roaring drunk and bitterly angry. Tony Smith, one of Pollock's few New York friends Lee allowed in the studio, recalls Pollock telephoning him one night in a drunken rage threatening to kill himself. Smith drove out to Springs, by which time Pollock was even more drunk but had forgotten the phone call and the thought of killing himself. Instead he was on the point of burning down the house, having filled the stove with so much fuel that flames were touching the beams. Smith tried to calm things down by suggesting they do a painting together.

Between slugs of whiskey and drags on cigarettes, Pollock and Smith spent the night heaving paint at the canvas, flinging it from buckets, shooting it from glass basting syringes, dripping it from brushes and sticks, and finally tramping through it in bare feet. Each time a syringe became clogged with dry paint, Pollock would hurl it down on the concrete floor and watch the shards of glass fly across the canvas. When the two men walked through the paint they cut themselves on the glass, and blood joined the whirls and swirls of paint. Pollock and Smith finally left, exhausted, and Pollock slept off another binge.

Although the Bonackers were convinced that Pollock's paintings were representations of his drunkenness, his biographers Steven Naifeh and Gregory White Smith claim Pollock's technique had another source. As a child, Pollock, who for some reason had been taught to urinate sitting down, watched his father urinate on a rock, making swirling patterns as he did so. This image—and a fascination with urinating in public places—never left Pollock. Even when a more private place was available, he preferred to empty his bladder by the side of the road, against the side of a building, or on the wheels of parked cars. He also routinely urinated in his own and other people's beds. According to Naifeh and Smith there is a psychological connection between this fixation and his technique of pouring, flinging, and dripping paint. He may even have urinated on many of his most famous paintings.

The drip paintings were first shown in 1947. They ultimately catapulted Pollock from relative obscurity to international notoriety. Greenberg exulted in them and found numerous pseudo-intellectual ex post facto justifications and interpretations for them. But it was *Life* magazine that gave them the seal of approval.

In the spring of 1947, Peggy Guggenheim gave up her gallery and her support of Pollock and other artists and returned to Europe. Lee Krasner persuaded a reluctant Betty Parsons to take Pollock on at her gallery, but his paintings, even those that had been critically acclaimed, didn't sell. Without Peggy Guggenheim's money every month, Pollock and Krasner became virtually destitute. They started handing out paintings in payment for debts. When Dan Miller extended credit in return for a drip painting, his wife would not let him bring it into the house. Other tradespeople simply refused to have anything to do with the paintings.

Despite the hardships, the period from 1947 to 1949 was one of the most productive in Pollock's career. He worked hour after hour, drinking less and sleeping longer than he had in years.

In 1949, almost out of the blue, *Life* magazine proposed a feature article on this little-known painter, whom Greenberg had repeatedly called the greatest living American artist. *Life* had from time to time entertained its readers by excoriating a nonrepresentational painter. Even harsh criticism by *Life* translated into sales, however, so Pollock was ecstatic at the thought of any coverage. There had already been snide references to Pollock in *Time* magazine in the context of lambasting modern painting in general and avant-garde critics like Greenberg in particular. *Time* said a Pollock painting looked like "a child's contour map of the Battle of Gettysburg."

Pollock agreed to be interviewed and photographed. He was so broke that he tried to borrow $150 from the photographer, then tried to sell him a painting. He was monosyllabic during the interview, but the resulting article changed his life—and the world of art.

The *Life* article claimed that Pollock had "burst forth as the shining new phenomenon of American art." It actually wasn't quite true until *Life* said so. Pollock certainly looked like the greatest living American artist. He was pictured leaning defiantly, arms folded, against one of his drip paintings, a cigarette drooping from his lower lip. He appeared part Hemingway with a paintbrush, part Humphrey Bogart; quintessentially American, unique and original.

On the eve of the biggest boom in art sales since the Renaissance, Pollock was suddenly a star. Pollock took advantage of his newfound fame almost immediately. His next show was scheduled for November, three months after the *Life* article appeared. Instead of the usual large canvases, which were time-consuming and exhausting, he produced many smaller paintings, which could be offered to first-time buyers at knockdown prices. The show, at Betty Parsons's gallery, was an unequivocal financial and critical success. Everyone wanted a small painting by that fellow profiled in *Life* magazine, and critics from the mainstream press were quick to jump on *Life*'s bandwagon. Only *Time* stayed severely critical of Pollock, but its distaste added to his aura. Pollock sold more paintings in one night than ever before. Within a year he went from penury to having the highest sales of any living artist in America.

He began working on large canvases again, churning out drip paintings and shipping them off to Betty Parsons. He was suddenly invited everywhere, from fashionable parties and openings in Manhattan to summer mansions in East Hampton and Southampton for dinner. His appalling manners and drunken escapades—he once asked an elderly Hamptons hostess what she did for sex, then proceeded to trash a room full of antiques—only added to his appeal.

In another example of his escapades, Pollock was driving with a friend, Roger Wilcox, when they came to the East Hampton mansion of a wealthy businessman, William Seligson. The estate stood out because of a vast, finely manicured lawn, like a golf green, which went on for ten acres with not a bush or a tree or a weed or a plant of any kind. Pollock compared it to a huge green canvas and said he wanted to paint on it.

Several days later, when the Seligson lawn was wet with heavy rain, Pollock drove his car across it, reversing, skidding, swerving, and circling, until it was covered with deep ruts rapidly filling with rainwater. Seligson confronted Pollock, who told him it was the biggest Jackson Pollock on the planet and offered to sign it. Seligson threatened to sue for $120,000, but it was obvious Pollock couldn't raise the money.

His own mythic image quickly became more important to Jackson Pollock than any artistic creation or ideal. He became extravagant, making pilgrimages to New York City and East Hampton to buy the finest clothes he could find. He bought a Cadillac convertible and renovated the Springs house. He took to appearing in bars where he might find artists with whom to pick fights.

He tried to outmaneuver Betty Parsons by getting commissions for which he would have to pay her no fee. He would hold court at parties and gatherings at his home, telling people, "I'm really the only artist worth looking at right now. There really isn't anybody else." At a family reunion at the Springs house with his mother and brothers, he read his own newspaper clippings out loud, with particular emphasis on one that compared him favorably with Picasso. The reunion ended acrimoniously.

Although the *Life* magazine story and numerous reviews of his work since then had made him a star, the backlash was soon to follow. People outside of the cloistered community of dealers, collectors, critics, and artists did not know what to make of Pollock and suspected they were being fooled. Peggy Guggenheim had impetuously given away Pollock's mural to the University of Iowa and tried unsuccessfully to get it back after he became famous. It hung high above a gallery in the rafters, where sparrows that made nests in the rafters left droppings on it. Students and faculty members remarked derisively that it got better and better each day. Occasionally there were protests against Pollock at Betty Parsons's gallery. But the worst criticisms came from Pollock's more obscure fellow artists who were jealous of his success.

Pollock was well aware of the criticisms and was stung by them because deep down he feared they were right and the Clement Greenbergs were wrong; perhaps he was a fraud. The fear made the prospect of an upcoming show all the more daunting. Then, in the early fall of 1950, the photographer Hans Namuth, who had taken still photographs of Pollock and established a good rapport, persuaded him to allow a film to be made of him at work.

Few artists of any stature had ever allowed the creative process to be filmed, and Pollock believed that the project would give him some form of immortality. It would allow people to witness something of what he experienced in his studio. If he did not look like a fraud while he was painting, he might not look a fraud on canvas.

However, Pollock underestimated the process of film production. It seemed every action had to be shot and reshot, even seemingly meaningless simple actions, like throwing away a cigarette or flipping off his shoes. Then Namuth said he wasn't satisfied with the finished product. He wanted to try a new approach. He would shoot Pollock's drip technique from a canvas-eye view by placing the camera beneath a sheet of glass and Pollock on a scaffold above it. It had to be done in the open air because the studio was too small.

If the earlier shoots were tedious and unsatisfying for Pollock, these were ten times worse. Filming had to stop for long periods while the sheet of glass was cleaned. The days grew short and cold. There was more endless repetition of gestures and movements. Pollock, directed by Namuth, painting and not painting on cue, began to feel that he was a fraud after all and that the film might expose him.

Shooting finally finished on a bitterly cold Thanksgiving weekend. A number of Pollock's friends from New York and the Hamptons had gathered at the Springs house for dinner. Namuth was in celebratory mood, but when he and Pollock came in, it was clear to everyone that Pollock was tense and depressed. He found a bottle of whiskey and quickly downed two tumblers full. After months of taking orders from Namuth, the time had finally come to rebel. He attacked the photographer, calling him a phony. Namuth responded with more orders—stop doing this, stop saying that. Pollock kept on repeating throughout dinner, in a stage whisper, "You're a phony!" Finally he grabbed the edge of the dining table and turned it over, sending all the food and dishes flying, then staggered out into the night. It was the start of another binge.

Pollock never had another period as productive as the one that immediately followed the publication of the *Life* magazine article. That year's show, for most of which Pollock was incoherently drunk, was a disaster.

Most people came only to stare at Pollock and not to buy. The paintings were all too large to sell and, at several thousand dollars each, overpriced. Only one sold and that at a discount to one of Pollock's friends. Pollock succeeded in alienating even those who were gracious about the show. He called one critic who gave it a favorable review at three A.M. and shouted, "If you like my fucking paintings, why didn't you buy one?"

Pollock now began a long and dreadful alcoholic decline. He routinely insulted every friend and ally. At a show at East Hampton's Guild Hall, a wealthy socialite complimented him on his work. "Bullshit! Bullshit!" he roared. A day would routinely begin at Dan Miller's store, where he bought beer for drinking "by the neck," meaning from the bottle. The beer gave him the confidence to face Jungle Pete's. If he was still on his feet he might make it out to the bar of the East Hampton Hotel, where he would throw chairs and tables if anyone told him he had had enough. At the Elm Tree he would lapse into unconsciousness until one of his Bonacker cronies carted him home and left him on the porch for Lee to sweep up.

He continued to work, but two shows, one in Paris and one at a new gallery in New York, were flops. The new darling and rival for the Greatest Living Painter title was Willem de Kooning, who had opened a new studio at Bridgehampton. Pollock and de Kooning were deadly enemies, and Pollock was rarely invited to gatherings at Bridgehampton, except as a potential floor show. He often turned up uninvited, and on one such occasion de Kooning wrestled him to the ground and broke his ankle.

Intermittently, at Lee Krasner's insistence, Pollock would try cures of various kinds for his alcoholism, balking at the most obvious one:

abstinence. A gaggle of therapists worked with him to limited effect. He poured scorn on Alcoholics Anonymous after one or two visits to meetings in Southampton.

He twice checked into rehab clinics, sabotaging their programs in advance by smuggling in bottles of whiskey, which he hid in the toilet tank. Inevitably, the more Pollock drank, the more he abused his wife, usually verbally, but sometimes physically as well. Pollock felt threatened by Krasner because the less he worked the more she worked. Her paintings had matured from claustrophobic little efforts on scraps of canvas to large, bold, colorful works, and people were beginning to take notice of her work over his for the first time.

Pollock began weekly trips to New York to see a therapist, but the visits served as a truck stop on a darker journey. After therapy he would roll into the Cedar Tavern, a Greenwich Village artists' hangout, to get drunk, grope at some young woman, and pick a fight with a painter over some imagined slight. It became so routine that Pollock's antics became part of the Cedar's mystique; the place filled up when Pollock was expected to be there.

Clearly, Pollock was losing his mind. Krasner had suspected that he was prone to insanity years before. Pollock had suggested they try to have children, but she refused point blank, because, she said later, it would have been irresponsible to have children "with someone that crazy."

Hand in hand with his deteriorating mental state went thoughts of suicide. He bought a bow and arrow and shot it inside the house. He would lock himself in his studio and play jazz records full blast for hours on end in a trance. He walked down the center of the road daring traffic to hit him, and he once leapt out of a moving taxicab.

While Pollock was doing little to further, or even rescue, his career, help came from an unlikely source: *Fortune* magazine. At the height of fifties prosperity, art became big business. Prices for works by collectible artists were rising so fast that they ceased to be status symbols and became investments.

In 1955 David Rockefeller bought a Cézanne for $500,000. *Fortune* confirmed the trend by publishing a guide that divided the art world as Wall Street stocks were divided: gilt-edged, blue chip, and growth issues. The gilt-edged were Old Masters; the blue chips included Cézanne, Manet, and Gauguin. The growth issues were living American painters and included Pollock and de Kooning. Suddenly the Cedar crowd couldn't sell their work fast enough.

Some artists are said to have backdated their paintings by ten years or more to give them a phony provenance. Critics like Clement Greenberg became dealers. Wealthy young collectors headed for Greenwich Village, SoHo, and the Hamptons looking for paintings. The big ones were especially highly prized. One dealer even sold by the square yard. Drunk as he was, Pollock was not oblivious to this boom. He was sought after and prosperous once more. But he wasn't going to live long enough to enjoy its full fruits.

It was on one of his binges at the Cedar that the forty-three-year-old Pollock ran into a voluptuous twenty-five-year-old art student and Garment District model named Ruth Kligman. Drawn by Pollock's mythic status, dissolute existence, and reputation as a wayward genius, she waited patiently at the Cedar night after night until he came in. She sat down with him and introduced herself. When his drinking brought him close to collapse, she took him back to her apartment a few blocks away and put him to bed. When he woke up next morning to find her naked beside him, the previous night a distant veil of noise and shadow, she convinced him they had had sex, although in his general physical condition it was unlikely. A lifetime of drinking had left him routinely impotent, and he and Krasner had not slept together for years. Eventually, however, Ruth was able to coax from him some degree of sexual response.

It was the beginning of an affair he paraded in front of the other artists at the Cedar and did little to conceal from his wife. A few weeks after their first meeting, Ruth Kligman found a job at an art school in Sag Harbor and moved out to the Hamptons to be near Pollock. Pollock disappeared for days and nights at a time, still drinking excessively, but crawling home to Ruth rather than Lee Krasner. When he returned to Springs there were scenes about his absence, but while Krasner knew of Ruth's existence, they never confronted the issue.

Then one night Krasner heard noises coming from the studio and went down to investigate. She found Pollock and Ruth Kligman together. There was an apocalyptic scene. Krasner threatened to leave him, and Pollock put his arm around Ruth and told Lee to go ahead. The last thing Krasner really wanted was to surrender Pollock to Ruth Kligman. She had tried to ignore the affair, hoping one or the other of them would tire of it. Now she retreated and left on a vacation alone to Paris. Almost as soon as she was gone, Ruth Kligman moved into the Springs house.

Life with Jackson Pollock soon became very different from life as

Pollock's mistress. He immediately began to miss Lee Krasner and became bored with the younger, more attractive woman. Even her habit of moving around the house nude or wearing only panties, which had seemed so exciting when he visited her, palled when he was at home seeking an escape from not painting. He began berating her in public as he had often done with Krasner. He ignored her when they were with the few friends who would allow her into their homes. He even beat her in public, slapping her to the ground. After only three weeks together, Ruth Kligman left for New York, and in Paris, red roses started to arrive at Lee Krasner's hotel.

Pollock was alone for three weeks. He stayed quietly drunk most of the time. When he visited friends, he spoke of Lee Krasner and began weeping. He seemed in a daze. One friend saw him, staggering and confused, bloated and pale, wandering around East Hampton, apparently uncertain of exactly where he was. Friends feared he might die or kill himself.

In mid-August 1956, Ruth Kligman called him from New York and told him she was coming out to visit him for the weekend and bringing a friend. The friend, Edith Metzger, was recovering from an affair with an older, married man, and Ruth brought her to the Hamptons so she wouldn't have to spend a midsummer weekend alone in the city. The night before her arrival, Pollock visited the home of a fellow artist in East Hampton and was unusually complimentary about his paintings. He ran his hands over the painted surface of one canvas like a blind man reading braille and talked wistfully about the feel of the paint.

"Life is beautiful," he said. "Why is it that all I can think about is death?"

Ruth Kligman and Edith Metzger arrived by train the next morning. Pollock was sullen and began drinking early, but he drove them out to Montauk, visiting friends who were so appalled by Pollock's physical deterioration and the two flighty young women that they found an excuse to cut the visit short.

They returned to Springs, where Ruth and Edith changed into bathing suits and spent the afternoon in the garden while Pollock drank gin. That evening after dinner, they drove to what for Ruth and Edith was an exciting night: a society gala at the Creeks, the East Hampton mansion of wealthy art collector Alfonso Ossorio. On the way, Pollock's driving became erratic and he appeared to be dozing at the wheel. He stopped the car and was soon being questioned by a passing policeman. The police officer recognized Pollock and let him go on his way.

They drove to a bar where Pollock could have some coffee and solid food to sober him up. After eating, Pollock was ready to get back on the road, but Edith, who had been terrified of Pollock and his white-knuckle driving from the beginning, refused to get back in the car with him. This put him into a fearful rage, and after she was persuaded to get in, he rocketed down the road with a screech of rubber.

As they sped along, Pollock continued to accelerate. Even Ruth, who had experienced his wild driving before, became frightened and screamed at him to stop. Edith Metzger was shouting, "Let me out! Let me out!"

Pollock started to laugh, and his eyes opened wide as he approached a sharp bend. Ruth stood up in the convertible but was pushed back in her seat by the force of their speed. Pollock misjudged the bend and veered across the crown of the road. The car careened off the road into a group of saplings and somersaulted.

All three were thrown out. Edith Metzger hit the ground and was killed when the car fell on top of her. Ruth Kligman landed in the soft underbrush and survived. Jackson Pollock was propelled fifty feet, head first, into an elm tree.

The news of Pollock's death was broken to Lee Krasner in Paris in the early hours of the morning. She had witnessed his escapades at the wheel before and characterized at least two other episodes of furious driving as suicide attempts. Other friends also realized the suicidal element in the accident. Days before, he had begun returning long-borrowed items to friends as if he were trying to tidy up odd elements of his life.

Pollock was buried in Green River Cemetery in one of three plots Lee had bought years earlier. Clement Greenberg refused to read the eulogy unless he could mention Edith Metzger, the innocent bystander Pollock had taken with him in his last act of self-destruction. Instead, the eulogy was read by a stranger, a local Presbyterian minister. A large rock from Pollock's back yard was placed over the grave, but later Lee Krasner feared it was small enough to be stolen. She had it replaced with a forty-ton boulder found at the East Hampton town dump, and a copy of Pollock's signature was carved on it.

Immediately after his death, the value of Pollock's work skyrocketed. Gallery owners called buyers trying to repurchase, at two and three times the price, paintings that they had sold days or weeks before. Eager dealers and collectors fanned out across the Hamptons looking for paintings he had left in Bonacker bars and stores in exchange for credit.

Dan Miller sold one of his for $7,500. Several paintings are reputed to have mysteriously disappeared from the studio. Peggy Guggenheim sued Pollock's estate seeking pictures that had been painted while he was under contract to her gallery and had never been given to her.

Even the graveyard where he was buried became a sought-after commodity. Plots near Pollock's grave were snapped up by wealthy Hamptonites, and Bonackers complained they had been priced out of a decent burial.

In 1972, sixteen years after his death, the painting that Pollock had begun in a drunken rage with Tony Smith became one of his most famous. Titled *Blue Poles*, it was eventually sold for two million dollars, at that time the highest price ever paid for a work by an American artist.

CHAPTER 2

Monroe, Miller, and a Secret Love Affair

AT THE END OF MAY 1957, Marilyn Monroe and playwright Arthur Miller, her husband, climbed into a white Lincoln convertible waiting outside their apartment at 444 East 57th Street and headed for the Hamptons for the summer. It was to be one of the most tumultuous periods of Marilyn's life—an emotional roller coaster ride with moments of near-perfect happiness, love, passion, and darkest despair.

Although Miller owned a large farm in Connecticut, where they spent most weekends, they chose to rent a rambling, weatherbeaten old farmhouse, with paint peeling from the shingles, in Amagansett. Today it is owned by Alec Baldwin and Kim Basinger. It was by no means lavish, but it was secluded, in a peaceful setting close to the beach, and, best of all, protected from unwelcome attention by shifts of local policemen who kept a twenty-four-hour watch on the lane leading up to the house.

The Millers' summer home, known as Hill House, was one of several small homes clustered around a large farmhouse, Stony Hill Farm. It faced broad green fields but was only a short walk from the ocean. The main house was owned by Jeff and Penny Potter, who rented out Hill House, which had been a caretaker's cottage, in the summer, as well as other cottages in the compound. They were amazed when the realtor introduced them to their new tenants, the screen legend and her controversial husband.

It was not Marilyn's first summer in the Hamptons. In 1955 she had been on a photo shoot in Prospect Park, Brooklyn, with photographer Sam Shaw when they were caught in a sudden torrential downpour. Shaw called his friend Norman Rosten, the poet, to ask if he could drop by to dry off. Rosten and his wife welcomed Shaw and at first missed the name of his companion when she was introduced. They thought she had said her name was Marion. It was only when Hedda Rosten asked her what she did for a living that she told them their unexpected guest was Marilyn Monroe.

The chance meeting led to a long and valued friendship, one of the most important, open, and constructive of Monroe's life. Monroe virtually became a member of the Rosten family. She was a guest at their rented home in Springs a number of times that year and the next. Her dressed-down appearance usually convinced locals that the striking blond woman was just another New York tourist, but sometimes the disguises failed to work.

One Saturday afternoon in July 1955, she was sunbathing on the beach near the Rostens' summer home when a crowd began to gather. She was wearing a large straw hat, dark glasses, and a black bathing suit and had been sitting under a huge umbrella. She had been there for a while without being noticed, but somehow news began to spread that Marilyn Monroe was on the beach. The crowd of sunbathers—men and women—began to press closer.

Some began to shout, "Hey Marilyn! Hey Marilyn!" Monroe leapt up and threw away the straw hat, revealing her unmistakable hair, and there was a gasp from the crowd. It really was Marilyn. She ran into the surf, calling Norman Rosten to come in with her, and began swimming furiously. Most of the crowd appeared to follow her in, shouting her name over and over. She swam and swam and swam, until she became cramped and exhausted. Only a passing speedboat saved her from being drowned. The exhausted star was hauled aboard.

Rosten had been helping her get her senses back for some minutes when he noticed the boat was plowing through its own wake. He looked up and saw that the young man at the wheel had his neck craned back at Marilyn and could not take his eyes off her. He did not realize he was taking the boat around in circles.

Another stay had equally dramatic but less public consequences. Marilyn had a love affair with a younger man who worked as a lifeguard, groundskeeper, and handyman at a large Southampton mansion. Marilyn was twenty-nine. He was not yet twenty-two.

In August 1955, Michael Byrne was walking on a secluded beach near Montauk when he noticed a striking woman walking through the edge of the surf, ankle deep in the water. It was the middle of the week, and the beach was deserted; and there was a strong and bracing breeze coming in off the ocean. The woman was kicking at the incoming surf every few yards as if she were place-kicking an invisible football.

She was wearing what at first sight seemed to be a baggy blue dress but on a closer look was revealed to be a man's shirt. She had dark glasses on, and a print headscarf was tied under her chin. Byrne, athletic and handsome, had a stable of girlfriends on the beaches of the Hamptons. He struck up a conversation with her.

"I just asked her the usual questions and talked awhile. I had no idea she was Marilyn Monroe or I would never have had the courage to try to talk to her. She said her name was Kelly and we talked about Grace Kelly. We talked about Brando. She said he was her favorite actor. We talked about the summer and the big houses and about East Hampton village, which she said she loved. We walked for a while, and she suggested we go for a swim. I thought it was too cold, but I was hooked by this time.

"I told her the place where I worked was just about deserted. The family was all at some picnic or someplace and wouldn't be back for hours. On the drive over to Southampton she took off the scarf, and I told her she looked just like Marilyn Monroe. She said, 'That's not Marilyn. This is Marilyn'—and she sort of 'became' Monroe, pout, breathy voice, wiggle. Everything. In an instant.

"It turned out she was wearing nothing but that baggy man's shirt. We skinny-dipped in the pool at the house, and we dried each other off in the pool house. There was an empty guest house close by the pool, and we made love in a bedroom there that afternoon. She had this wonderful, almost luminous skin, and she was very giving as well as responsive. I couldn't believe what was happening. An hour or two earlier I was some schmo on the beach. Now I was in bed with Marilyn Monroe."

Byrne's love affair with the legend lasted a little less than two weeks. Byrne worked most of the day, but they met for walks on the beach and ocean swims and picnics. They sneaked into his employers' guest house or crammed themselves into Byrne's tiny servant's quarters to have sex.

"One day, she told me she was going back to New York City and I should write and sometimes she would too. She was kind and loving—

but she was saying it was over. She was older and rich and famous. It was a wonder to me she had any time for me at all," Byrne recalls. "Everyone thought she was dumb—me too—but boy, she was smart. She always had some book with her—poetry usually. And she could talk about anything.

"She said being famous was like a drug that she had to have. Sometimes she wanted to kick it and leave it behind. Sometimes she felt she had kicked it. But then she needed to be Marilyn. It was a craving. She had to have someone recognize her, and that was like having her drug—a fix, you could call it."

Byrne kept quiet about his affair for decades. "I didn't think anyone would believe me, so I said nothing to my friends at the time. I didn't want them to start to follow me if they did believe me. After that summer I heard she was out in the Hamptons again, this time with Miller. By then I had moved on, and I didn't try to contact her. I figured she had forgotten me."

But Marilyn had not forgotten him. Years later she told her business manager, Inez Melson, about "a wonderful young man" she had met strolling on the beach in the Hamptons and why she had cut the affair short.

"I couldn't have done that to him—brought him into my life," she told Melson. "He would have wound up hating it and hating me for it."

By the time of Marilyn's passionate fling with Byrne, her relationship with Miller was already under way, and Marilyn was convinced they would get married despite numerous obstacles. Not least of them was the fact that Miller was already married. He was also a controversial figure, suspected in those paranoid times of being a Communist, and had many enemies in Hollywood, Washington, and the conservative press.

Miller had first met Marilyn Monroe in January 1951, and they had struck up a brief friendship. Miller was in Hollywood hawking an original screenplay, *The Hook*, which Elia Kazan had agreed to direct and which they were trying to sell to Harry Cohn, head of Columbia. Kazan and Miller both met her on the set of *As Young as You Feel*, which was being directed by a friend of Kazan's, Harmon Jones. She was depressed over the recent death of her agent, benefactor, and lover, Johnny Hyde, and could not get through her limited part without crying. The meeting led to a brief affair with Kazan, but it had far-reaching consequences for Miller.

They had a number of outings together. On one, to a bookstore where she bought several books on Miller's recommendation, Miller noticed that another customer was staring at her and masturbating. He never forgot the image. Marilyn exuded an urgent sexuality even when she wasn't being Marilyn. Miller and Marilyn had an unspoken, unacknowledged, but definite attraction. Later Miller said there was "something secret—a filament of a connection" between them, although he must have been aware of her relationship with Kazan. Kazan certainly knew of her attraction to Miller and complained later that she could not stop talking about him.

Miller left Hollywood for New York. He and Marilyn exchanged numerous letters, then lost touch, but each was still haunted by the unfulfilled promise of a romance. It was to be four more years before they were to meet again, but Marilyn kept his picture at her bedside— alongside one of Abraham Lincoln. She told friends, even before she married Joe DiMaggio in 1954, that she would one day marry Arthur Miller.

Miller, thirty-nine, and Marilyn, twenty-nine, met again in 1955 at a cocktail party to which Marilyn had been brought by the Rostens. Hedda Rosten was a former classmate of Miller's at the University of Michigan.

They talked for an hour, but it was two weeks before Miller called the Actors Studio, where Marilyn was studying under Lee Strasberg, and managed to get her number from Strasberg's wife, Paula. They arranged to meet at the Rostens' home in Brooklyn and made love for the first time that afternoon. For the next several months, Marilyn Monroe and Arthur Miller continued a love affair in absolute secrecy.

Marilyn was no longer married to Joe DiMaggio; their stormy relationship had been doomed to end. Even so, DiMaggio visited her in New York. He had not given up hope of winning her back. The sexual attraction was still there. The one thing right about their marriage was their sex lives. "If that's all it took," Marilyn was to say years later, "we'd still be married." At one point that spring, by some miracle of scheduling, she was sleeping with DiMaggio, Miller, and a number of other men.

Miller's own marriage was stagnating when he began his affair. He bought a bicycle, and on the pretext of needing more exercise he would ride to remote corners of New York City—Coney Island, Sheepshead Bay, Far Rockaway, and Staten Island—with Marilyn at his side. Some intimates, including the Rostens, were in on the secret, and Marilyn and Miller even hosted dinner parties as a couple at the Rostens' home.

While their mutual friends agreed that Miller and Marilyn were in love, it is also true that she had intimate relationships around that time with both Marlon Brando and wealthy dress manufacturer Henry Rosenfeld, who had arranged a suite for her at the Waldorf-Astoria Hotel during her stay in New York and even proposed to her. Miller was not aware of the other relationships, although he did know that DiMaggio continued to pursue her throughout most of their courtship.

In January 1956, Miller decided to seek a divorce, "Marilyn or no," but it was not going to be easy. Miller checked into the Pyramid Lake Guest Ranch, a motel outside Reno, Nevada, for two months to establish residency for a Reno divorce. He was registered under the name "Leslie," and every day Marilyn, on the set of *Bus Stop*, called him there using the name "Mrs. Leslie." They had taken the names from a novel they had read together, *About Mrs. Leslie* by Vina Delmar.

Nevada law required unbroken residency, but Miller made a number of secret trips to Los Angeles while he was supposed to be at Pyramid Lake. Had that been known to authorities at the time, his divorce, and therefore his marriage to Marilyn, might have been deemed invalid. While living in Nevada, and just as his relationship with Marilyn had become public, he was served with a subpoena to appear before the House Un-American Activities Committee.

Miller had long been a target of the extreme right because of the clear left-wing slant in his plays. He had been investigated for a variety of reasons, on numerous occasions, including surveillance by the FBI and also by private detectives acting on behalf of movie studios. He had pulled movie scripts from production when he found out they were to be reworked with an anti-Communist theme. He had broken with his friend Elia Kazan for cooperating with the committee. And Miller's 1953 play *The Crucible*, based on the Salem witch trials, was clearly a comment on the committee's activities and other features of the anti-Communist witch-hunts of those days. Yet it was Miller's relationship with Marilyn, as much as anything he had written, that brought him to the attention of the committee.

Reports of their love affair and even the possibility of marriage had begun to appear in newspapers in the first weeks of 1956. By the spring it was an open secret in Hollywood. Congressman Francis Walter, chairman of the committee, whose political fortunes were flagging, saw in Miller an opportunity for a high-profile investigation. It's claimed he acknowledged that Miller's relationship with Marilyn was responsible for drawing him to the committee's attention by offering Miller a deal: if he could arrange for Marilyn to pose with Walter for photographers, the committee would softball Miller at the hearings. The playwright indignantly refused.

At the committee hearings, Miller refused to name others he had met at gatherings of Communists and left-wingers and left himself open to a charge of contempt of Congress. This refusal, prompted behind the scenes by Marilyn herself, was to lead to two years of exhausting legal battles before Miller was finally vindicated.

At one point, Miller, whose passport had expired and who had applied for another, was asked about his travel plans. He was planning to go to England in the near future, he said, and he would be with "the woman who will then be my wife." Later, confronted by reporters, he told them he would marry Marilyn Monroe. It was news to her. "He just told the world he's marrying Marilyn Monroe. He never even asked me," she told Norman Rosten as reporters began to besiege her home on Manhattan's Sutton Place. Loyally, she confirmed they planned to marry.

The pair discussed getting married at the Rostens' Hamptons summer house. It might have taken place there but for a tragic incident. Marilyn and Miller had been tailed by reporters on the winding roads to his Connecticut home, and one car carrying a *Paris Match* reporter had crashed into a tree, all but decapitating her. Desperate to bring the media circus to a swift end, they slipped across the state line into New York that night and were married in the courthouse in White Plains by a judge who interrupted a dinner party to officiate. Two nights later, there was a second, Jewish ceremony, under a chuppah at the home of the literary agent Kay Brown.

Within two weeks, Miller and Marilyn were in England where she was to shoot *The Prince and the Showgirl* with Sir Laurence Olivier. Marilyn's emotional problems, profoundly introspective dramatic technique encouraged by the Strasbergs' coaching methods, and her increasing dependence on barbiturates to relieve chronic insomnia all led to her being an unreliable costar for Olivier. For her part, Marilyn believed Olivier was condescending. "It was like he was slumming," she claimed later. His attitude, or her perception of it, fueled her insecurities.

Shooting the movie quickly became an ordeal for all concerned. Marilyn was repeatedly late on the set and often ill prepared. Miller, to Marilyn's dismay, appeared to take Olivier's side against her. The two men became comrades in arms. Each was in an emotionally consuming marriage to a beautiful, promiscuous, disturbed, addicted superstar— Miller to Marilyn, Olivier to Vivien Leigh. They identified with each other. Marilyn found some jottings about his feelings during the shooting that expressed his disappointment with her and sympathy for Olivier, and she was deeply wounded. It has been suggested that at this time Marilyn was already being unfaithful, with her longtime business manager Milton Greene.

When Miller and Marilyn moved into Hill House for the summer of 1957, it was in part an attempt to restore the love for each other that had been badly shaken in England. They had had only one other break together since *The Prince and the Showgirl,* a two-week trip to Jamaica. Miller, who had done virtually no writing since their marriage the previous summer, resolved to work during the sojourn in the Hamptons while Marilyn rested.

At first all went well. Their nearest neighbors were a reclusive artist and his wife who jealously guarded their own privacy and so left them alone. Job Potter, the six-year-old son of the owners of the cottages, found any excuse to visit them, but Marilyn had a natural affinity for children, so the visits were never a nuisance. Marilyn decided she wanted to learn how to cook. She started practicing on spaghetti. Miller found her hanging the pasta over a chairback and drying it with a hair dryer. She did manage to master thick steaks, which they supplemented with angel food cake and ice cream from the local general store. Miller even put on a considerable amount of weight, twenty-five pounds by his own admission.

They took long walks along the beaches and chatted amiably with the local commercial fishermen who hauled their nets up from the ocean with winches on trucks parked on the beach. Marilyn amazed the locals by running up and down the beach frantically trying to throw back the so-called junk fish that the fishermen had used as bait or considered unsuitable for market and left struggling on the sand. Marilyn was trying to save their lives.

Miller was used to her obsession with any living thing. He had once seen her weeping because some wildflowers had been cut when the lawn had been mowed and had to restrain her from pushing the stalks back into the ground. She became almost violent when there was talk of hunting deer. Another time she came across two schoolboys trapping pigeons in a park and paid them to stop; each week she returned to pay further ransom.

But even Miller was astonished by Marilyn's obsession with the stranded fish. "Some of them may live and grow old and be alive when their children grow up," she reportedly told him. One day she became so obsessed with her mission to save the fish that she risked exhausting herself, and once again Miller had to intervene to stop her. He based the short story "Please Don't Kill Anything" on the incident, and "The Misfits" owes something to her obsession.

There were less unnerving pursuits. Marilyn cut Miller's hair in the farmyard. She abandoned her Hollywood wardrobe, wandering about the house naked and wearing only Miller's shirt when they went out. They swam nude in the ocean at night and made love on the beach. Miller records that she appeared like Botticelli's Venus emerging from the waters, her body reflecting the sun in the same way and "with the same salt-water-washed, sea-emergent stare."

"I don't think I ever saw two people so much in love with each other," says Jim Proctor, a close friend of Miller.

They had pet names for each other. She called him "Poppy" or "Pa." He called her "Penny Dreadful" and "Gramercy 5." The origins are obscure. Occasionally their idyll was interrupted by the banal demands of her screen career. Miller returned to Manhattan with her for the New York premiere of *The Prince and the Showgirl,* which received bleak reviews.

Then, in July, Marilyn had an announcement. She was pregnant. According to Miller, Marilyn desperately wanted a child. "A child of her own was a crown with a thousand diamonds," Miller says in his autobiography, *Timebends.*

Yet Marilyn had by that stage had at least seven, and by one account thirteen, abortions, the most recent in the summer prior to her marriage, when she was seeing several lovers. Some of them had been performed in less than ideal circumstances by unskilled surgeons. The procedures had probably exacerbated a condition that made it difficult to have children, endometriosis. In this condition the lining of the uterus develops in other pelvic organs, including the fallopian tubes and ovaries, causing cysts and blockages. She is also reported to have suffered from pelvic inflammatory disease, a sexually transmitted disease which often has severe effects on the reproductive system.

Despite her unpromising medical history, Marilyn became excited by the prospect of at last having a child. Miller warned her that she should wait to see how the first crucial weeks of the pregnancy went before throwing herself into motherhood. He was also worried about becoming a father at what at that time was considered late in life. Nevertheless, Marilyn's enthusiasm for her future role was infectious, and Miller soon set aside his reservations. She seemed to develop a fresh confidence, what Miller called "a quietness of spirit that I had never seen in her."

Disaster and disappointment lay ahead, however. Marilyn began to feel dizzy and weak. She developed what she thought was a stomach bug and was in severe intestinal pain. Then one afternoon Miller heard a piercing scream from Marilyn in the garden—a cry of fear, it seemed, as much as pain—and he found her unconscious and bleeding. She was taken to Doctors' Hospital in Manhattan, where the pregnancy was diagnosed as ectopic. The fetus had begun to develop in the right fallopian tube.

She had surgery to end the pregnancy and repair the damaged fallopian tube. When Miller visited her, he found her deeply depressed, lying in total darkness even during the day and expressing fears that he would leave her if she couldn't have children. In fact children had never been part of Miller's vision of their life together, but she would not be comforted.

She expressed similar feelings of worthlessness to Jim Haspiel, a fan with whom she was on good terms, and to Susan Strasberg, who came to see her to try to cheer her up. The photographer Sam Shaw, who had first introduced Marilyn to the Rostens, also visited her and one night walked with Miller to his apartment. *Esquire* had recently published Miller's short story "The Misfits." Shaw suggested that it would make a great movie and could provide a breakthrough role for Marilyn.

"The Misfits" told the story of twentieth-century cowboys in Nevada who trap wild horses for a living and their relationship with a free-spirited woman to whom all life is sacred. Miller had been planning to write a remake of the Marlene Dietrich movie *The Blue Angel* for Marilyn, but he was so taken by Shaw's idea that he started work on *The Misfits* instead.

When Marilyn had sufficiently recovered, an ambulance drove her and Miller back to Amagansett. She continued to be despondent, probably more so now that, while she was no longer pregnant, Miller was busy from breakfast to dinnertime working on *The Misfits* screenplay. Miller's mother came out to visit; Marilyn had become close friends with Miller's father and responded well to his two children, who had also visited them in the Hamptons, but his mother was a different challenge. She was superstitious about sick people and so was the last person who should have been around Marilyn at this time, when she was both physically and emotionally drained. There was friction, and Miller's mother cut short her visit. Miller himself suggested, a little cruelly, that the two did not get along because Marilyn was unable to use her sexuality to win his mother over.

There was further pain for Marilyn after she again announced that she was pregnant. She probably wasn't, but when it became obvious that she was not, she decided she had had a miscarriage. Sinking deeper into despondency, she turned increasingly to barbiturates assisted by alcohol and blamed herself for losing another baby. Miller finished work on the screenplay one night and found Marilyn asleep, naked, in an armchair. He did not disturb her at first, but after some time noticed that her breathing had become heavy and labored. He counted the barbiturates that were left—there were few—and checked the sherry bottle that lay at her feet. He realized she was headed into a coma.

Paramedics were summoned from Southampton. She had her stomach pumped and was given more drugs to revive her. Had no help been summoned, she might well have died. She had no explanation for the incident and no longer remembered taking handfuls of pills and washing them down with sherry. Some of her close friends, including the Rostens, who had discussed her emotional instability with Miller, feared that it had been a suicide attempt.

She had barely recovered when she agreed to return to New York for a publicity stunt for *Life* magazine. The publishers were so eager to get her to appear at a charity event that they sent a helicopter to Amagansett to pick her up in a field near their home and deposit her there again a few hours later. Miller was as awed as the locals—Job Potter particularly—at the sight of the helicopter descending to pluck her out of one world and take her into another. Miller confessed to being frightened by her hold over that world and its hold over her.

As work on *The Misfits* progressed, it became a source of friction. Marilyn loved the story and the male characters and, Miller says, laughed out loud at some of their lines. But she seemed less and less enthusiastic about what would be her own role, Roslyn. A character unmistakably based on Marilyn, Roslyn is a lonely woman who comes to Nevada to seek a divorce and falls in love with a rugged, older cowboy. Marilyn would not give a commitment to play the role, even though it was being written for her. Miller rationalized her hesitation— it was his gift to Marilyn and therefore hers to play or not—but he later admitted he was deeply hurt.

Miller and Marilyn so loved their home in the Hamptons that they discussed buying or building a permanent place there. Marilyn had grandiose ideas that went far beyond Miller's concept for a simple country life. She pressed him to allow Frank Lloyd Wright, the legendary architect, to design a home for them, either in Roxbury, Connecticut, where Miller already owned a house and some land, or in the Hamptons.

Despite Miller's warnings to Wright that they liked to live quite simply and felt no need of impressing the whole world, Wright came up with a lavish and palatial scheme. It featured a circular living room sixty feet in diameter, supported by five-foot-thick stone columns and with a domed ceiling. It looked out on a seventy-foot-long pool. It had only one bedroom and a small guest room, but it featured a conference room where, Miller says dismissively, Marilyn would sit holding court like the queen of Denmark.

The renderings showed a vintage limousine with liveried chauffeur arriving in the driveway and a flag atop the dome signaling that the owners were home. Wright was notorious for ignoring costs, as was Marilyn. Miller guessed that Wright's estimate for the total cost might just pay for the pool, whose twenty-foot-high retaining wall would require feats of engineering. Miller recalled, "It would have been useful as a hideaway for corporate executives to plot illegal stock deals and illicit mergers." The Wright home was never built, neither in Connecticut nor the Hamptons.

Marilyn and Miller closed their summer home a few days before Labor Day 1957 and left the Hamptons. They returned the following year, but this time their idyll was cut short by the demands of shooting *Some Like It Hot.*

Their stay had had a profound effect on them. Neither knew it at the time, but it was the high point of their happiness together. They had become closer and had seemed to heal the wounds in their marriage caused by Marilyn's infidelities and Miller's jealousy. However, Miller had become more afraid of her emotional instability and more aware of her vulnerability than ever and had begun to have doubts that he could cope with them.

The marriage began to deteriorate the following year, 1958, as Miller fled to a place within himself and Marilyn, in response, began to publicly ridicule and humiliate him. *The Misfits,* which Miller began writing in Amagansett, eventually became Marilyn's final complete movie. It is also the only one in which she was able to demonstrate her full dramatic range. But what began as a Valentine for Marilyn and a gift to celebrate her recovery also coincided with the final chapter of their marriage. By the time shooting started in the Nevada desert in

1960, their union was disintegrating. Soon after shooting ended in November, they announced their separation.

Marilyn never forgot the heady few months in the Hamptons when she was in love and believed she was going to be a mother. Years later, Susan Strasberg and other friends said they believed motherhood might have been the only thing that could have saved her. Morbidly, she marked the anniversary of losing the child there each year after. She was to die on that anniversary in 1962.

CHAPTER 3

Steinbeck:
An Iconoclast's Tragic Journey

Author John Steinbeck and his third wife, Elaine, began looking for a country home to escape the enervating distractions and assaults of New York City in the winter of 1955. Steinbeck, then fifty-three years old and a hulking bear of a man, had grown up in Salinas, California, about eighty-five miles from San Francisco. As a child he vacationed every year at Pacific Grove on Monterey Bay. He wanted another home near the ocean.

At various times they had discussed Nantucket, which they judged to be too far from New York, Rockland County, which appealed to Elaine but was not near the ocean, the Jersey Shore, and central Long Island, which Steinbeck insisted was too full of city folk. They spent days in rented cars driving to summer resorts shrouded in nagging rain and winter gloom. It was depressing work, and they couldn't agree on any of the houses they had seen. They had even started to argue about each other's tastes.

In 1953 the Steinbecks had spent a month in Sag Harbor in a rambling house rented for them by a Broadway producer, Ernest Martin, who had a summer home in East Hampton. Steinbeck had finished a novel, *Sweet Thursday*, in the house, a project he began in order to get him through the postpartum depression that took hold of him when he finished what was to be his last major work, *East of Eden*.

The Steinbecks had enjoyed their brief stay in Sag Harbor and decided it was at least worth looking at some rental homes there for the following summer. Elaine wanted a garden; John wanted a beachfront. They found a newspaper advertisement that offered a house to rent in a cove a mile from Sag Harbor, and together they drove out to see it. They quickly realized that it was unsuitable but continued on the house tour out of politeness to the agent. John Steinbeck glanced out of a window and noticed a house sitting on a steep headland on its own triangular promontory with its own dock. Steinbeck turned to the agent and shouted, "This isn't the house I want! That is!"

"But it isn't for sale!" the agent told him.

"Just ask," Steinbeck pleaded.

As it turned out, the owner of the house had decided to sell that morning. That afternoon a giant of American literature was standing at the door asking the price. John and Elaine Steinbeck agreed to buy the house without even looking inside.

It was just as well they didn't because the place was badly in need of renovation. A single fireplace was the only source of heat. The house had no insulation and little ventilation. Previous owners had made improvements, but the standard of workmanship was generally low. It had been inadequately winterized, and the ravages of the season had damaged parts of the walls and roof.

Steinbeck was already relatively wealthy, and the cottage was much more modest than a man of his means could have afforded. But they had fallen in love with the location—two acres of land with an oak-shrouded garden for Elaine, a bay for Steinbeck, and in a community that reminded him of his beloved Pacific Grove. They had some major work done on the house almost immediately, including turning a screened-in porch into a living room, and the large family room with the fireplace and a vaulted ceiling into a library and study. He placed a powerful telescope there so he could keep an eye on happenings in the harbor. Steinbeck also built, some distance from the main house, a small studio to work in undisturbed. It was a strange-looking building with eight sides and a steep roof and stood like the top of a buried turret or lighthouse poking up out of the ground. It had windows on all sides and a spectacular view of the bay and the harbor beyond. He called it Joyous Garde, after a castle in Malory's *Morte d'Arthur*.

Sag Harbor had once been one of the three greatest whaling ports in the world and the first port of entry into New York. It had been established in 1730, when colonists were still employing Indians on whalers to tow harpooned whales to the beaches for slaughter, something the local Indians had been doing with naturally beached whales for hundreds of years.

Sag Harbor grew into a raucous, rowdy, colorful, and cosmopolitan port, with sailors from all over the world crowded into its noisy, heaving, downtown looking for recreation or a place on a whaler leaving on voyages of up to four years. It had its own red-light district featuring brothels and taverns populated by Indian, European, African, and even Polynesian and Oriental prostitutes. The sailing ships, some of them built from the white oak of nearby Shelter Island, stood three abreast in the port.

The author James Fenimore Cooper lived in Sag Harbor and outfitted his own whaling expedition; he used his experiences to write *The Sea Lions* and *The Spy*. Herman Melville had visited Sag Harbor at the high noon of its whaling days; in *Moby-Dick* Melville had his character Queequeg spend time there, only to conclude, from how the Christian sailors behaved, that it was better to "die a Pagan."

Sag Harbor's fame reached as far as Japan. Trade with the closed society of Japan had been opened by whalers from Sag Harbor in the mid-nineteenth century. Sag Harbor had been a place where the rich shipowners and middle-class tradesmen lived cheek by jowl with the underclass of whaling men.

The streets were a jumble of large fashionable homes—with win-dowed rooms overlooking the bay cut into the roofs so owners could spot returning ships—lowly taverns, music halls, churches, and boarding-houses. After 1847, Sag Harbor's most productive year, the whaling industry and Sag Harbor went into a steep decline from which they never recovered. It was partly due to overkill by the whalers, partly the supplanting of whaling products by petroleum products, and partly the discovery of gold in California, which appeared to offer richer, quicker gains to the hard whaling men. The last whaler left Sag Harbor in 1871 and never returned.

Steinbeck studied Sag Harbor's short, colorful history and was fascinated by the local populace, the thick-skinned, straight-talking descendants of the whalers and coopers and shipwrights of Sag Harbor's glory days. He was later to use Sag Harbor as the model for New Baytown, the setting of what was to be his final novel, *The Winter of Our Discontent*.

The America that had evolved in the first decade following World War II was very different from the America that Steinbeck had built his considerable reputation writing about. There was an unimagined prosperity for a growing middle class. The year Steinbeck bought his Sag Harbor house, the automobile plants of Detroit turned out eight million cars—four times as many as in the twelve months following the war. Only a few thousand families had owned televisions in 1946, but by 1955 stores could not keep up with the demand and manufacturers were making 250,000 per month.

Steinbeck was depressed by the changes. The America he knew was disappearing—the good with the bad. He believed the new medium was already eroding literacy. The man who had written classics of American literature—*Tortilla Flat, Of Mice and Men, The Grapes of Wrath, Cannery Row,* and *East of Eden*—and who had himself become a legend in the process believed he was in danger of becoming an anachronism. Although those works would ensure his literary reputation for generations to come, Steinbeck was terrified by the prospect of trying to match them and never succeeding.

Steinbeck had met Elaine in 1949 when he was in Hollywood finishing the script of the movie *Viva Zapata!* and had recently ended a passionate affair with Paulette Goddard. One night he asked the actress Ann Sothern on a date, and she brought Elaine Scott, wife of the actor Zachary Scott, as a chaperon. Several dates with the two women followed within a week, then Ann Sothern dropped out, leaving the field to Elaine.

He had originally asked Ava Gardner for the date before calling Ann Sothern, but she had been busy, so he thereafter attributed his marriage to Elaine, the mainstay of his last years, to Ava Gardner. Steinbeck had already had two disastrous marriages to volatile women. Elaine Scott's marriage was already effectively over. The Steinbecks were married in December 1950 and made their home in New York City. His new happiness was reflected in a productive period in his creative life. In 1952 he finished *East of Eden.*

On a lengthy trip to Europe in 1954, the year before he took the Sag Harbor house, Steinbeck, then fifty-two, had collapsed with the symptoms of a stroke and been rushed to the hospital. The cause was never discovered. When he moved to Sag Harbor, he was deeply depressed and haunted by the fear that his best work—indeed all of his worthwhile work—might be behind him.

He was unable to bring himself to write much more than magazine articles for *Punch* and *Saturday Review* and short stories for *Atlantic Monthly* that first summer, so the Steinbecks concentrated on becoming part of their new community. Bob Barry, who owned a marina and whose family were prominent Sag Harbor citizens, befriended the Steinbecks and eased their way into acceptance.

Steinbeck soon developed the habits that were to be routine for the next decade. He would rise early, drive into town with his dog, pick up the newspaper and his mail, stroll along Main Street window-shopping, then breakfast with the regulars at a coffee shop before returning to Joyous Garde to write. In the evenings he would drive back into town to meet Bob Barry or other friends for beer at the Black Buoy or Sal and Joe's.

Often when he was not writing he would take his boat out, sometimes with Barry, who was an accomplished fisherman. That year he wrote of taking his boat beyond Montauk Point, some thirty miles away, to fish: "We bring them home alive, and we cook them while they are still kicking and they are delicious. The Atlantic is very much richer...than the Pacific. Lobster, crabs, clams, oysters and many kinds of fish. I really love it out here." Steinbeck never did catch many fish, but he loved exploring the Hamptons' shallow coves and hidden inlets.

That first summer, Steinbeck organized a party at his home for all the Sag Harbor citizens and a handful of Hamptons literati that he had gotten to know in the few weeks he had lived there. He called it the "Sag Harbor Yacht Club Dry Regatta," but it was only dry inasmuch as it was held on land. It left Steinbeck and, it is said, scores of others in Sag Harbor in bed with epic hangovers for two days. He preferred the company of his Sag Harbor neighbors and a small number of literary friends and visitors to the Hamptons social set.

He routinely turned down invitations to social gatherings in Southampton and East Hampton, although his fame ensured that the invitations would contine to arrive. He even turned down an invitation to a party for Britain's Princess Margaret that socialites were feuding over attending. Two of his closest friends were John Fisher, an interior decorator from Bridgehampton, and his wife, Shirley, who was a literary agent. The couples established a routine of spending Fridays at the Fishers' house and Saturdays at the Steinbecks'.

Although the cottage was still only fit for occupation in the summer, the Steinbecks stayed in it part of the following winter and his depression lifted. He wrote to a friend: "I get the old sense of peace and wholeness [here]. The phone rings seldom. It is clear and very cold but the house is warm. Elaine is ecstatically happy out here.... You can't imagine the change in disposition and approach in all of us. And it seems to be getting into my work. I approach the table every morning with a sense of joy."

Steinbeck worked on an experimental novel that he eventually discontinued and a poorly received satire, *The Short Reign of Pippin IV,* that his publisher, Viking, tried hard to persuade him not to release. Then he began work on what he believed would be a relatively straightforward project: a translation into modern prose of Malory's *Morte d'Arthur*. The classic tale of King Arthur had always been close to Steinbeck's heart. It was one of the first books he had read, and he returned to it again and again. But the task of capturing it in modern prose while retaining the color and appeal of the original haunted him for the rest of his life.

He traveled to England to read and copy original manuscripts and toured places Malory would have been familiar with. He bought a microfilm reader to work from copies of rare manuscripts of *Morte d'Arthur* in Sag Harbor, and even discovered a lost original manuscript and a lost fifteenth-century work of scholarship on Arthur. He intended to write an introduction to each story and to publish a journal as a running commentary, as well as copious annotations. He invested so much time and energy and money in the project that friends suggested he was trying to avoid working on anything else. Steinbeck, however, believed it would be the climax and the monument of his career.

After several unsatisfactory drafts, he unhappily put Arthur aside to work on *The Winter of Our Discontent,* a story about an honest man's crisis of conscience in a town where he witnesses numerous examples of profitable corruption. It was set in a town clearly modeled on Sag Harbor and used several neighbors and local acquaintances as well as himself and his family as characters. The story's events took place between Easter weekend and July fourth, and Steinbeck meticulously incorporated even the day-by-day Sag Harbor weather during that period into it.

The late fifties and early sixties were the height of "nuclear jitters." The fear of imminent nuclear Armageddon was almost universal, and it was fueled by routine civil defense drills in which schoolchildren practiced diving under desks to escape atomic flashes. Cities designated underground parking lots and skyscraper basements as nuclear shelters and stocked them with water and crackers. Nuclear testing was commonplace and sometimes used to manipulate political crises. Suburban families installed underground shelters in back yards and built sandbag emplacements in their dens and basements. People even bought a variety of firearms to defend their shelters from others who lacked their foresight and to "keep order" after the war.

Steinbeck was skeptical about the ability of U.S. politicians to avoid a nuclear war and created his own plan to survive it with his circle of family and friends. He decided the Hamptons was safe from nuclear attack, and he issued invitations to those of his New York friends he wanted to join him when the bomb dropped. Steinbeck reconnoitered the entire route from New York City to Sag Harbor and chose a series of hiding places for a relay of vehicles, starting in Queens. The Steinbeck refugees were to swim the East River, search for the vehicles using a map Steinbeck had provided, and struggle out to the Hamptons. He even stressed that the refugees were to drink and eat nothing until they had crossed the Shinnecock Canal into the Hamptons, as everything west of that line was likely to have been contaminated by radiation.

Steinbeck's fears about nuclear war came to a head during the Cuban missile crisis of October 1962. Steinbeck, like millions of other Americans, believed only a miracle could prevent the confrontation from escalating into war, and he followed the evolving crisis closely. He turned on the television news one morning for the latest developments and heard something that stunned him almost as much as a declaration of war.

A news anchor was announcing that John Steinbeck had been awarded the Nobel Prize for Literature. The telephone began to ring almost immediately; after each call it would ring again, so that it became almost impossible to call anyone. Afraid that Sag Harbor was about to be invaded by an army of reporters, Elaine put the breakfast she had been cooking, still in the frying pan, into the refrigerator, and they set off for New York City and a press conference at Viking.

Back in Sag Harbor the next day, Steinbeck came back down to earth. The *New York Times* slammed the Nobel Prize Committee for awarding Steinbeck literature's most coveted accolade. "The award of the Nobel Prize for Literature to John Steinbeck," the *Times* said in an editorial, "will focus attention once again on a writer who, though still in full career, produced his major work more than two decades ago.... Without detracting in the least from Mr. Steinbeck's accomplishments, we think it interesting that the laurel was not awarded to a writer—a poet or critic or historian—whose significance, influence and sheer body of work had already made a more profound impression on the literature of our age."

The assault was the first of many. Almost all the major newspapers and magazines came out against the award because Steinbeck had never, in his critics' eyes, matched the achievements of *The Grapes of Wrath*. *Time* magazine, which had made attacking Steinbeck almost a tradition, joined the chorus, and it did not die down in the days that followed. On the eve of the presentation of the prize itself, an article in the *New York Times* suggested the Nobel Prize Committee had given the award to a writer whose "limited talent" was "watered down by tenth-rate philosophizing."

Steinbeck became a recluse in Sag Harbor while the battle raged, trying to compose an acceptance speech that would serve as a rejoinder. What hurt most about the stinging criticism was Steinbeck's own inner fears that it might be correct. He was also acutely aware that the prize had brought a curtain down on the careers of earlier recipients William Faulkner and Ernest Hemingway. Steinbeck hated public speaking and public appearances generally, and the thought of having to make a speech at the Nobel Prize award ceremony, particularly in circumstances this controversial, terrified him. He sought help from speechwriters, friends, and politicians, but they had little to offer.

Steinbeck composed his final draft the night before he left Sag Harbor for the journey to Stockholm. He did not refer to the avalanche of criticism over the award, but he did speak of literary critics as "a pale and emasculated priesthood singing their litanies in empty churches" and a "cloistered elect, the tinhorn mendicants of low-calorie despair." On the way home, Elaine accidentally put the Nobel Prize check in the garbage and had to retrieve it.

A few months later, in May 1963, Steinbeck awoke in great pain and unable to see out of one eye. He was taken to Southampton Hospital, where he underwent an operation to repair a detached retina. The period of recovery was more of an ordeal than the surgery itself. He had to lie blindfolded and immobile for several weeks. His friend, the writer John O'Hara, whom he had met years before when O'Hara was commissioned to dramatize a Steinbeck novel, came to read to him every day.

Even after his release from the hospital, recuperation was slow and painful. For many more weeks he had to wear blindfolds with pinholes to gradually acclimatize to light and to retrain his damaged eye.

After his recovery, Steinbeck was recruited into one of his few forays into politics. Steinbeck's work was highly political—one reason why it was so controversial and criticism of him so bitter—but he generally shied away from the politics of committees and organizations. He had supported Eisenhower, then switched his allegiance to Adlai Stevenson primarily in admiration of his elegantly composed speeches. He also supported Stevenson over Kennedy, largely on the basis of his disdain for Kennedy's father, Joseph P. Kennedy. However, a Kennedy apparatchik, economist John Kenneth Galbraith, was a friend of Steinbeck's and had persuaded him to attend Kennedy's inaugural ball.

In 1963, Edward R. Murrow persuaded the sixty-one-year-old Steinbeck to join a number of other writers on a United States Information Service tour of Eastern Europe and the Soviet Union. The Americans wanted Steinbeck because he could be shown off as a liberal who had criticized the U.S. government and its policies and received accolades, in stark contrast to the treatment of Soviet writers who criticized the Communist regime. Indeed, the writings of Steinbeck had been widely used in the USSR to paint a negative picture of the United States and capitalism. It was, of course, an incomplete picture, which focused on a particular period in U.S. history, the thirties.

The Soviets wanted him, too; because Steinbeck had been an outspoken critic of life in the United States in the past, any discussion of his books with other writers was bound to lead to a repetition of those criticisms, which could be used to support the official Communist line. As a result, Steinbeck walked a tightrope throughout the tour and found himself being used as a Cold War pawn. During the trip he expressed his fury at the Soviet authorities for pirating his books. His major novels were all bestsellers in the USSR, and he had never received a cent in royalties. He even discovered that one of his books was being produced as a play without his permission.

While the Steinbecks were away, President Kennedy was assassinated, and on their return to Sag Harbor, they wrote two letters. One was to Jackie Kennedy, whom they had met at Kennedy's inaugural ball, offering their condolences. The other was to President Lyndon B. Johnson offering their best wishes and support. Elaine Steinbeck had known Lady Bird Johnson at college.

The letter to Jackie resulted in a visit with the widowed First Lady at her house on N Street in Washington—her first home after leaving the White House. It was an emotional scene. Elaine Steinbeck was so upset by the assassination and her meeting with the president's widow that Jackie asked her to leave for a while because if there was any crying, she, Jackie, would fall apart and she was trying to hang on to her composure. The trio talked about the Hamptons, as all of them knew the area well, and Jackie described her childhood in East Hampton. Then Jackie made an astonishing request. She asked Steinbeck if he would write John Kennedy's biography and offered to make all his personal papers, diaries, and whatever presidential documents she could available to him, as well as smoothing the way for interviews with his family, friends, and staff.

The conceit that the Kennedy years had amounted to a heroic moment in American history—Camelot—had already been established by Jackie Kennedy. Only a week after the assassination she had given an interview at the Kennedy compound in Hyannis Port to Theodore White, who was writing an article about the Kennedy administration for *Life* magazine. She had compared the Kennedy White House to Camelot—not the Camelot of Arthurian legend but the Camelot of the Broadway show, which had been a favorite of the president's.

Now, coincidentally, she was asking Steinbeck, who had struggled to retell the *Morte d'Arthur* in modern prose, to lend his literary skills to securing the modern Camelot myth. The idea appealed to Steinbeck, and over the next several months they discussed the project several times in letters, phone calls, and meetings. However, the book was never written.

Jackie eventually asked William Manchester to write a definitive account of the assassination, and he suspended work on another book to complete it. Prior to its publication by Harper & Row and its serialization in *Look* magazine, Jackie and Bobby Kennedy sought an injunction to prevent publication. She had said things of a personal nature during long emotional interviews that she now regretted. It has been claimed that she had been drunk during some of the interviews.

Steinbeck, now sixty-two years old, found he was unable to do any satisfactory work and threw himself into daily life in Sag Harbor. He became involved in the planning for the Sag Harbor Old Whalers Festival, which celebrated the town's raunchy past. He brought action and spice—and tourist dollars—to a civic celebration that until then had amounted to not much more than a parade. He organized an annual debate between Nantucket and Sag Harbor on which of the two whaling ports had had more significance, founded an annual international whaleboat race, and organized an extravagant fireworks display—which, as Sag Harbor's own living legend, he set off himself with some panache. He also tried to persuade President Johnson to attend the festival. Instead, Johnson sent a naval vessel.

Most of the literary, artistic, and academic establishment who had been close to Kennedy had ignored Johnson, whom they regarded as an intellectual lightweight in comparison to Kennedy. Steinbeck's simple gesture of support in the first days of his presidency and Elaine's college connection to Lady Bird sparked a close friendship between the Johnsons and the Steinbecks.

It was this friendship and Steinbeck's personal loyalty to Johnson that led Steinbeck into one of the most controversial and uncharacteristic campaigns of his distinguished career. Johnson first invited the Steinbecks to the White House in 1964 to talk about his trip to Eastern Europe and for Lady Bird to renew her acquaintance with Elaine. The evening went well, and afterward President Johnson spontaneously walked the Steinbecks to their hotel, as horrified Secret Service agents scattered along Pennsylvania Avenue.

The Steinbecks became frequent visitors at the White House thereafter. When Johnson was elected to the presidency in his own right in 1964, Steinbeck helped draft his inauguration speech, and Johnson appointed him to the Council for the National Endowment of the Arts.

Johnson's liberal policies, his realization of Kennedy's civil rights program, and his war on poverty were overshadowed by his escalation of the Vietnam War. The war dominated all news broadcasts and front pages, obscuring Johnson's real achievements. Many creative people had abandoned their support for Johnson because of Vietnam, and Steinbeck stood out as one who had not. Johnson had little time for poets and novelists; his friendship with Steinbeck was a striking exception. Without any prodding at first, Steinbeck began to defend Johnson and his Vietnam policies in print, condemning antiwar protesters he would almost certainly have supported, or at least defended, at an earlier time in his life. His campaign began with a column in the Long Island newspaper *Newsday*.

Then, in 1966, Steinbeck's son John wrote to him from boot camp, where he was completing basic training, and asked Steinbeck to use his influence with the president to ensure that he was sent to Vietnam in a combat role and not protected because he was Steinbeck's son. Although he feared for his son's life, Steinbeck agreed to help. Later he received a moving letter from the president expressing admiration for the younger Steinbeck's bravery. "I shall pray for his safe and swift return to you," Johnson wrote, adding: "Your own wise words of encouragement are a great source of comfort to me." Steinbeck, now with a personal interest, took the remark as a cue.

The Sag Harbor house became the headquarters of a personal prowar propaganda campaign as Steinbeck stepped up his defense of the war in print, in letters to friends, and in conversation. Just as loud was his conspicuous aloofness from other writers' condemnations of the war. He called the antiwar protesters "sour-smelling wastelings [with] ill-favored and barren pad-mates." They were "Vietnicks," and their attempts to stop the war were "shuffling, drag-ass protests" that gave him "a shiver of shame." The soldiery in Vietnam, however, gave him "a quick glow of pride...in just belonging to the same species as these men."

There was widespread criticism of his stance and his proximity to Johnson. It came from as far away as Moscow, where the Russian poet Yevgeny Yevtushenko published a poem condemning Steinbeck. It was translated and published in the *New York Times*. He referred to a remark Steinbeck had made to dissident writers in Moscow in 1963: "Little wolves, show me your teeth."

> *Understand, I cannot remain silent and isolated.*
> *Yes, we are little wolves.*
> *But John, you're an old wolf.*
> *So show your teeth.*
> *The teeth of Steinbeck.*

Steinbeck sent Yevtushenko a reply condemning what he said was China and Russia's responsibility for the war because of their arms shipments to the North Vietnamese. He defended American bombing of North Vietnam, which he maintained was limited to oil depots, transportation, and military installations, despite irrefutable evidence to the contrary. A heavily edited version of the letter was published in Moscow—the Russians had not admitted giving military aid to North Vietnam—alongside a *Life* magazine picture of Vietnamese victims of American napalm bombing.

The more loudly Steinbeck was criticized for his views, the more entrenched his position became and the more vociferously he expressed it. In fact, he was naive about some of the crucial aspects of the war, having ceased to watch what he believed were biased television reports. He was jolted by a letter from his son in Vietnam, who told him that the war was not as simple an exercise in defending democracy as he had thought nor as clearly justified as he, Steinbeck, was saying. Steinbeck resolved to go to Vietnam to see for himself.

Steinbeck got himself and Elaine accredited as correspondents in Vietnam for *Newsday,* and they left for the war zone in December 1966, stopping in Hawaii on the way to mark the twenty-fifth anniversary of Pearl Harbor. While Elaine attended press conferences and briefings in

Saigon, Steinbeck, then sixty-four years old, threw himself into frontline reporting.

At that point in the war an important U.S. offensive was in progress. Accompanied by a major in the Military Office of Information, Steinbeck went on combat missions, deep reconnaissance patrols, air strikes, and ground assaults, traveling for days at a time, returning to Saigon for a day or sometimes less, then setting off again for the action. Some of the missions were so hazardous that the military men involved were volunteers.

One night, Steinbeck and his son found themselves together on a mountainside, defending a military outpost, with Steinbeck armed with an M-79 covering his son from an unprotected position above him. It would all have been a grueling experience for a man twenty years younger. His time in Vietnam lasted for six weeks.

If his defense of the war in dispatches from Sag Harbor seemed hawkish, then his bellicose dispatches from the paddies and hamlets of Vietnam sounded like belligerent enthusiasm. He had always been fascinated by weaponry and military hardware and could not resist describing weapons in admiring detail. That fascination and his real affection and respect for the young men who were fighting the war permeated his reports. His impressions were underlined by photographs showing Steinbeck in combat gear, sometimes toting an M-16 or peering along the business end of an M-60. In contrast with the gallantry of American troops, the Viet Cong were portrayed as terrorists, devoid of support among the people whose hope of freedom lay solely with American escalation of the war.

Steinbeck also went on classified military missions into Laos and discovered that the United States had been secretly bombing villages the Viet Cong were using as bases. At that time, the American public was unaware that the war had been spread to neighboring Laos and that a supposedly neutral country was being bombed. Steinbeck did not write about the discovery or the secret military missions.

His dispatches caused an uproar in the United States. Antiwar activists accused him of treason to his own past. It was not uncommon at gatherings of writers and journalists for fistfights to break out when Steinbeck's name came up.

Back in Sag Harbor, Steinbeck defended his visit to Vietnam and his prowar dispatches. He wrote in *Newsday:* "I have been accused of being a war-monger, of favoring war and even celebrating it.... What I have been celebrating is not war but brave men."

But his support of the war and his disdain for the antiwar movement proved more visceral. He was dismayed by what he saw, or thought he saw, America becoming. He wrote from Sag Harbor to a friend who was returning from Vietnam: "The long-haired men and short-haired women who prowl the streets make the V.C. look like friendlies. If you have any regard for your personal safety you will stay where you are."

Steinbeck was invited to the White House to discuss his trip to Vietnam. President Johnson had read and, understandably, approved of his dispatches. Steinbeck made numerous suggestions. The Viet Cong used captured American ordnance, and Steinbeck wanted U.S. shells booby-trapped and left for capture. He believed a complex series of massive bombing missions would draw the North Vietnamese to the conference table, and he had ideas about persuading Viet Cong deserters and prisoners to fight for the United States. His ideas were transcribed, classified "Secret—Eyes Only," and discussed by Defense Secretary Robert McNamara and General William Westmoreland.

Steinbeck was exhausted by his foray into Vietnam, disheartened by the hostile reaction to his stance, and weakened by back problems—he had slipped a disc helping someone lift a heavy load. Heavily medicated, forced to rest, and unable to sit up to write, Steinbeck spent weeks in Sag Harbor that spring and summer of 1967 with little else to do but think on the complex drama he had witnessed and the escalating protest back home.

Gradually he came to believe that U.S. involvement in Vietnam was a mistake, not because it was morally wrong—he retained his admiration for the soldiers doing the fighting—but because the war was unwinnable. This view is reflected in letters to friends from Sag Harbor. He refrained from publishing his new position partly out of embarrassment at appearing to ally himself with "doves" that he despised, and partly out of loyalty to Johnson, but he made plans for a new novel, set in Vietnam.

Steinbeck's health quickly began to deteriorate, however. He underwent a grueling operation on his back and shortly following recovery, he had a minor stroke and was admitted to Southampton Hospital. Soon after that he had a heart attack, and during the course of his treatment it was discovered that the sixty-five-year-old Steinbeck had emphysema. Also, his arteries were so clogged that the main vessels from the heart had been reduced to the width of a sewing needle.

He was offered a bypass operation, common today but still being developed in the sixties, and he turned it down. He told his doctor that it

was his time to die. In August 1968, Steinbeck left the hospital and
returned to Sag Harbor. Elaine Steinbeck had taken a crash course in
nursing to see him through what they both knew were his final weeks.
He was no longer able to work. Several times a day he would have to
take oxygen from canisters strategically located in the house. There
were few outings, but twice a week he went to Southampton Hospital
for examinations. In the evenings he would watch television with the
sound turned down and make up the dialogue. Many nights there were
breathing problems, which Elaine nursed him through. Usually the
Steinbecks returned to New York in October, but they stretched the
season as long as they could. In mid-November, Steinbeck was so weak
that he needed expert daily attention. They closed up the Sag Harbor
house and returned to New York, Steinbeck taking one final look back
at the idyllic retreat where he had spent the last thirteen years. He knew
he would never see it again. Five weeks later, on December 20, 1968, he
died in his sleep in his New York apartment with Elaine lying beside
him.

CHAPTER 4

The Rise and Fall of Truman Capote

Truman Capote floated lazily on his back in the sky-blue waters of the spacious swimming pool of Gloria Vanderbilt's sprawling Southampton mansion. He was describing in detail the men and women who had been models for the characters in a novel Capote passionately believed would secure his literary reputation for generations to come. The listener, who had read parts of the manuscript Capote had not yet completed, was his friend Gerald Clarke, a journalist with *Time* magazine.

Gloria Vanderbilt and her fourth husband, Wyatt Cooper, were conveniently in Paris. Capote, who lived in much less imposing style in nearby Sagaponack, had brought Clarke with him to avail himself of her hospitality in her absence while at the same time gleefully detailing his betrayal of her and others. Clarke, who would later recount the incident in his monumental biography of Capote, listened intently to the names of the friends Capote had used and abused in his manuscript.

"All the plots are real," Capote insisted. "I haven't made up a thing. And it's going to be easy. It's all in my head."

"But Truman," Clarke said after Capote had finished listing his dramatis personae, "they're not going to like this."

"Nah," replied Capote as he floated, gazing serenely into a cloudless sky. "They are too dumb. They won't know who they are."

The novel that Capote and Clarke were discussing was to become one of the most controversial works of fiction in American publishing history: *Answered Prayers*. It was a novel Capote had been planning for years: a gossipy, sordid, malicious roman à clef, detailing the deepest secrets of Capote's wealthy and socially prominent friends, many of whom lived in the Hamptons' great houses—from Gloria Vanderbilt, whose Southampton pool he was floating in so serenely, to CBS founder William S. Paley, for whom Capote had developed a secret and violently jealous hatred.

The title came from a quotation from St. Teresa of Ávila: "More tears are shed over answered prayers than unanswered ones." He had been planning the book for seventeen years, virtually his entire literary life, mentioning notes and outlines for plots as early as 1959.

Capote had become an international figure at the age of twenty-four with the publication of his first novel, *Other Voices, Other Rooms,* in 1948. The New Orleans–born author went on to write a number of short stories, movie scripts, and novellas while systematically developing an astonishing circle of rich, powerful, and famous friends.

He was a witty and entertaining guest at the best dinner tables in Manhattan and the Hamptons; he was fashionably in demand for parties, for weekends, for seasons in the ritziest resorts, and long cruises on immaculate yachts. He shared gossip and secrets, primarily with the wives of his wealthy hosts. He was part court jester, part lapdog, part friend, but after virtually every function, every event, every soiree, if he was sober enough, he made fresh entries in diaries and journals for later use.

In the summer of 1957, Capote and his friends, Jack Dunphy, who was to be his closest companion throughout the rest of his life, and Oliver Smith rented a large Victorian house in Bridgehampton. It stood in the shallow, booming surf on stilts; when the tide was in, the water came up so high that the house looked as if it were about to sail away— and, in fact, the owners had dubbed the home Sailaway. The three worked above the water all summer on their various projects—Dunphy on a stage play, Oliver Smith on some set designs, and Capote on *Breakfast at Tiffany's.*

Breakfast at Tiffany's was published the following year in *Esquire* after *Harper's Bazaar* had deemed it too risqué, even after considerable rewriting. Although it is chiefly remembered today for the 1961 film version starring Audrey Hepburn, the novella became a small classic, cemented his literary reputation, and made him a fortune.

In 1964, having rented Sailaway and other summer homes for years, Capote bought two neighboring houses in the Hamptons village of Sagaponack, one for himself and one for Dunphy. Capote's home was a small boxy structure in a field about a hundred yards from the ocean. It had a large, open living room with a high, vaulted ceiling and a small bedroom downstairs. A spiral staircase led to three tiny upstairs rooms, which Capote later turned into one room. It was because the house was so claustrophobic that he bought the neighboring home, shrouded by trees and bushes, for Dunphy. It gave them the security and intimacy of living together and the privacy of living apart. Capote, in a gesture of generosity, gave Dunphy the deed to both houses.

By the time he purchased the Sagaponack homes, Capote was finishing work on the book for which he is most famous, In Cold Blood, the detailed, haunting account of a bloody and senseless crime that first caught Capote's imagination when he read a short news item buried in the New York Times. For six years, helped by Harper Lee, author of To Kill a Mockingbird, Capote had followed the case of the two young criminals, Perry Smith and Dick Hickock, who had brutally murdered a wealthy farmer and his wife and children in a small Kansas town. He ultimately witnessed their grisly executions by hanging.

Capote's work on the murders first appeared as a series of articles in the New Yorker and the book, In Cold Blood, was published early in 1966. It combined the techniques of fiction, the skills of a screenwriter, and the disciplines of journalism. It was one of the most thoroughly hyped publishing events of the century. Capote is said to have made two million dollars in 1966, the first year of publication. That year was to be both the pinnacle of his success and the start of his steep decline. Early in January 1966, Capote signed a contract for Answered Prayers which gave him a twenty-five thousand dollar advance and two years to finish the book. In Cold Blood immediately soared into the best seller lists where it was to stay until the fall, selling 300,000 copies that year. It ultimately sold five million copies worldwide.

Capote was on the cover of every news magazine and became a talk-show celebrity and a sought-after lecture-circuit speaker. He also became an instant expert on the criminal justice system in all fifty states, although he actually knew very little about the subject. If he was a star before In Cold Blood, he reached almost legendary status after its publication. "People didn't invite Truman to lunches or parties or for weekends," says one close friend. "They literally beseeched him to come." By the spring, Capote's face, frame, gait, and high-pitched nasal drawl were as familiar to people who had never read a word he had written as to those who had.

Basking in this glory, Capote dreamed up an event that was to be part celebration of his success and part public prank on his rich and powerful friends. His oldest friend was editor and publisher Eleanor Friede, and, lying by the pool at her home in Bridgehampton one summer afternoon, he came up with the idea for what was to be the social event of the decade: the Black and White Ball.

The idea was to stage a lavish ball for five hundred people, all of them personally approved by Capote, not primarily because he admired them, but because they admired him. They would be an eclectic mix, reflecting the spectrum of Capote's social circle: members of his family, or rather the few he kept in touch with, farmer friends from Sagaponack, politicians, business tycoons, TV, movie, and Broadway stars, socialites, literary lions, European aristocrats, and doormen from his apartment building. He chose as the setting the grand ballroom of the Plaza Hotel, and as guest of honor he selected Katherine Graham, the owner of the *Washington Post,* then just emerging as a social and political force.

The point, for Capote, was to stage a party so chic and so apparently exclusive that people would be begging him for invitations. It was to be a masked ball, an antiquated concept in which, at least theoretically, people would mix socially and perhaps even more intimately without ever knowing the identity of their partners. He maintained total control, insisting that the men wear black and the women white or black and carry a fan, a concept inspired by the "Ascot Gavotte" scene in *My Fair Lady,* which had been designed by Capote's friend Cecil Beaton. Invitations were for one: no one was allowed to bring a companion or date unless he or she had been individually invited to the ball. Wives were invited without husbands, if Capote felt like it, and husbands without wives.

Using Friede's home in the Hamptons as a sort of battle HQ, Capote spent the summer gleefully exercising absolute power: a multimillionaire would be excised from his guest list with a sweep of his hand; a handsome young waiter's name would be added. He even controlled the preball dinners, down to who would sit with whom. Such capriciousness might have been expected to turn off most of his guests. It merely added to the party's social luster. By the end of the summer, as Capote predicted, people were prepared to donate kidneys if necessary for an invitation.

One Hamptons socialite who had been left off the guest list

threatened to stage a rival party with Jacqueline Kennedy as guest of honor in an attempt to siphon off guests from Capote's ball, but she quickly backed off. Even the presence of the widowed First Lady, who in any case was not in New York that week, was unlikely to be much competition.

The party was staged on November 28, 1966. The first guests to push their way through a press of photographers, society reporters, fashion critics, and television news crews were announced at the entrance to the ballroom: the maharajah and maharani of Jaipur. In the next thirty minutes, in one of the most diverse social gatherings in history, hundreds of celebrities were announced at the door: from Frank Sinatra to Rose Kennedy; from historian Arthur Schlesinger Jr. to Jerome Robbins; from Gloria Vanderbilt to Lynda Bird Johnson. Katherine Graham danced with the doorman of the UN Plaza apartment building; a famous television actress went home to bed with a bouncer she thought was a glitterati guest. And Capote, overseeing the proceedings, was in his element.

But there was an underlying hostility in the organization of the ball that betrayed Capote's ambivalence toward the people whose friendship and patronage he had courted and with whom he had surrounded himself. That deep-rooted hostility was fueling his plans for *Answered Prayers*.

Those plans kept being pushed back. His 1968 deadline came and went, and in 1969 his contract was renegotiated for a 1973 delivery. This was later renegotiated again for 1974 and again for delivery in 1977. Although Capote began to sift and file and index his copious notes and detailed journals in 1968, he did not get around to writing a word until 1972. Throughout this time, Capote continued to write other, quite insubstantial articles, short stories, and novellas, some of which had been dug up from his files of unpublished material and none of which added to his literary reputation. His distractions were many, including an escalating drug and alcohol habit and a number of tempestuous homosexual affairs. He installed one of his lovers, a married former banker, in a rented house in the Hamptons.

Late in 1974 he began showing a small circle of trusted literary friends individual chapters from his long-planned book. He published one of these chapters in *Esquire* in 1975 to wide acclaim. Having promised more, he plucked another chapter, called "La Côte Basque," from his unfinished manuscript and gave it to *Esquire*. That's when the roof caved in.

"La Côte Basque" is set in the chic Manhattan restaurant of that name on East 55th Street. The action takes place over lunch with P. B. Jones, the novel's protagonist, and Lady Ina Coolbirth, an American socialite married to a British aristocrat, gossiping about their friends and acquaintances. Various real people make cameo appearances: Princess Radziwill, Jackie Kennedy, Gloria Vanderbilt, Carol Matthau, and many others. The "fictional" characters are so clearly defined that, even if they were as dumb as Capote said they were, they could not fail to recognize themselves.

Lady Ina Coolbirth, for example, had grown up on a western ranch and, now in her forties, was married to an English knight, the latest of a string of husbands. She is unmistakably "Slim" Keith, one of Capote's oldest and closest society friends, who happened to have been raised on a western ranch and was married to an English knight. Lady Coolbirth entertains Jones with several short and pithy observations about their society friends and with two long anecdotes.

One is the bawdy story of Sidney Dillon, a married tycoon with powerful political contacts. Dillon, who is portrayed as a Jew with WASP pretensions, has a brief affair with a the wife of a former governor of New York. He finds he has to scrub the evidence of his infidelity from the bedsheets "like a Spanish peasant" and bake them in the oven to dry because he is expecting his own wife back next morning.

The Sidney Dillon character is recognizably CBS founder Bill Paley. Capote describes Dillon's deceived wife, Cleo, as "the most beautiful creature alive"—a phrase he used to describe Paley's wife Babe. Capote resented Paley's wealth and political power and was intensely jealous of his marriage to Babe and incensed at what Capote imagined was his mistreatment of her.

More vicious still, and more tragic in its consequences, is the other anecdote that Lady Coolbirth tells Jones. For years Capote had been fascinated by a society scandal from the 1950s that had reverberated through New York and Hamptons society: what *Life* magazine had described as "the Shooting of the Century."

Billy Woodward, the scion of a wealthy New York banking family and the owner of a popular and successful race horse, Nashua, had married a beautiful, seductive former model, Ann Crowell, who came from a poor Kansas family. The marriage was frowned on by Billy's mother, Elsie Woodward, a New York, Hamptons, and Rhode Island social grande dame whose family had helped found some of the Hamptons' social institutions. It also triggered fits of jealousy and outrage among the society women who had failed to interest Billy Woodward enough for him to marry one of them.

The marriage was volatile, not least because violent arguments became a kind of foreplay for the Woodwards. They slept apart, but they would have sex in the afternoons, often after some loud and physical disagreement. They each also had affairs—he with a European princess, and she with Britain's Lord Astor and the Aly Khan.

In October 1955 the Woodwards, who were then living in a mansion on Long Island's North Shore, attended a lavish dinner party given for the duke and duchess of Windsor. After returning home, Ann Woodward shot her husband dead and told police she had been disturbed by a prowler and fired blindly down a dark corridor separating their bedrooms.

Although she was cleared by a police investigation and by a grand jury, the suspicion that Ann Woodward had murdered her husband, and the guilt she in any case felt at having killed him, overshadowed the rest of her life. She left her children in the charge of her mother-in-law and went into a social exile. She roamed the earth's rich playgrounds, awaking in an alcoholic haze in the beds of a succession of both wealthy and poor men, each more unsuitable than the last. The shooting had virtually been forgotten when Truman Capote, obsessed with the sordid details of Ann Woodward's peripatetic sex life for twenty years, resurrected it.

He is alleged to have actually run across Ann Woodward only once. In a bar in Biarritz—it's St. Moritz in some versions—someone pointed out Truman Capote to Ann, and she replied, "That faggot!" in his hearing. In retaliation, Capote is said to have made a pistol with his finger and thumb and gestured as if to fire at her.

His actual shot, in "La Côte Basque," portrays Ann—he didn't even bother to change her given name—as a former prostitute and sexual adventuress whose career follows an upward path through various beds until she reels in the big fish, one of society's most eligible bachelors. Her husband discovers she never legally dissolved a marriage she had contracted as a teenager. Rather than be left destitute, she kills him and makes up a story about a prowler. Her mother-in-law stands by her for the sake of the grandchildren and the family name. Lady Coolbirth, who tells this story to P. B. Jones, concludes with a rhetorical question about what the two women talk about when they are alone.

Capote, who had boasted that none of the events in *Answered Prayers* had been invented, seemed to believe, or at least asked others to believe, that his version of the Woodward story was the truth. However, for years he had told stories about Ann Woodward that were pure fantasy. At one dinner party at Gloria Vanderbilt's Southampton mansion, he claimed Ann had snared Billy Woodward with Byzantine sexual techniques she had learned in a brothel. He claimed that he alone had discovered the motive for the murder: that she had been married to a police officer in California and was still legally married to him, making her marriage to Woodward invalid.

In fact, Capote's version of events—like a later fictional version, *The Two Mrs. Grenvilles* by Dominick Dunne—ignored crucial facts of the Woodward case. Not only had there actually been a prowler at the Woodward home and other North Shore mansions that night, he had been caught and confessed to having fled the house when he heard the fatal gunshot. Paul Wirths had served a prison sentence for burglary.

What Billy Woodward had discovered about his wife's impoverished past was not a husband but a father. She had told everyone her estranged father was dead, but Billy found he was a streetcar conductor and so far removed from his daughter's life that he thought his long-lost offspring was the actress Eve Arden. Not the stuff of divorce and murder. However, even today, the Capote and Dunne versions are usually accepted as being closer to the truth than the more mundane facts of the case.

Ann Woodward happened to be in New York when she was given an advance copy of *Esquire*. After reading Capote's warped account of the shooting and realizing that the incident she had spent twenty years living down was to be regurgitated in such a libelous form, she committed suicide with an overdose of Seconal. The consequences for Capote were less extreme but in a way equally tragic. When the magazine was published in November, Capote's social world collapsed around him. Capote's friend Slim Keith—"Big Mama," as he called her—had been warned that she was portrayed in "La Côte Basque," but she had expected some sort of valedictory cameo. She was horrified by her portrayal as Lady Coolbirth, who gossiped so relentlessly and so cruelly.

"I was absolutely undone," she said later. "I was staggered that he could be sitting across from me at a table and then would go home and write down everything I had said." Joshua Logan, whose parties are the butt of one of Gloria Vanderbilt's witty asides in "La Côte Basque," called Capote "that dirty little toad." Gloria Vanderbilt took an oath that if she ever saw Capote again she would spit in his face. The number one gossip columnist in America, Liz Smith, summed up the outrage that rang from Manhattan's East Side to East Hampton: "Never have you heard such gnashing of teeth, such cries for revenge, such shouts of betrayal, and such screams of outrage."

Even those who were not lampooned in "La Côte Basque" were offended by its tone and by the realization that Capote, whom they had imagined as one of them, was an interloper after all—and one filled with venom. In an instant, relationships decades old were ended. Doors that had been open and welcoming were slammed shut; calls that were once instantly returned were ignored.

Capote was in Los Angeles when, as a Sagaponack neighbor put it, "the chic hit the fan." Naively, Capote had supposed that one or two of his friends would be annoyed by their portrayals, those he intended to offend would be offended, and the others would think it marvelous fun. "What did they expect?" he kept saying as he stumbled around Joanne Carson's house, where he was a guest. "They all know I'm a writer! What did they expect?"

Returning to Sagaponack, Capote tried to repair some of the damage. He called Slim Keith, but she refused for days to speak to him. He had one of his lovers call her and beg her to forgive Capote while he listened on an extension.

"Truman thought it would make you laugh!" he said.

"Well, it didn't," she said. "It's just junk." She heard Capote's breathing on the other end of the line and hung up. Later Capote sent her a telegram: "Big Mama, I've decided to forgive you—Love, Truman." She did not respond. Later she told people that she had decided to behave as if he had died. "I took a cleaver and chopped him out of my life," she said.

However, she actually did contact him once more, years later: a relative of Capote's had written a largely invented account of Truman's childhood notable for a malicious portrayal of his mother, and Slim Keith sent him a note in Sagaponack saying, "It was so amusing to read of your pathetic antecedents."

Capote also called Bill Paley, whom he had intentionally offended, but Paley feigned ignorance. "I started to read it but I fell asleep. Then the magazine got thrown away," he told him. Babe Paley, who was seriously ill, was distantly polite when she ran into Capote, but she refused the entreaties of middlemen to make up. "I'll never forgive him," she told Jack Dunphy at the Paley estate in Southampton, where he had gone to try to smooth things over. "Never!"

Others, never mentioned in "La Côte Basque," cut Capote out of respect for, or fear of, those who had been offended. When Babe Paley's brother-in-law, the artist Jim Fosburgh, relented and had lunch with Capote, Babe found out within hours and berated him for his disloyalty.

Capote began threatening to put people in the book if they were not nicer to him. However, the next chapter, "Unspoiled Monsters," published in the May 1976 edition of *Esquire,* and featuring Tennessee Williams as one of its targets, failed to have the impact of its predecessor.

Capote claimed to have written more of *Answered Prayers* and even claimed at one stage that a chapter had been stolen from his Sagaponack house. Rumors circulated that more chapters lay hidden beneath the floorboards, but the house, now owned by Hamptons artist Ross Bleckner, has been extensively remodeled and no lost manuscripts have been found.

Capote later realized that publishing a number of loosely connected chapters had been a mistake; he should have waited to publish the finished novel. "They were very misleading as to what the book was really about," he told one interviewer. Even so, he claimed to feel no guilt about what he had done and stuck by his claim that he had invented nothing.

The furor over *Answered Prayers* left the fifty-one-year-old Capote isolated, if not entirely alone. He continued to trek from place to place—Verbier in Switzerland, Palm Springs, Sagaponack, New York City—drinking large quantities of vodka and slipping more and more under the control of prescription and street drugs. Cocaine, on which he spent by his own estimate sixty thousand dollars in a single year, became his champagne, Valium and Librium an aperitif, Seconal his digestif.

His drug use was especially dangerous because he already used large doses of phenobarbital, a powerful barbiturate, and Dilantin to control epileptic seizures. His drunkenness and drug abuse became public entertainment. He was removed from a stage at the University of Maryland after just five minutes of a speaking engagement because he was incoherent. He was coherent, but conspicuously drunk, during an appearance on a New York TV talk show. He was twice arrested in the Hamptons for drunken driving and had to sober up in a jail cell. He intentionally risked being jailed by angering the judge in one of those cases by turning up in court in shorts and sandals.

In reclusive periods in Sagaponack, he was so slovenly about his appearance that he would sleep in his clothes night after night. He became so lazy that he wouldn't even bother to find his way to the bathroom and would simply open the door and urinate on the back step. On several occasions, he staggered out into the night shouting obscenities and was discovered next morning, lying in a pool of his own urine and surrounded by the shattered glass of a bottle.

He repeatedly tried to stop drinking and abusing drugs but could not do so for more than a few weeks at a time. He checked into one rehab clinic and not only absconded but persuaded other patients he met there to leave with him. Heading for another clinic, he had to stop on the way for a bottle of vodka. The Sagaponack house became a pharmacy of illegal substances. Bags of cocaine were hidden between the pages of favorite books, and loose pills and capsules and brown plastic bottles of tranquilizers littered the shelves. He began checking into hospitals the way he once spent weekends in splendid homes. In 1981 he collapsed outside the Sagaponack general store and was taken to Southampton Hospital, where he stayed for a month. He told people he had died twice and been resuscitated. Just a few days after his release he suffered another seizure in Manhattan.

He was admitted to Southampton Hospital four times in 1981, seven times in 1982, and sixteen times in 1983, and Southampton was only one hospital where he was a regular. He was hospitalized in several other states in the same period. Usually the problem was a seizure or an overdose, sometimes simply an anxiety attack. Occasionally he would be having hallucinations and would run to neighbors' homes begging to be sheltered from some pursuer. Doctors each had a similar refrain: stop drinking and taking drugs and you will live many more years; don't and you could be dead in six months.

Sagaponack ultimately became a source of deep unhappiness. His relationship with Jack Dunphy was suffering because of Capote's pathetic circumstances; he could no longer drive his red Mustang convertible in the Hamptons because he had lost his license, and he believed his former society friends had conspired with police to have him arrested if he ventured out in the car. When he did get out, the hidden mansions and private beaches were a reminder that the world he had once frolicked in no longer welcomed him.

He finally closed the Sagaponack house in August 1984 and never returned. He flew to Los Angeles to stay with Joanne Carson. By her original account, he was tired and ill during his stay, and when she went to rouse him on the morning of August 25, he was dead. But in a conflicting account, published in Gerald Clarke's biography, Capote took a cocktail of drugs, including a massive dose of Valium. Slipping peacefully away, he asked Joanne Carson not to summon medical attention, and he kept talking and gossiping until the end. He was one month away from his sixtieth birthday, but years of substance abuse had left him looking twenty years older.

CHAPTER 5

To Hell and Back:
The Saga of Andrew Crispo

THERE WAS A DEEP-THROATED, full-bodied roar followed by the sound of shattering glass and the crackle and snap of a raging fire. The earth trembled for half a mile around, and the explosion could be heard as a distant clap of thunder ten miles away. In moments a column of dense, black, acrid smoke spiraled hundreds of feet into the air above Gin Lane in one of Southampton's richest and most fashionable neighborhoods— over the homes of former White House Chief of Protocol Angier Biddle Duke and his wife Robin, heiress Gloria Vanderbilt, the painter Roy Lichtenstein, Jackie O's sister, Lee Radziwill, the actor Alan Alda, the financier Felix Rohatyn, and the news anchor for NBC's New York flagship station, Chuck Scarborough.

Scarborough heard the blast and felt it shake his whole home. One glance from his window told him whose house had been destroyed. He knew at once that the lead on that night's evening news was unfolding just yards from his summer home. Scarborough ran to a relative's house a short distance down Gin Lane and returned with a Canon home video camera. He got as close to the fire as he could and began shooting.

It was great stuff: tongues of flame, columns of smoke, scurrying hose-toting firemen, crowds of spectators, piles of blackened debris. The three-million-dollar home had been blown off its foundations and reduced to rubble in seconds. Now an uncontrollable fire was sweeping through the remains like an angel of vengeance.

Inside the remains of the Mediterranean-style brick-and-stucco beachfront home, a collection of paintings and sculptures worth millions of dollars was being consumed—works by Georgia O'Keeffe, Fernando Botero, Robert Motherwell, David Hockney, and Lowell Nesbitt. Exquisite porcelain, antique furniture, Oriental carpets, rare books, and other treasures were being destroyed. What had not been splintered in the explosion was being blistered and burned by flames. What the flames could not reach was being turned charcoal black by smoke and soot. Everything else was being drenched by the hoses of the men trying to keep the blaze from spreading to nearby homes.

Scarborough called his New York office and insisted on their sending a helicopter to his home to pick up the videotape. It arrived as firemen were still fighting the blaze among the ruins of the eviscerated house. Scarborough handed the video to the pilot, then rushed back into his house for something else. The devastated home had been featured in that month's *Architectural Digest*. Scarborough emerged with a copy. There were photographs inside of how the house and its owner's art collection had looked just an hour or so earlier.

What made the explosion on Gin Lane worthy of the lead on the evening news was not simply that it had happened in a spectacularly affluent neighborhood and been witnessed by a gossip-column-ful of the rich and famous. It was not even the knowledge that some near-priceless paintings had been destroyed in the blaze. What made the explosion a big story was that Chuck Scarborough, like other journalists across the country, knew the identity of the home's owner, his bizarre history, and the outlandish stories—fact and fantasy—that swirled around his house in the Hamptons.

Andrew Crispo was born in 1945 in Philadelphia, the son of an immigrant Italian woman and her French lover. He was abandoned to the care of a Catholic orphanage as an infant. It is claimed he turned tricks in Philadelphia as a teenager. In 1964, aged nineteen, he arrived in New York trying to break into the art world, encouraged to do so by a high-profile lover in the Philadelphia art community. He worked as a window dresser, a salesman in an antiques store, and a courier for 57th Street galleries.

He became an art connoisseur, not in terms of an object's or work's beauty or intrinsic value but in terms of its monetary worth. Like George Bernard Shaw's classic cynic, he knew the price of everything and the value of nothing. Working as a courier for art galleries gave him the contacts and opportunities to deal on the side for relatively small profit. He eventually landed a prestigious job with a top gallery—a step up the ladder to his own gallery.

A dark, strikingly handsome, cherub-faced, robust man, he was not above giving sexual favors to those who could help him. His lovers are said to have included Liberace, the politically powerful attorney Roy Cohn, and Henry McIlhenny, the chairman of the board of the Philadelphia Museum of Art. In 1975 he had enough backing to open the Andrew Crispo Gallery on 57th Street.

Success, wealth, and fame literally walked in through his door one day in the shape of Baron Heinrich "Heini" von Thyssen-Bornemisza, the wealthiest and most voracious individual art collector in the world. Crispo would eventually replace the baron's primary dealer—who was also the baroness's lover—Boris Rappetti, who hurled himself out of a Manhattan office building to his death.

The baron's dealings with Crispo over the next several years totaled some $90 million for four hundred nineteenth- and twentieh-century paintings that caught his—or Crispo's—eye. Just as important, Crispo was able to use his connection with von Thyssen to connect with other wealthy clients. In 1978 Crispo bought the Gin Lane house in the Hamptons for only $167,500. Over the next ten years the house would increase in value to fifteen times its purchase price. He also bought a luxury co-op overlooking the Hudson River on West 12th Street in New York's Greenwich Village—just a short walk from the gay bars and clubs that Crispo and his circle of friends frequented.

One of those clubs was a basement space where the drinks were cheap. Located on a seedy, isolated block on West 14th Street, the place was known as the Hellfire Club or just Hellfire. It was not a strictly gay hangout. Heterosexuals, gay men, and lesbians knew Hellfire. Some nights would be exclusively the preserve of gays; others were set aside for heterosexual devotees of bondage and discipline. And there was always a smattering of "tourists"—straight people who came simply for a chance to stand on the edge of the inferno and watch.

In the seventies and eighties, Hellfire was to the New York sex underground what Studio 54 was to disco. Women in flimsy red lingerie would make grand entrances with their men on leashes and walking on all fours, wearing only a pair of leather briefs. Dominatrixes holding whips would stand, elbows on the bar, chatting to slaves dressed only in a studded neck collar and a pouch held on by a thong. A tire hung from the ceiling on a rope, and inevitably, as the evening wore on, someone would climb into the tire so that his or her buttocks could be exposed and paddled remorselessly.

Behind a partition was a series of stalls where men or women could be chained to a wall and abused. Men who wished to watch their wives have sex with one or more strangers would screen burly, tattooed recruits from among the night's clientele. In various corners couples would engage in sex while passersby watched or participated by pawing one or the other of them. The more outré sexual diversions took place in a closed room off the main floor. Anything went at Hellfire. Only laughter was forbidden.

Andrew Crispo was a Hellfire regular and by his own admission a sadomasochist. He would recruit willing gay victims and take them back to his apartment or gallery or invite them out to the Hamptons for the weekend. There they would be subjected to violent and prolonged physical and sexual assaults.

Crispo did not only recruit from the often jaded denizens of Hellfire. He had lists of the numbers of strategically located pay phones in Manhattan and the Hamptons. One was on the corner of West 4th Street and Sixth Avenue, where a solitary passerby might be prepared to risk an invite to a "party." Another was in the vestibule of the Ramrod Cafe on West Street.

For some reason, Crispo also had the number of a pay phone perilously close to the Southampton Town police headquarters. One night, he is said to have called that pay phone and unwittingly invited a rookie cop to a sex party. The police considered organizing a sting operation against Crispo's Gin Lane estate but ended up letting the matter drop. In the light of later events, it was a fateful omission.

One of Crispo's circle of friends and an employee at the 57th Street gallery was a disturbed young man named Bernard LeGeros. LeGeros's parents, John and Raquel, owned a sprawling estate overlooking the Hudson River in Rockland County, north of New York City. John LeGeros had a high-profile job at the United Nations administering aid to the third world. Bernard LeGeros had twice tried to commit suicide—once threatening to leap from an East Side apartment building until he was talked down by police, and once swallowing a small amount of cyanide. LeGeros was obsessed with the military and with firearms and owned an automatic rifle, which he kept in his Manhattan apartment.

Crispo referred to LeGeros as his bodyguard and sometimes, it is claimed, as his "executioner." He was a regular weekend guest at the Hamptons house and an active participant in Crispo's S&M parties. When they were not at the Hellfire or other gay hangouts, Crispo and LeGeros were often seen at the Limelight, the former Church of the Holy Communion on Sixth Avenue and West 20th Street that had been converted into a chic Manhattan nightclub. From the late seventies on, Limelight had been one of New York City's most popular clubs.

Movie stars, rock musicians, writers, artists, gossip columnists, socialites, and hangers-on packed Limelight's dance floors, gyrating beneath stained-glass windows and on what were once altars, aisles, and naves. Outside on 20th Street, there were always as many people waiting to get in as there were inside. The inner sanctum of Limelight was the VIP room, where celebrities and favored customers could gather among their own kind. The man who ran the VIP room for the club's owner, Canadian businessman Peter Gatien, was Fred Rothbell, whose ability to spot candidates for the VIP room—and, just as important, noncandidates—was legendary. Crispo knew Rothbell well, and Crispo and his companions' path to the VIP room was always cleared.

Rothbell had enemies, and one was a man in Crispo's circle named Edo Bertoglio, a photographer and another Limelight regular. Gatien lent Rothbell his luxurious villa in Puerto Rico's exquisite Palmas del Mar resort, and when Rothbell got there he found that Gatien had also allowed Bertoglio and his girlfriend, Lynn Smith, to use it. There was some petty tension during the vacation between Lynn Smith and Rothbell, and Bertoglio harbored a long-standing grudge against him.

Bertoglio talked about avenging himself on Rothbell, but he apparently did not want to go much further than punching him on the nose. He did badmouth Rothbell among his friends and acquaintances, who included Bernard LeGeros. When LeGeros heard about Bertoglio's distaste for Rothbell, LeGeros went a lot further. He told Bertoglio they should kill him. Bertoglio wasn't interested and told him so, but LeGeros kept ruminating about the possibility. For the next several days it was all he could think about.

On February 22, 1985, a week or so after his conversation with Bertoglio, Bernard LeGeros was in Hellfire with Andrew Crispo and another man, Billy Mayer. They watched as a naked man put his head and arms through the tire to be spanked with a large paddle by a heavy-breasted blond woman dressed in black leather. As they emerged into the unseasonably mild night, Bernard LeGeros, fired by the violence he had just witnessed, began to talk about killing Fred Rothbell. According to Rockland County prosecutor Kenneth Gribetz, Crispo began to egg LeGeros on. "This would be a good night to kill him," Crispo is alleged to have said. LeGeros agreed.

Crispo, according to Gribetz, began to go into more detail. They should lure Rothbell away from Limelight on the pretext of going to a party, take him up to the LeGeros spread in Rockland County, and eventually shoot him in the head and dispose of the body there. The three caught a cab on Greenwich Avenue and talked further about Fred Rothbell as the taxi negotiated the noisy, narrow, milling streets of the West Village and headed uptown to Limelight.

In a quiet, book-lined room where pastors once studied theology books and prepared Sunday sermons, Crispo, Mayer, and LeGeros passed cocaine around and tried to convince Fred Rothbell to join them for a party. Fortunately for him, he told them he could not get away. Crispo, apparently undaunted, told Mayer and LeGeros he would work on Rothbell and said they should meet him back at Hellfire in an hour.

LeGeros and Mayer hung out for a while at one of the Limelight bars, went to LeGeros's apartment, where he collected his car and an assault rifle, then made their way back downtown to Hellfire. They watched the swingers, bondage freaks, dominators, and subservients for a while, and it soon became obvious that Crispo had stood them up. LeGeros and Mayer then headed over to Crispo's apartment on West 12th Street.

There is no doorman at the co-op complex, and visitors are buzzed up after identifying themselves over an intercom. Crispo was apparently reluctant to let them up at first, saying he had company. Then he relented and pressed the buzzer. When LeGeros and Mayer entered the apartment, they found Crispo wearing black leather shorts and a black T-shirt and fondling the frayed tip of a black leather whip. Fred Rothbell was not in the apartment. Instead, Crispo's guest was a tall, well-proportioned, blue-eyed blond in his twenties, with the Nordic good looks of a fashion model. His beautifully cut clothes had been tossed casually on the rug. He was lounging on the sofa, naked. His name was Eigil Vesti.

Eigil Vesti was a student at the Fashion Institute of Technology. He had been raised in Oslo, studied in Norway and Denmark, and taught himself English by shipping out on cruise ships catering to English and American tourists. He eventually made his way to America to follow his dream of becoming a fashion designer. He had been at FIT since 1982 and was just a few weeks away from graduating.

He had developed a wide circle of friends in both the fashion industry and the gay community. A well-known fashion designer used to lend him clothes to wear. Another friend was the successful photographer Stephen AuCoin, with whom he shared an apartment on West 26th Street and who had used him as a model. Yet another was a party promoter named Dallas who kept Vesti up to date on the latest gossip and gave him invitations to parties and openings, so Vesti's datebook was always full.

Vesti had spent February 22, 1985, working on a resumé, planning a vacation in Florida which he was combining with a modeling assignment set up for him by AuCoin, and browsing around the Metropolitan Museum. In the evening he had dinner in Chelsea with his friend Dallas and returned home at midnight. Apparently the evening had ended too early for him, so either bored or lonely, he headed out again and ended up at Hellfire, where he ran into Andrew Crispo. He was now on Crispo's sofa and about to take part in a sadomasochistic trip from which he would never return.

First, according to the version given by LeGeros to the Rockland prosecutor, Crispo invited both Mayer and LeGeros to whip Vesti. Vesti, at least at this point, is said to have been a willing, even eager participant. Mayer brought the whip across Vesti's buttocks and handed it to LeGeros. LeGeros, who had played combative roles in these events before, laid into Vesti with more enthusiasm. Mayer, who had apparently seen enough for his appetite, left. LeGeros followed him out to try to convince him to come back and returned alone. The S&M party continued with LeGeros, Vesti, and Crispo until it was decided to head up to Rockland County. According to LeGeros, Crispo taunted Vesti on the journey upstate, telling him, "You're going back to Norway in a fucking box."

A little over three weeks later, on St. Patrick's Day 1985, five teenagers out hiking in the Hudson Valley were crossing the LeGeros property when they came across what looked like the entrance to a cave. In fact it was an eighteenth-century smokehouse not far from the LeGeros house. One of the boys looked inside. What he saw made him recoil. The others peered in, then they too shrank back in horror.

Inside was indeed a gruesome spectacle. It was a body, but the flesh had been burned, and most of it appeared to have been eaten by animals. The shoulders of what was now little more than a skeleton were topped by a horrific black leather mask with slits for the eyes and nose and a zipper across the mouth. It was covered with blood.

But for the teenagers' curiosity and that gruesome mask, the fate of

Eigil Vesti might never have been discovered. In another few weeks, the animals and the elements would have made the remains unidentifiable, and detectives from the Stony Point police, state police, and Rockland County prosecutor's office would have had nowhere to start.

When the mask was removed by medical examiner Dr. Frederick Zugibe, the head and face were almost intact. It was easy to establish the cause of death: the victim had been shot twice in the back of the head with an assault rifle. There were no reports of missing persons in Rockland County that matched the description of the victim, so a description and photographs were sent to police departments all over America.

When Eigil Vesti had disappeared, his friend Dallas had alerted the police and Vesti's family; he had also distributed flyers around Chelsea, Greenwich Village, FIT, and Vesti's known hangouts. One of Vesti's sisters had traveled from Norway to help find her brother, bringing with her his dental records and numerous photographs. The family had hired a private investigator who had dug up some information on Vesti's patronage of various S&M clubs, including Hellfire.

Within twenty-four hours of the discovery of Vesti's body, the New York Police Department's Missing Persons Bureau told Rockland investigators they had a shrewd idea they could identify the body. The dental records confirmed the identification. Detectives began by questioning Raquel and John LeGeros and their sons, David and Bernard. Bernard LeGeros at first professed to know nothing of the crime, but he drew attention to himself by contacting police with unsolicited theories about how and why the murder had been committed. He told them he owned an assault rifle, which he kept at the Rockland County house. Maybe it was the murder weapon and was missing, he told them. Perhaps it had been stolen from the house and dumped in the woods around the property after the murder, he suggested.

Then there was the mask. He knew about masks like that, he told detectives. They were used in S&M parties, he said, to hide the identity of either the master or the slave—most often to dehumanize the slave. The killer could be a psycho who hated gays and cruised gay bars looking for victims. Even more helpfully, he recited a list of gay and S&M bars in New York where they might pursue such an investigation. Detectives asked LeGeros to come down to headquarters.

When detectives asked LeGeros what he did on the weekend Vesti disappeared, he was able to give a detailed account—names of his companions, times, places, witnesses—omitting, of course, meeting with the murder victim at Andrew Crispo's apartment. He told them that on Sunday morning, twenty-four hours after the murder, he and Crispo had traveled to Crispo's house in the Hamptons. He even remembered the name of the limousine service. But when detectives asked him about the following weekend, he was unable to give them anything like as much detail. That in itself was suspicious. Partly to intimidate LeGeros, who seemed buoyant and confidant, and partly as a precaution in case LeGeros became a suspect, Detective William Franks of the Stony Point police read him his Miranda rights.

LeGeros said that he didn't kill Vesti and had no idea who the killer might be, but his mood had changed visibly. Franks and the other detectives let him wait for a while in another room. By the time they resumed the interrogation, LeGeros said he was ready to tell them everything. He said his friend Billy Mayer was the killer. Mayer had picked up someone in a bar, borrowed LeGeros's car, brought the victim to Rockland, taken LeGeros's gun, committed the murder, and then driven back to New York and told Bernard LeGeros all about it. It seemed an unlikely scenario.

Then LeGeros made an even more detailed statement. This time he put himself at the murder scene. He, Vesti, and Mayer had driven upstate after meeting Vesti in a bar. Once upstate, Mayer had subjected Vesti to some S&M activity, then blown him away with the assault rifle. They had both burned the body, then LeGeros had returned alone and tried to burn the body a second time.

Still suspicious, Franks had LeGeros go through the story all over again. New details of the S&M session appeared, but the basics remained the same. Franks warned LeGeros that his story wouldn't hold up for five minutes if Mayer could prove he was somewhere else.

Now LeGeros changed his story again. This time it wasn't Mayer who was involved, but Andrew Crispo. He said Crispo had supervised the S&M session and had sex with Vesti. LeGeros admitted that it was he who had shot Vesti twice in the back of the head. They could find the gun in an airshaft at Crispo's gallery. A pair of handcuffs and other items that had been used in the S&M ritual had been thrown out of the car on the journey back to New York. The detectives charged LeGeros with murder and set about trying to confirm each element of his story. A key witness was Billy Mayer. He not only confirmed seeing Vesti at Crispo's apartment, he said LeGeros had confessed to him a week after the murder, showing him a flyer seeking information on Eigil Vesti and telling him, "That's the guy I killed."

"When you kill," LeGeros allegedly enthused, "you can't be angry or upset. You have to kill as if you were just lighting a cigarette."

A search of Andrew Crispo's gallery produced the murder weapon precisely where LeGeros said it would be. Aided by LeGeros, detectives found clothes that Vesti had been wearing the night of the murder; they had been thrown away on the Palisades Parkway in New Jersey.

Andrew Crispo dropped from sight and refused through an attorney, Robert Kasanof, to answer any questions without a guarantee of immunity. But it did not take long to compile a dossier on his lifestyle. Rockland County prosecutor Kenneth Gribetz became convinced Crispo was involved in the murder. He was not alone. Rumors about what went on behind the high walls and thick hedges of Crispo's Southampton home swept the Hamptons. LeGeros had been a regular guest. He was with Crispo in the Hamptons the Sunday following the murder. They appear to have had a quiet weekend, considering what was alleged to have happened at Stony Point. They traveled out by limo, ate at the Driver's Seat restaurant, and saw the movie *Witness*, returning to New York City on Monday.

But the Suffolk County and Southampton Town police departments believed other weekends had not been so quiet. Crispo was said to have pointed out an Oriental sculpture in the grounds of his home to one weekend guest and remarked, "That's where I bury my enemies." Crispo denied it through his attorney but continued to refuse to speak to detectives. To prove that Andrew Crispo had been involved in the murder of Eigil Vesti, prosecutors would need more than the confession of LeGeros.

Although LeGeros was the only living witness to the murder, his testimony could only be used against himself, not Crispo. Under New York State law, uncorroborated accomplice testimony is inadmissible. Even if LeGeros could have been used as a witness against Crispo, a good defense attorney would have demolished him. He had given other statements to the police that were clearly lies, including one accusing Billy Mayer of playing the role he now attributed to Crispo.

Prosecutors had no evidence to link Crispo to the crime. Hoping to uncover some, within a week of LeGeros's indictment for the murder of Vesti, Detective Sergeant Anthony Oleander of the Southampton police led a search party of dogs, spade-wielding police officers, and bulldozers to dig in the grounds of the Southampton house. The searchers found nothing, but the stories of sadomasochistic orgies in the Southampton house, the Greenwich Village apartment, and the 57th Street gallery persisted. A number of men came forward to claim that they had been participants in such orgies, with Crispo, LeGeros, and others delivering whipping and beatings.

One of the men who came forward had a story that seemed strong enough for the Manhattan district attorney, Robert Morgenthau, to bring an indictment. An art student named Mark Leslie claimed that about five months before the Vesti murder, he had been lured to Crispo's gallery with the promise of cocaine and sex. Once there, he had been held by Crispo, LeGeros, and a number of violent young men he said were graffiti artists. At Crispo's direction, they had subjected him to several hours of beatings, humiliation, and sexual assault. LeGeros had held him at gunpoint. He had been forced to sodomize Crispo, he claimed, and Crispo had threatened at one point to kill him. They eventually let him go. Here was a living witness, a victim, not an accomplice. Crispo was indicted for assault.

There were other legal problems closing in on Crispo. He had been under investigation by the Internal Revenue Service, and his sudden notoriety gave his case a new importance in the eyes of federal prosecutors. The IRS gives particular emphasis to famous and infamous people suspected of tax evasion, because the publicity surrounding their cases is believed to discourage other would-be tax evaders. Fired by Crispo's new high profile, prosecutors indicted Crispo, claiming he owed $8 million in taxes.

LeGeros went on trial in Rockland County represented by a man who seemed singularly out of place in the netherworld of bizarre sex and gratuitous violence in which LeGeros operated. Murray Sprung was an upright old-school attorney in his eighties, a man in severe pain from arthritis. He had prosecuted Japanese war criminals in the Philippines, where he had become a family friend of John and Raquel LeGeros. His strategy was to try to convince the jury that Crispo was the prime mover behind the crime, that LeGeros was almost as much Crispo's victim as was Vesti. Crispo had enslaved LeGeros with drugs, sex, and the force of his personality, and although LeGeros had indeed pulled the trigger, his mental capacity was diminished.

Crispo himself was called to give evidence. He arrived at court surrounded by photographers and with both a lawyer and a bodyguard. He was dressed in Moss Bros. chic—a blue sports jacket, dove-gray trousers, a starched, gleaming white shirt, and a striped tie. He refused to answer each question by asserting his Fifth Amendment right to say nothing that might incriminate him. After the charade had been played out with a few questions, the judge ordered that Crispo be dismissed.

Crispo was more forthcoming with reporters outside the court. "I think this affair is a tragedy," he told them. "It's a tragedy for the LeGeros family. It's a tragedy for the family of Eigil Vesti—and for myself. I'm going to an acupuncturist to soothe my nerves. You take it a day at a time. Like a baseball game, a ball comes in, you bat it out. That's the way I handle it."

Edo Bertoglio and Bernard Mayer were also called. They testified that LeGeros had told them prior to the arrest that he and Crispo had murdered Vesti. "Don't tell Andrew I told you," LeGeros allegedly begged Bertoglio.

"He said that he and Crispo and the blond guy [Vesti] went to Rockland County," Bertoglio testified, "where he roughed up the guy and then took him out and had him kneel down, and then he told me he shot this guy in the back of the head two times. He mentioned that he cut open his chest, took his heart out, and then tried to burn the body."

The prosecutors agreed with the defense that Crispo had plotted the murder but argued that LeGeros was in full possession of his faculties. The jury likewise rejected the argument that LeGeros was merely Crispo's pawn. They found him guilty of second-degree murder, and he was sentenced to twenty-five years to life.

Within a few weeks, Crispo was in jail too. He pleaded guilty to tax evasion and was sentenced to seven years. He had deliberately falsified the invoices on dozens of sales to avoid income tax. He wound up his affairs by selling a sculpture, *The Muse,* a masterpiece by Constantin Brancusi, to the Guggenheim Museum for three million dollars. He then entered federal prison to serve his sentence.

In 1987 he went on trial in Manhattan Supreme Court for kidnapping, assault, and other charges. This time, LeGeros, his skin a shade of light gray from his year behind bars, testified against Crispo. The victim, Mark Leslie, also gave evidence. He claimed that he had met Crispo after answering a pay phone at a gay bar in Greenwich Villege. He went to Crispo's apartment and had willingly submitted to being beaten.

However, he claimed, Crispo later lured him with the promise of drugs to his 57th Street gallery. There, he said, Crispo had staged an elaborate show. LeGeros had played the role of policeman and arrested Leslie, placing him in handcuffs. Crispo then directed a weird ritual in which Leslie was sexually assaulted and abused. The jury, unconvinced that any real coercion had been used, found Crispo not guilty.

Crispo returned to federal prison to serve out his sentence. He was released in June 1989 after serving three years and, he says, went immediately to the Hamptons to recuperate. Returning to the Southampton house and his private collection was, he said, "like visiting his children." In *Architectural Digest* Crispo claimed that he kept his life as an art collector and his life as a dealer completely separate and apart. He made it a rule never to sell anything he had in his collection—even to buy something else. "There is no upgrading when you really love something," he said. Two weeks later, the house and collection were in ruins.

So Andrew Crispo found himself in court once more—this time suing the Long Island Lighting Company, claiming that the explosion and fire at his home had been caused by a gas pipe that had been laid too close to an electrical cable. The cable had shorted out, melted a section of plastic pipe, and ignited the gas. The defense claimed that Crispo was falsifying the value of the contents of the house, just as he had once falsified the value of his sales to evade taxes. Once again, the jury decision went Crispo's way. He was awarded $8.6 million.

Crispo returned to the world of art dealing—but with a much lower profile. He picked up the threads of his affluent lifestyle. The Greenwich Village apartment was lavishly remodeled. He bought another Hamptons house in the same neighborhood. He also bought a historic property in Charleston for two million dollars. He was never charged with the murder of Eigil Vesti, although the case remains open and if new evidence pointing to Crispo ever comes to light, he could still be tried.

Bernard LeGeros continues to serve out the long days and longer nights of his life sentence. From jail, he wrote a letter about Crispo that was published in the *New York Post*. "Crispo...belongs in hell," he wrote. "The only thing is, he would enjoy it."

PART TWO

High Life

Introduction

STEAMSHIP SERVICE from New York brought the first waves of summer visitors to the Hamptons, although the area's attractions had been known to British officers on leave before the Revolutionary War. The Long Island Railroad pushed out from New York to Greenport in 1844, then on to Westhampton Beach, and beyond to Shinnecock Bay, Bridgehampton, and Sag Harbor in 1870 and East Hampton in 1895, opening up the Hamptons to New Yorkers. New York City developers, believing the Hamptons could rival the preeminent resort of Newport as a summer destination for New York, had begun buying prime building sites in advance of the railroad's completion.

There were eight hundred summer visitors in the first year of train service to East Hampton. They have been coming in larger and larger numbers ever since. At first, the locals were suspicious and resentful of the summer visitors, but that did not stop many from renting out their guest rooms to them. In 1863, George McClellan, fired as commander of the Army of the Potomac, spent the summer licking his wounded ego in the Hamptons as a boarder at Mulford Farm.

In the late nineteenth century, New York was at the height of its Gilded Age glory. Wealthy New Yorkers had been building great estates for themselves on what was to become known as Long Island's Gold Coast. America's wealthiest dynasties—Morgan, Whitney, Vanderbilt, Astor, Woolworth, Payne, Payson, and DuPont—created private fiefdoms on up to a thousand acres of Gatsby-esque splendor.

They also built outposts of these fiefdoms in East Hampton and Southampton. Coyly called "cottages," which makes them sound like rustic retreats, some were spectacular shingled mansions of thirty rooms or more. A number were the work of the famed architect to the rich,

Stanford White, who also created an elegant Long Island estate for himself, Box Hill.

New York society was ruled over by Caroline Webster Schermerhorn Astor, the descendant of wealthy Dutch ships chandlers who had made a fortune in New York in the seventeenth century, and the wife of William Backhouse Astor Jr., grandson of John Jacob. Mrs Astor and her autocratic social arbiter, Ward McAllister, had arbitrarily reduced the definition of "society" to "the Four Hundred," which also happened to be the number of people who could fit comfortably into Mrs Astor's ballroom in her Fifth Avenue mansion. In fact, there were only 319 names, representing 169 families, on the official list.

Most of those 319 members of the social elite spent their summers in Newport, but once Southampton became accessible, a number, led by stockbroker Charles G. Francklyn, began to stray from the stifling formalities of the Rhode Island resort. They joined the wealthy descendants of the original colonists, who had made fortunes from Sag Harbor's industries, and others to form a distinct outpost of society in Southampton and East Hampton.

The Hamptons were by no means devoid of glamour prior to this time. Julia Gardiner, a descendant of Lion Gardiner, had become First Lady in 1844, marrying President John Tyler. A beautiful and strong-willed young woman, she had shocked people by agreeing to model for a store advertisement, which showed her strolling on Ninth Avenue in New York City in her finest clothes. In place of a pocketbook she was pictured carrying an ornate sign that read: "I'll purchase at Bogert and Macamly's—Their goods are Beautiful and Astonishingly Cheap."

Her father was a senator, and President Tyler invited both of them aboard the warship *Princeton* in February 1844. One of the *Princeton's* enormous guns exploded, killing the senator and several others. President Tyler carried Julia to safety. They were married the following June despite the thirty-year difference in their ages.

Julia became by far the most glamorous First Lady Washington would know until another born-and-bred Hamptonite, Jackie Kennedy, became First Lady in 1961. She introduced White House balls and began the tradition of playing "Hail to the Chief." The Gardiners' East Hampton home became a summer White House, and she was widely known as "the Rose of Long Island."

The estates built in Southampton were on a more modest scale than those in Newport and the Gold Coast. Few remain. In 1895, for example, Charles Steele, a partner of J. P. Morgan, built a thirty-room

Marilyn Monroe and Arthur Miller, with Miller's parents, Florence and Isidore in 1956 (*Associated Press Photo*)

Truman Capote and
Princess Lee Radziwill in
1967 (*The New York Post*)

Capote turns up at
Southampton Town Court
on a drunk driving charge.
He was scolded by the
judge for not wearing
socks or pants. (*The New
York Post*)

John Steinbeck at his home in Sag Harbor in 1962 (*The New York Post*)

(*Opposite*) Jackie Onassis' grandfather, John Vernou Bouvier Jr., with his daughter, Maude, (left), and Jackie's mother, Janet Lee Bouvier (*The New York Post*)

(*Right*) Dr. Rodney Wood and his wife Nancy leave court after pleading guilty to prostitution. (*Register Guard*)

(*Below*) Dr. Wood's funeral with the three Mrs. Woods—Nancy, left, Gael in the fur coat, and Sharon (*The New York Post*)

(*Inset*) Andrew Crispo (*The New York Post*). What was left of Andrew Crispo's house in the Hamptons after an explosion and fire. (*The New York Post*)

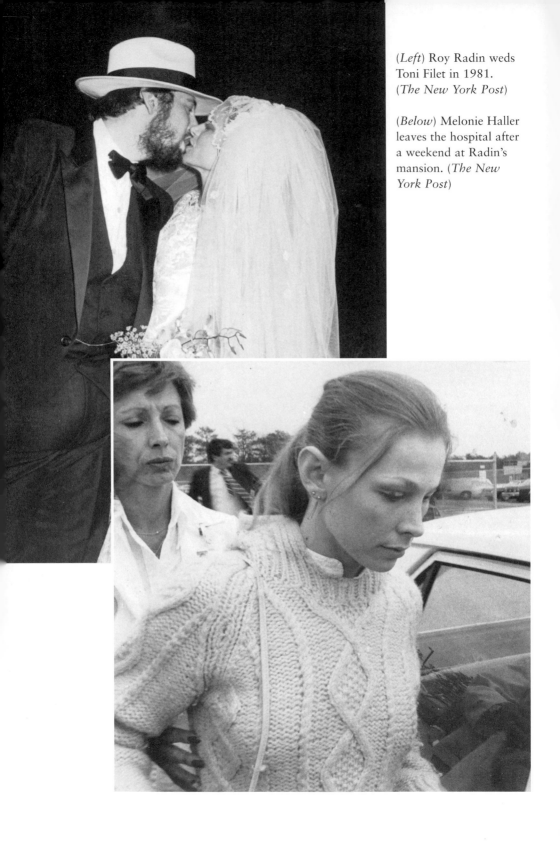

(*Left*) Roy Radin weds Toni Filet in 1981. (*The New York Post*)

(*Below*) Melonie Haller leaves the hospital after a weekend at Radin's mansion. (*The New York Post*)

English Tudor–style mansion on four acres on South Main Street in Southampton overlooking Lake Agawam, adding a ballroom for the debut of his three daughters into Southampton society some years later.

When one of those daughters, Kathryne, married F. Skiddy von Stade, the president of the Saratoga racecourse, and took over the house, it became known as the von Stade mansion and stood as one of the finest examples of turn-of-the-century "cottages" until it met an ignominious end in 1984. After lying vacant for years, it briefly bloomed as a designer show house, then was razed in the dead of winter; a postmodern shingle-style house was built in its place.

A wealthy developer, Arthur Benson, bought all the available land in Montauk for $151,000 in 1880. He formed the Montauk Association and commissioned White to build several ocean-front houses. The brilliant landscape designer Frederick Law Olmsted was engaged to landscape the estates. Seven of those houses, with bay windows, broad wraparound porches, gables, and cupolas, still stand. Although Hamptons realtors today routinely claim houses are "Stanford Whites," only about fifteen other genuine Stanford White–designed homes still exist in the Hamptons. One has been turned into million-dollar condos.

White also built the ornate clubhouse of the Shinnecock Hills Golf Club, one of the first golf clubs in America and a place that was to become a focal point of Hamptons society as golf grew to eclipse polo as the game of the rich. William K. Vanderbilt and Edward Mead had become interested in golf in Scotland and brought a prominent golfer, Willie Dunn, to America to help popularize the sport, then little known here. Dunn designed the first twelve-hole course at Shinnecock Hills.

White's career was sensationally cut short in 1906. He was assassinated in the original Madison Square Garden, which he had designed, by Harry K. Thaw, the disturbed husband of one of White's numerous young mistresses.

Austin Corbin, the president of the Long Island Railroad, planned a stunning era of development in the Hamptons. He wanted to build a harbor at Fort Pond Bay near Montauk as the first port of entry to the United States for transatlantic passenger ships. It would cut a day off the journey from Europe. After his tragic death in an accident in a horse-drawn carriage in 1897, the plan was never realized.

The complex social codes and hierarchy that had been established in Gilded Age society in New York and Newport were also established in the Hamptons. The Hamptons began to get its glamorous image through newspaper gossip columns during the era of what one gossip columnist called "Publi-ciety," when gossip pages focused on the wives or sons and daughters of wealthy entrepreneurs as intensely as they now focus on TV and movie stars.

The New York City gossip columns of newspapermen like Maury Paul, who wrote under the name "Cholly Knickerbocker," recorded every social move and scandalous twist in the lives of New York's heirs and heiresses in a never-ending daily soap opera. Often these were mere social notes of comings, goings, innocent romances, and extravagant balls, but there were darker themes.

One Southampton heiress elopes with a British army officer only to return to her family, the marriage over in all but name, after six weeks; she arrives home abused, disillusioned, and pregnant, amid dark accusations of "unspeakable behavior." A scion of a wealthy industrial dynasty falls from his polo pony and is rendered unpredictably violent, forcing his beautiful young bride of six months to commit him to an asylum. An East Hampton heiress is forced by her mother to undergo a sterilization procedure as a teenager because her father's will endowed her unborn offspring with the bulk of his estate.

Carl G. Fisher, who had been prominent in developing Miami Beach, foresaw the rise of the Hamptons as a weekend and summer destination—a sort of Miami of the North—in the twenties. He bought ten thousand acres of land in and around Montauk and built a luxury two-hundred-room hotel, the Montauk Manor, a golf course, polo grounds, and a marina before he ran out of money as a result of the stock market crash and the Depression.

By then, the concept of Hamptons weekends was well established. Hamptons weekenders and summer residents tended to be wealthy, including many stockbrokers, lawyers, bankers, and businessmen. Summer family life for these elite people centered on the Shinnecock Hills Golf Club and the exclusionary Meadow and Maidstone clubs. There were extravagant garden parties, picnics—or "fêtes champêtres," as they were pretentiously known—equestrian events, tennis, and golf. In 1928, two prominent Hamptons families, the Bouviers and the Lees, formed an uneasy marital alliance that was to have fateful consequences.

CHAPTER 6

Jackie and Black Jack: A Father's Heartbreak

THE *EAST HAMPTON STAR* called it one of the most splendid social events of the decade. It was certainly one of the last. Within a little over a year many of the guests were to find themselves financially ruined by the Wall Street crash, which caused some of those sipping champagne that summer's afternoon to die by their own hands. The event was the wedding of one of the Hampton's most prized heiresses to one of the Hampton's most notorious rakes.

The bride was Janet Norton Lee, twenty-one, one of three beautiful daughters of self-made millionaire James T. Lee, president of the New York Central Savings Bank. The groom was classically handsome thirty-seven-year-old John Vernou Bouvier III, better known as "the Sheik" or "Black Jack" for his dark complexion, voracious sexual appetites, and compulsive gambling on and off Wall Street. They were married on July 7, 1928, at St. Philomena's Church in East Hampton before five hundred of the richest and most prominent figures in New York and the Hamptons.

There was a good deal of whispering and suppressed giggling in the pews. Several of the wives of the attorneys, bankers, and stockbrokers among the guests—and one or two of their daughters—had been among the innumerable lovers used and cast aside by the groom.

And if the bride had held out against his advances, which had been part of her allure, she had not held so fast against those of the best man, his brother, Bud Bouvier, who had been her first choice as a husband. Bud Bouvier's alcoholism and chronic depression, and the fact that he was already divorced, had forced her to switch her attention to Black Jack. Many of the guests knew that; they also knew that Bud had been released from a drying-out clinic less than a week before the wedding. The following year Bud Bouvier finally drank himself to death.

There was also gossip about the bride's parents. Most in the wedding party knew that James Lee and his wife Margaret were secretly separated. Margaret was having an affair with a married New York lawyer who could not secure a divorce. The Lees had divided their spacious duplex on New York's Park Avenue into two apartments with separate entrances so that they might live at the same address without ever speaking to each other, and Margaret Lee only visited East Hampton if her husband was not present.

The guests gathered for the reception at James T. Lee's rented East Hampton estate on Lily Pond Lane. At one point in the afternoon, the noise of a loud and bitter argument between Black Jack and his new father-in-law could be heard above the music of the Meyer Davis orchestra. It was to prove the first of many, almost all about Jack's lack of money or moral restraint.

It was a bitter day for James T. Lee. He had disapproved of his daughter's relationship with Black Jack from the start but believed that it was better to let the marriage take place than to encourage an elopement by forbidding it. Even after they announced their engagement, he was advised by his friends on Wall Street who knew Bouvier's record that he would never marry her, as he had been engaged several times in the past and no wedding had taken place. By the time the realization that this wedding would take place dawned on Lee, the preparations had gone too far for him to deny his daughter's wishes without a scandal. Now he found himself the father-in-law of a man he deemed a gambler and a libertine.

Shortly after the raised voices had been quieted, Black Jack and Janet Lee Bouvier left for New York City to spend their wedding night at the Plaza Hotel. The following day, they embarked for a five week honeymoon in Europe aboard the Cunard liner *Aquitania*. The honeymoon began as it was to continue, with casual and obvious infidelity and bitter and violent recrimination. It was on board ship that Black Jack was first unfaithful. He met the tobacco heiress Doris Duke, then only sixteen years old, and charmed her into bed, triggering a display of Janet Lee Bouvier's violent temper. She trashed the corridor outside their stateroom.

Lee's distaste for his daughter's husband extended to all the Bouviers, who were among the Hamptons' most prominent families. The Lees claimed a distant relationship with the family of Robert E. Lee, although there is neither evidence nor any likelihood of such a link. The Lees were descended from Irish immigrants. James T. Lee's Irish mother-in-law, Margaret Merritt, lived in the Lee home in a position little better than that of a servant. She was never introduced to the Lees' rich friends because her Irish brogue gave away their origins. They made her do so much housework that some guests mistook her for a domestic.

The Lees' fantasies about their genteel Southern roots were as nothing compared to the genealogical fabrications of the Bouviers. They claimed descent from a family of French aristocrats with large estates near Grenoble. There was such a family named Bouvier, but they were not related. The Bouviers of East Hampton and New York were descended from a cabinetmaker and a serving maid. Michel Bouvier, who had fought as a foot soldier in Napoleon's Grande Armée, immigrated to America after the emperor's defeat at Waterloo in 1815.

Michel Bouvier made a fortune as a cabinetmaker in Philadelphia and later as a furniture manufacturer, thanks in part to the patronage of Joseph Bonaparte, the emperor's brother, who was in exile in Delaware. The Bouviers claimed the two were friends, but in fact they seldom met. Michel Bouvier also made huge profits speculating in real estate in Virginia. He built himself a grand house on Broad Street in Philadelphia and was able to leave each of his ten children a large legacy. One of them, Michel Charles, known as M.C., used his inheritance to buy a seat on the New York Stock Exchange. He became the patriarch of the family. He left his fortune to his nephew John Vernou Bouvier Jr., Black Jack's father.

John V. Bouvier Jr. multiplied the family's wealth and bought a large estate in East Hampton, where the whole Bouvier clan gathered on weekends and all summer long. Called Lasata, it covered fourteen acres close to the beach on Fuller Road. The main house was a sprawling, seven-bedroom, ivy-covered Italianate mansion with oak-paneled reception and dining rooms, a spacious solarium, and a red brick terrace overlooking a formal garden designed around a baroque fountain.

Lasata, which mean "place of peace" in the language of the Shinnecock Indians, was modeled on a sixteenth-century Florentine villa and was filled with eighteenth- and nineteenth-century French and American furniture, including many pieces made by the family patriarch. John Jr. set up court here and reinvented the Bouvier family history. Instead of being simply a cabinetmaker, Michel Bouvier became a heroic figure of the Napoleonic era who fled from France after Waterloo with a price on his head.

A whole gene pool of noble ancestors from Provence was invented or commandeered from the historical record. *Our Forebears,* a privately published book written by John Jr., detailing what purported to be the family history, was distributed to every member of the family. It became the foundation of the Bouviers' social mythology, confidence, and hauteur—and just about every important statement in it was a lie.

John V. Bouvier Jr. and his wife Maude had three children in five years: John V. Bouvier III or Black Jack, William Sergeant, known in the family as Bud, and a daughter, Edith. Ten years after Edith was born, Maude unexpectedly became pregnant again and gave birth to twin daughters, Maude and Michelle. Black Jack earned a reputation as a rake early. He was expelled from his prep school, Phillips Academy, for gambling.

At Yale his fellow students would see him disappear into his room with a woman late at night, and a different woman would emerge the next morning. After graduating close to the bottom of his class, he went into a stock brokerage firm, but his career was interrupted by America's entry into World War I. While his brother, Bud, enlisted immediately and was severely wounded in a gas attack, Black Jack waited until August 1917 before enlisting and spent the remainder of the war in camp in North Carolina. He boasted that during the remaining months of the war he saw service only in the local brothels.

After the war Black Jack returned to Wall Street. In 1919 he borrowed heavily from an uncle, his brother-in-law, and a friend to start his own brokerage business. It was successful, but Black Jack spent heavily, so no matter how much he earned he was always short of cash and continued to borrow.

He held almost nightly parties at his Park Avenue apartment, and each spring and summer saw him in East Hampton, either at Lasata or rented homes there. He owned four expensive automobiles, one of which came with a chauffeur whose uniform matched the car's maroon bodywork. He managed by carefully juggling IOUs while enjoying an occasional run of good luck either at the stock exchange or the card tables.

Shortly after Black Jack and Janet Lee Bouvier returned from their honeymoon, Janet announced that she was pregnant. The prospects of a grandchild mollified "Old Man Lee," as Black Jack called him, and for a time relations were cordial. Black Jack was also prospering in the market in the first year of his marriage.

Janet expected to give birth in the third week of June 1929, but the week came and went. Arrangements had been made for her to have the child in a Manhattan hospital, but Black Jack insisted that they continue to spend each weekend in East Hampton. It was at Lasata, six weeks later than expected, that Janet finally went into labor, and she gave birth at a hospital in Southampton on July 28. The eight-pound baby girl was named after her father, Jacqueline Lee Bouvier. A future generation would know her as Jackie Kennedy Onassis.

It was the last carefree summer of prosperity in America for some years. In October, the volatile stock market took a violent downturn, then nosedived. In the ensuing panic, vast fortunes were wiped out. The Bouvier finances continued to be secure because M. C. Bouvier, Black Jack's great-uncle, carried very little debt, had a substantial cash reserve, and invested heavily in municpal bonds, which were not affected by the crash. Even so, he lost several million dollars in one week, about 50 percent of his fortune. His nephew, Black Jack's father, actually made money in the first few days of the crash, but this was quickly swept away in an avalanche of selling.

Black Jack himself was left at the mercy of Old Man Lee. His own family agreed to lend him only twenty-five thousand dollars and to pay for a long-term lease on a house on Egypt Lane in East Hampton, appropriately named Rowdy Hall, so Black Jack reluctantly turned to his father-in-law for further help. James T. Lee forced Black Jack to give up three of his cars, move into a rent-free apartment in a Manhattan building the Lees owned, agree to stay away from high-risk investments, and submit to a humiliating monthly audit of his spending.

Black Jack's answer was to keep borrowing secretly elsewhere to finance his vices. He continued his womanizing and gambling, often at the Maidstone Club, a country club on Further Lane and the locus of East Hampton society since its founding in 1891. He also took women to the Egypt Lane house when Janet wasn't there and to the Manhattan apartment when she was. The golf caddies at the Maidstone Club knew that Black Jack rarely went more than nine holes of the course; and after making a putt on the ninth, he would dismiss his caddy to keep an assignation with a woman in the nearby groundsman's hut. One caddy, quoted by C. David Heymann in *A Woman Named Jackie*, says he would double back to watch through the window of the hut as Black Jack had sex with whichever member's wife he was with that afternoon.

In March 1933, a few hours before Franklin Delano Roosevelt was sworn in for his first term, Janet gave birth to her second child, Caroline Lee Bouvier. Although both Jacqueline and her younger sister had the maternal surname, Lee, as a middle name, Caroline was forever known simply as Lee. Jackie and Lee spent almost six months of the year in East Hampton. Their parents and the servants stayed at Rowdy Hall but entertained at Lasata. To save money, they eventually sold Rowdy Hall and Black Jack's father gave him another house, called Wildmoor, which had been in the family before Lasata was acquired.

Jackie quickly took to country pursuits. She showed pet dogs when she was only two years old. She learned to ride at the East Hampton Riding Club, which was close to Lasata. She would arrive for her lessons in her grandfather's chauffeur-driven Duesenberg, and a nanny would be standing by to brush the dirt from her riding habit with a stiff whisk. Jackie was soon competing determinedly in equestrian events and riding to hounds with her mother, who was an accomplished horsewoman and a junior master of the local hunt, the Suffolk Fox Hounds. Lee, on the other hand, who had been traumatized in an early riding accident, took no further interest in her sister's and mother's all-consuming passion for horses.

The tension in her parents' marriage was obvious to Jackie. She could hear loud arguments every weekend in East Hampton. She would climb out of bed and listen to the raised voices outside her parents' bedroom. Her cousins and friends also knew of the state of the marriage, from overhearing their parents gossiping, and teased her unmercifully. By 1935 Janet had become so humiliated by Black Jack's philanderings that she rarely agreed to be seen out with him, because she believed everyone was whispering about his latest conquests. This attitude only gave Black Jack a freer rein for his infidelities, but to Janet that didn't matter. He rarely missed an opportunity even when they were together.

Once, at a party at Lasata, Black Jack was seen walking off into a remote corner of the gardens with his arm around the wife of another guest. On another occasion, Janet actually caught him making love with one of her friends from the Suffolk Fox Hounds. Janet also found a woman's bathing suit in the shower at the Bouvier cabana at the Maidstone Club, which she took to be further evidence of his infideltiy.

The most flagrant of all Black Jack's affairs had an audience of millions. One of Black Jack's nine-hole golf partners with whom he had sex at the groundsman's hut was a Hamptons socialite named Virginia Kernochan. One summer afternoon, while Janet competed in an equestrian competition, Black Jack and Virginia Kernochan disappeared together for several hours. They returned in time to watch Janet competing in the final events. Several press photographers were present and one of them, working for UPI, photographed Janet sitting on a fence in her riding habit. To Janet's right, also on the fence, sat Virginia Kernochan. Black Jack, standing a few feet from his wife and not realizing he was in the shot, was stealthily clasping Virginia Kernochan's hand in an unmistakably affectionate manner. The photograph was published the following day in the *New York Daily News*.

James T. Lee was even more outraged than Janet at the public humiliation and pressed his daughter to get a divorce, but still she persisted in trying to repair the marriage. Finally, at the end of the summer of 1936, she told Black Jack she wanted a trial separation.

Jackie was seven years old and adored her father, so the news of the separation came as a particularly hard blow. Black Jack moved out of the apartment and into a Manhattan hotel and for the next several months only saw his daughters on weekends. The dynamics of the separation only increased the children's preference for their father. Janet Bouvier became the disciplinarian as well as the person who, from the children's point of view, had thrown their father out. Their father was associated only with fun and excitement, with weekend outings, indulgences, and gifts.

It was around this time that the Bouvier cousins began whispering about the family's darkest secret. Jackie and Lee, but particularly Jackie, were being abused by their mother. Janet had always had a vicious and violent temper, and she would beat the children at the slightest pretext, often with no apparent motive at all other than to help slake her own rage. As is often the case in child-abuse histories, Janet had been physically abused by her own mother.

Jackie was the primary target of the abuse. One obvious reason was that she was the eldest. Another reason was that she never made any secret of her preference for her father, which infuriated Janet. Then there was Jackie's physical appearance; she was fast growing into Black Jack's double.

Black Jack himself was aware of the abuse and gathered evidence from witnesses for a custody and divorce case. The sworn affidavits are still held by the Bouvier family. In one, a governess, Bertha Kimmerle, said both children were beaten regularly.

"I had not been in the home more than ten days when when Mrs.

Bouvier gave Jacqueline a very severe spanking because the little girl had been too noisy in her play. She would spank Jacqueline quite frequently...for no reason that I was able to see," Kimmerle said. On another occasion, another governess, stepping in to stop Jacqueline from being struck by her maternal grandmother, was struck herself. She also testified that Janet Bouvier told her to spank the children if they cried for their father.

After six months apart, Janet and Black Jack agreed to a trial reconciliation for another Lasata summer, but it did not work. They began living apart again, and Janet became determined to find another husband. Her search became full-time employment, and she continually left the children with a nanny. This only increased Black Jack's access to them.

In an attempt to limit Black Jack's presence, Janet took a house in unfashionable Bellport, Long Island, and refused to let the children stay with their father at East Hampton. But Jacqueline spent most days of that summer riding at Lasata. Riding had ceased to be a common bond with her mother and had become both a means of escape from the conflict and a way of securing her father's approval. She won equestrian events in the Hamptons so often that she was reproached by her own trainers for trying too hard.

Janet tried to compete with the hold Lasata had on the children by forcing them to spend more time with their maternal grandparents. They found the Lees' home too dreary, and they were confused by their grandfather and grandmother's bitter relationship—a mirror of Black Jack's with Janet—and by their treatment of Janet's Irish grandmother. The gambit only led to more demands to spend time at Lasata with their father.

The cycle of abuse became self-perpetuating. The more Janet slapped and beat the children, the more they showed a preference for their father. The more they showed their preference for their father, the more Janet abused them. She had also begun to show signs of severe depression. She was drinking heavily, taking sleeping pills, and staying in bed until lunchtime.

Not that everything at Lasata was ideal. The Bouviers were a competitive bunch. Mealtimes inevitably produced wrangles between Black Jack and his father or sisters, often in front of or even over the grandchildren. Black Jack's constant boasting about Jackie's equestrian achievements made her Bouvier cousins jealous, and they sought their revenge by constantly teasing Jackie and Lee about their parents' separation.

Janet finally decided on a divorce in the summer of 1939. She hired an attorney who began a lengthy investigation of Black Jack's infidelities in the Hamptons and in New York. For weeks he was followed by a team of private detectives who were so indiscreet in their work that Black Jack became aware that he was being shadowed. He would play tricks on the detectives, such as seeking them out to say hello. A striking blond woman was even hired to seduce Black Jack—no difficult task—but he recognized her as a honey trap planted by his wife's camp.

Even so, Janet was soon armed with a thick dossier of Black Jack's marital misdeeds, which included photographs of him with various women. A prominent New York socialite, Marjorie Berrien, was named as his current mistress, and there were accounts of out-of-season trips to East Hampton with his male friends and their mistresses. Janet filed for divorce in New York in January 1940 and leaked some of the details of his infidelities to the press.

The resulting publicity was damaging to both Jackie and Lee. Divorce still carried a severe social stigma at that time, and a public and messy divorce with allegations of sexual misconduct played out in the press was even more scandalous. Black Jack had a weapon in reserve, however. He was armed with sworn affidavits from Janet's household staff about her abuse of Jackie and Lee, her drinking problem, and her drug taking. Janet had also been seeing other men since the separation, so she was vulnerable to allegations of sexual misconduct too. A bargain was struck: the New York divorce case was dropped, and Janet instead sought a more discreet, unopposed divorce in Reno, Nevada. It took six weeks of residency—with Lee and Jackie—and a twenty-one-minute hearing, and Janet was free.

Janet's husband-hunting had become a Bouvier family joke. One of her companions was named Zinsser, and Black Jack's sisters told people Janet had been going through the alphabet and finally reached Z. The joke took on a life of its own, for when Janet and Zinsser broke up, she was next seen on the arm of an investment banker whose name began with A, and the Bouviers said that she had started going through the alphabet again.

The joke, however, was on Black Jack. Janet's Mr. A was Hugh D. "Hughdie" Auchincloss, a multimillionaire whose fortune was greater than that of the Lees and Bouviers combined. His family was related by a complex web of marital alliances to some of the most powerful and best-connected families in America, including the Vanderbilts, Whitneys, and Rockefellers. He was forty-two, seven years younger than

Black Jack, and as unlike him in character as it was possible to be. He was mature, solid, industrious, even stodgy.

He was also far removed from the New York–Hamptons social scene. His power bases were Washington and Newport. He was already twice divorced when he met Janet, so he had no reservations about marrying a divorcée, and as he had three children of his own, he welcomed a marriage to a woman who already had children.

For Janet, one of the attractions of the match was that it enabled her to remove the children from the control of their father. Hugh Auchincloss owned two palatial estates, Merrywood, a forty-five-acre spread on the banks of the Potomac in Virginia, and Hammersmith Farm, near Newport, Rhode Island. At these two retreats, the children could be entertained on a scale beyond the reach of the Bouviers at Lasata.

In June 1942, twenty-four hours before Hugh was about to take up a post with the U.S. Office of Naval Intelligence in Jamaica, Janet and Hugh married on impulse. A few months later he was reassigned to the Pentagon, and the couple were reunited.

Black Jack's first reaction to the marriage was a towering rage followed by uncontrollable jealousy, not over Auchinclosss marrying his ex-wife per se, but over his becoming Jackie's stepfather. According to the divorce settlement, Janet retained the right to remarry and relocate anywhere, even if it interfered with Black Jack's rights of visitation every other weekend. Black Jack began defaming Auchincloss on the stock exchange, repeating "Take a loss with Auchincloss" to anyone who would listen.

What Black Jack did not know was Hugh Aucincloss's real area of vulnerability. Auchincloss was a voracious collector of pornography of the most grotesque kind—books, slides, photographs, and other material showing the darkest, most recondite corners of human sexuality, which he kept in a library at Merrywood. In addition, he pursued his esoteric lusts in person in the brothels of Washingon, D.C. Had Black Jack known this, he might have been able to force Hugh and Janet to surrender custody of Lee and Jackie.

Jackie and Lee spent part of that summer at Hammersmith Farm, the Auchincloss estate in Rhode Island, and the latter half was spent with Black Jack and the other Bouviers at East Hampton. By then, Black Jack had his own connection with the Pentagon. He was having an affair with the wife of a British army colonel who was working as a liaison officer in the Defense Department.

Anne Plugge was spending July and August in the Hamptons while her husband worked in Washington, D.C. Within days of her arrival she had moved in with Black Jack. Jackie and Lee got on well with her, but for the first time they had a rival for their father's affection. Because he no longer had the restraints of marriage, he was able to pursue this affair as indiscreetly as he wished. The whole of East Hampton society was talking about their public displays of affection. John Davis, Jackie's cousin and family biographer, says he walked in on them when they were making love in the shower of the Bouvier cabana at the Maidstone Club. "They made love wherever they found themselves," Davis recalls.

The love affair continued intermittently until the following spring, when Anne Plugge returned to England with her husband. Later she wrote to Black Jack that she had given birth to twins who were beyond any doubt his children. The existence of Jackie's English half-brother and half-sister was to remain a secret for decades.

In the fall, Jackie, thirteen, and Lee, nine, left to live at Merrywood. To Black Jack's dismay, Jackie fell in love with the place. She began a process of playing her stepfather and father off against one another. If one refused her something, the other was sure to grant it. If one gave her something, the other tended to top it. Janet had successfully turned the table on Black Jack. Hughdie's Merrywood and Hammersmith Farm became the girls' preferred venues.

Black Jack began to drink more heavily than ever over what he considered to be the loss of his daughters to Auchincloss. The loss was magnified by the children's decision to spend the following summer in Virginia. Black Jack was plunged into despair. His drinking became so heavy that his friends, most of them heavy drinkers themselves, persuaded him to check himself into a detox clinic, the same sanatorium where his dead brother had spent some time many years before. It was the first of a series of leaps on and off the wagon that continued until his death.

When Jackie returned to the Hamptons in the summer of 1944, she had blosomed into a beautiful, alluring adolescent. She was fifteen but looked twenty, with sensual lips, large, expressive eyes, and a thick halo of hair, and she had taken up adult affectations, including smoking cigarettes through a long holder.

Black Jack found he had new rivals. Most were the teenaged sons of East Hampton's summer social set; they pursued Jackie relentlessly, but she showed no interest. Instead there was another, more controversial figure in her life.

He was Prince Serge Obolensky, a White Russian emigré who was older than her father. They went on many outings together, including long drives to Montauk Point. Obolensky's family had had close ties to the czar, and Obolensky regaled her with stories about life in imperial Russia. How far the couple went in consummating the relationship cannot be known, but it was certainly romantic, if not physical. She was well under legal age, and he was close to sixty.

When Black Jack reproved Jackie and pointed out that the prince was old enough to be her father, even her grandfather, she made a signifcant counterthrust. She fired back that most of his girlfriends were also young enough to be his daughters. Black Jack's emotional hold on Jackie had begun to slip.

According to her cousin John Davis, Black Jack's love for his eldest daughter was somewhat unhealthy. He says that Black Jack was "in love" with her instead of simply loving her as a daughter, so he was unable to bring about his emotional separation as she moved to adulthood. He became obsessed with the thought that she might be sleeping with men. Over the next several years he wrote numerous letters warning her to stay away from sexually unscrupulous men, men very like himself, in fact.

This obsession intensified after Jackie was named Queen Debutante by gossip columnist Igor Cassini. Black Jack believed the title made her a sexual target for every Ivy League undergraduate who wanted to boast of having slept with the Deb of the Year. In fact, Jackie appears to have remained chaste at least until her twenties and did not take her first lover until she was living in Paris. According to a completely unsubstantiated story, she surrendered her virginity to some presumably hasty embraces in the open-cage elevator of a Paris apartment building as it rode up several floors. It was Lee who, unknown to Black Jack, had a sexual outlook more like his own.

The era of idyllic summers in the Hamptons was coming to an end for the Bouvier family, although few if any of them realized it. In January 1948 John Vernou Bouvier Jr., Black Jack's father and the family patriarch, died at the age of eighty-three. It was more than just the loss of a beloved head of the family; the nucleus of the family, its very core, had gone, and the others were left floundering. Black Jack could not take his place. He had neither the capacity nor the respect of the others.

Then there was the question of money. Just about everyone had assumed that Black Jack's father was wealthy. The family, and Black Jack in particular, was stunned to discover that the estate was worth less than a million dollars, which taxes would reduce by one third. The Hamptons lifestyle had been cutting slowly into the Bouvier capital for years, and no one had been adding to it. The wealth that Michel Bouvier had made, which might have been built into one of America's greatest fortunes, had been lost. Black Jack had once boasted he would make five million dollars and retire before he was forty to live on a yacht crewed exclusively by women. Now his last chance of real wealth seemed to have vanished. He got a hundred thousand dollars, and his debts to his father were waived. Lasata had been left not to Black Jack but to his younger twin sisters, who promptly put it up for sale. John V. Bouvier Jr. was barely in his grave in St. Philomena's Cemetery in East Hampton when the wrangling began.

Partly because the estate was so small and no one could be satisfied, there were some very bitter arguments among the Bouviers over their inheritance. Black Jack wanted as many of the heirlooms, paintings, and antiques as possible sold so that he could have more cash. The things that were of little or no monetary value he wanted thrown away. The others wanted the most valuable items kept away from Black Jack so they might stay in the family.

In the end, a raiding party of Bouviers entered Lasata while it was being cleared for sale and rescued family treasures, including diaries, letters, and other documents going back over a century, just minutes before they were to be taken away. Black Jack had had most of them marked for destruction. They form the basis of most of the detailed information available about the family's history, and as Jackie's legend grew, they increased in importance. They were eventually passed to the writer John Davis, Jackie's cousin.

The family patriarch's demise increased Jackie's emotional dependence on the Auchincloss family for a sense of belonging, and therefore accentuated her distance from her father. It also made her more financially dependent on them. She had expected a substantial inheritance, but all she got was three thousand dollars, which Black Jack, struck with a sudden preference for conservative investments, insisted be put into U.S. bonds.

Jackie had always been cash poor. It would have been beneath her to work while at college—she was now at Vassar—and she was still dependent on her father for a meager monthly allowance. She now realized that she would inherit very little from her own father and would always be short of money, unless her stepfather took care of her or she married a rich man.

This was an issue for her for many years to come. Her entire attitude to men was colored by a powerful need for financial security. Her father had already fixed in her mind the relationship between affection and money. He would withhold money from her if he thought she wasn't paying enough attention to him and reward her with cash when she visited him or wrote him a long and affectionate letter.

The lesson was clear enough by the time she was in college. The increasing distance between Jackie and her father was emphasized the following summer when she refused to stay with him in East Hampton. She could not bear to be there now that Lasata was empty and up for sale. She went on a trip to Europe with her college friends instead, over her father's objections. For her the Bouviers' Hamptons idyll was over.

On a visit to the Hamptons in 1949 for a friend's wedding, Jackie was told by her host, Charles Bartlett, that there was someone at the reception she ought to meet. He was a young congressman from a wealthy Masschussetts family. On the way to be introduced she ran into the boxing champion Gene Tunney and spent several minutes chatting with him. When she was once again free, Bartlett could not find the man he had wanted to introduce her to. He had been talking to a striking blonde and had apparently disappeared with her. It was another two years before Bartlett finally managed to introduce her to John F. Kennedy.

The decline of the Bouviers and a shadow of what might have been was brought home to Black Jack at the wedding of his younger daughter, Lee, to Michael Canfield, in 1953. Canfield was the adopted son of Harper Brothers publisher Cass Canfield, and there is a good deal of circumstantial evidence to suggest that he was a bastard child of a member of the British royal family, the duke of Kent. Lee was only twenty, and while Canfield was not rich, she saw the marriage as an escape from the conflicts in her own family, including the tug-of-war between Black Jack and Janet over her and Jackie. It had the added advantage that Canfield had just taken a diplomatic post in London, so the couple would most likely be away for several years.

Canfield believed he was marrying an heiress to a significant fortune and the setting of the lavish wedding, Merrywood, certainly lent itself to that misconception. Black Jack was on his best behavior and gave the bride away. Later he toured Merrywood's green pastures and enormous Georgian mansion and understood for the first time the lifestyle that Janet and Hugh Auchincloss had been able to give Jackie and Lee and the chasm between his wealth and theirs. Returning to East Hampton after the wedding, he became profoundly despondent.

At the time of Lee's wedding, Jackie was already seriously involved with John F. Kennedy. Black Jack had mixed feelings about the romance. He liked Kennedy personally. They had, after all, a lot in common. Both were womanizers, both were charismatic figures in their own spheres, and both adored boisterous, manly pursuits. Black Jack had Kennedy over to his New York apartment and to his East Hampton home without Jackie, and they had a riotous time together.

However, he despised Kennedy's father, Joseph P. Kennedy, and had for many years, dating back to the elder Kennedy's days at the Securities and Exchange Commission under Franklin D. Roosevelt, when he instituted banking regulations that severely hampered brokers like Black Jack. In addition, the Bouviers were all dyed-in-the-wool Republicans.

This hatred of Joe Kennedy was one of the few things Black Jack had in common with his former father-in-law. Having won over Black Jack, Kennedy tried to win over Jackie's maternal grandfather by trying to arrange a meeting while on a visit to East Hampton to see Black Jack, but he was warned by both Janet and Jackie to stay away.

Old Man Lee's hatred of Joe Kennedy was so intense that it extended to the entire family. He could not stand the idea that his descendants would be Kennedys. Ultimately he disinherited Jackie over her marriage to JFK. He rarely spoke to her afterward and refused to attend the presidential inauguration in 1960. No one knows why Lee despised the Kennedys so. It cannot be explained solely by anything Joe Kennedy did as chairman of the SEC. More likely, they had a personal feud over some business deal that went against Lee. There is speculation that the answer to the mystery lies in the records of Joe Kennedy's financial dealings, which remain sealed at the Kennedy Library in Boston.

Jackie's engagement was announced in June 1953. She was twenty-three, Kennedy thirty-six. There was an immediate wrangle over where the wedding would be held. Black Jack wanted it held in East Hampton, although he was hardly in a position to pay for it. The Kennedys wanted it held in Hyannis Port. Janet believed that would be a humiliation and insisted it take place at Hammersmith Farm. She won.

The wedding, set for September 12, 1953, was to prove the last great battle between Janet Auchincloss and Black Jack. The ceremony was certain to attract national attention. Joe Kennedy's publicity machine had managed to get the engagement covered by *Life* magazine, and he had made sure that dozens of reporters, photographers, and columnists had invitations.

Now sixty-two, Black Jack spent the entire summer at East Hampton preparing to give Jackie away. He stopped drinking. He dieted religiously. He ran daily along Maidstone Beach and swam in the cool waters of the Atlantic to get fit. He lay on the beach for two hours a day, turning himself every fifteen minutes, to perfect his deep tan. He took saunas at the Maidstone Club. He became obsessive about his weight and kept meticulous records for his tailor, who was already working on the formal gray morning suit he would wear to the wedding. He dug out a precious Bouvier family heirloom, a century-old diamond-and-pearl pin that had belonged to his grandfather's brother, M. C. Bouvier. His determination to cut a spectacular figure at the wedding was intensified by the repeated snubs in the weeks leading up to the wedding orchestrated by Janet on one side and Joe Kennedy on the other.

He was pointedly not invited to the engagement party or any of the half-dozen dinners, parties, and weekends hosted by Hugh Auchincloss and Joe Kennedy to celebrate the coming nuptials. Black Jack knew about these events from the other Bouviers who were invited. What he did not know was that Janet had heard all about his preparations to give Jackie away and was determined on one last act of vengeance for everything that had gone before. The morning of the wedding saw Black Jack at the Viking Hotel in Newport. The most recent snub had come the previous day, when he was not invited to the bride's eve-of-wedding banquet. It had offended him so much that after weeks of abstinence he started drinking again. He had tried to contact Jackie, but Janet had managed to have a member of her household staff block all phone calls.

According to Jackie's cousin John Davis, when Black Jack's two brothers-in-law, John E. Davis and Harrington Putnam, arrived at the Viking to take him to the church, they found him in his room half dressed, with a half-finished bottle of scotch on his bedside table, but still coherent. As they helped him finish dressing, a call came through from Janet Auchincloss to check on Black Jack's condition. When she heard that Black Jack had been drinking, she told Jackie that her father was in no condition to give her away and Hugh Auchincloss would step in.

Davis and Putnam managed to get Black Jack dressed and believed he could make it to the church, but by then Janet was adamant. The last thing she wanted was a confrontation at the church door in front of dozens of reporters and photographers, seven hundred guests, and thousands of spectators. Janet told his two sisters to insist that Davis and Putnam keep Black Jack in his room—by force if necessary.

Janet's maneuvers to keep Black Jack away from the wedding, and the complicity of Davis and Putnam and their wives in the plan, caused bitterness in the Bouvier family for years afterwards. Jackie wrote a conciliatory letter from Acapulco, where she and JFK were honeymooning and visited him in New York after their return. However, she had less and less time for him from then on. She had effectively swapped a naturally polygamous father for a womanizing husband.

Black Jack went into a slow decline after the debacle of the wedding. His confidence shaken by his wife's ultimate victory over him, he became reclusive. Both Jackie and Lee saw him only seldom over the next four years, unaware, as Black Jack was, that he was dying.

In July 1957, Black Jack made the usual arrangements to spend the summer in the Hamptons but he could not summon the energy for more than one or two weekends. Jackie visited him and found his morale low; nevertheless, she left to join her mother in Newport.

Black Jack checked himself into Lenox Hill Hospital at the end of that month and was diagnosed with liver cancer. Within a month he had lapsed into a coma and died. Jackie was summoned to his bedside but arrived too late. The last word Black Jack uttered, according to Jackie's cousin Miche Bouvier, was "Jackie."

Jackie took control of the funeral arrangements. She wrote the *New York Times* obituary herself and had JFK ensure that it was published exactly as she had written it. Black Jack's funeral took place in St. Patrick's Cathedral in New York City, and he was taken to the family plot in East Hampton for burial.

Before allowing the casket to be closed, Jackie had placed a bracelet her father had given her as a graduation gift into his hands. According to one account, a Long Island Railroad train gave a long, mournful whistle just as the coffin was being lowered into the grave. It was a sound Jackie and Lee had heard many times, signaling her father's arrival on summer weekends—weekends that now seemed long, long ago.

CHAPTER 7

After Camelot:
Jackie and Her Sister, Lee

JACKIE ONASSIS and her sister, Lee Radziwill, returned to the Hamptons because of an event that happened on Aristotle Onassis's island, Skorpios, in 1971. Lee and her husband, the Polish prince Stanislas Radziwill, known as Stas, were among several summer guests, but while most had come for Ari and Jackie's lavish hospitality, Lee had come to convalesce. She had recently had a hysterectomy, and while she had recovered physically, she found emotional recuperation more difficult.

Soon after the Radziwills' arrival, Jackie introduced Lee to another of her guests, the photographer Peter Beard. It was one of those rare meetings of two people who believe they are meant to be together and recognize the fact at the same instant. Other people present saw that Beard and Lee were immediately and violently attracted to each other.

Since their childhood in the Hamptons, Jackie had become one of the most celebrated women in the world. Her marriage to John F. Kennedy, the shining moments of Camelot, her controversial remarriage to Aristotle Onassis, and her much-publicized spending and indulgences had made her an icon of wealth and beauty.

Lee's marriage to Michael Canfield, who some claimed was the illegitimate son of British royalty, had taken her to London. A woman of ethereal beauty, fashionably gaunt and with more angular features than her sister, Lee had had numerous affairs. She eventually left him for Radziwill, whose family had been leading Polish aristocrats until the Nazi invasion forced them to flee to England. They had two children. Lee had also had affairs during her marriage to Radziwill, including one, which the prince was aware of, with Onassis prior to his marriage to Jackie. There had been another with a leading British socialist politician that could have destroyed his career. The marriage was already troubled when the Radziwills came to Skorpios, but the death blow was to be delivered by her affair with Beard.

Beard is an international adventurer and photographer best known for documenting African wildlife and its destruction by the encroachments of man. He was once described as part Byron and part Tarzan. He was fast becoming a legend, his long, lonely forays in Africa punctuated with jet-set affairs with beautiful women. He had once endured twelve strokes of the cane in a Nairobi prison. Beard and Lee began an affair, which they were able to keep secret even on the tiny island with only a handful of guests and servants. They would meet in his room in the Onassis villa, close to the apartments where her husband and children slept.

Aristotle Onassis enjoyed Beard's company—both were very much men's men—but there was an undercurrent of macho rivalry. Onassis made a childish bet that he could hold his breath underwater longer than Beard. Beard accepted it, stayed under water for four minutes, and won ten thousand dollars.

The affair with Peter Beard eventually gave Lee Radziwill, then thirty-eight, the emotional strength she needed to leave her fifty-seven-year-old husband and return to the United States. The ten thousand dollars was put into a project that Lee's account of her childhood in the Hamptons had inspired. Beard would be documenting the disappearance of wildlife, but of a very different kind.

It was several months before Beard, Lee, and Jackie were in New York together. Beard arranged a dinner with artist Andy Warhol and an underground filmmaker, Jonas Mekas. Warhol had become the most celebrated of the pop artists of the sixties with canvases of Campbell's Soup cans and multiple Marilyns. When he met Jackie and Lee, he had become famous for other reasons. He had survived an assassination attempt and had become an omnipresent, if slightly incongruous, figure at all kinds of social gatherings and events and a gossip column staple. He had launched *Interview* magazine and created the Factory, a studio that provided a base for all kinds of avant-garde projects.

Andy Warhol and his business partner, Paul Morrissey, had recently bought an estate in the Hamptons in Montauk, at the easternmost point of Long Island. It was a secluded compound in a dramatic setting at the end of a long, narrow, winding private road. Five clapboard houses, the largest known as the lodge, were set on twenty acres of open land facing the Atlantic and perched close to sheer cliffs.

Built in the thirties, it was known as the Church Estate, after a wealthy family who had owned it and used it only a few weeks a year as a base for bass fishing. Morrissey and Warhol were not so much interested in the compound as a retreat, for they were welcome at any of dozens of more palatial Hamptons homes every weekend, but they were very shrewd investors and got in before real estate prices in the Hamptons skyrocketed. They paid $235,000 for the estate. Within a few years it would be worth thirty times that amount.

A caretaker and his wife lived in one of the houses. Nearby was a farm and stables where horses could be rented to ride the remote dunes and beaches. Neighbors included TV host Dick Cavett, who owned two of a cluster of magnificent houses created by architect Stanford White. (Tragically, Cavett's homes burned down in 1997.) Another neighbor was Peter Beard, who had a small stone cottage near the Coast Guard station. Lee and Beard's affair was still supposed to be a secret, although it was now more widely known, and it was still as violently passionate as when it first began on Skorpios.

Between them, Peter Beard and Andy Warhol persuaded Lee to rent the main house, which had five bedrooms for herself, her children, and weekend guests, who included Jackie and her children. It would be an emotional return for Lee, who felt more nostalgic about her childhood memories of eastern Long Island than her sister did. She had not been back since her father's funeral.

Warhol and Morrissey visited on weekends and stayed in one of the smaller houses. Mick and Bianca Jagger, another celebrated couple who were among Warhol's astonishing circle of friends, would stop by.

Warhol was fascinated by Jackie and Lee and pondered framing the toilet seat from the main house as a pop art artifact because Jackie, Lee, Bianca, and Mick, had sat on it. (Later Elizabeth Taylor added her luster to this select group, after persuading Warhol to let her use the estate for free.) Lee and Warhol had a trait in common: they loved juicy gossip, and between them, they knew everyone. They sat together for long periods exchanging rumors and anecdotes.

That summer, Jackie, Lee, and Peter Beard embarked on the project for which Aristotle Onassis's hasty bet had provided the seed money. Lee planned a documentary film with Beard about her childhood, which would coincide with a book she was writing on the same subject. Although Jackie was ambivalent about publicity—she seemed to resent it and be obsessed with it at the same time—she endorsed the project.

Coincidentally, an element of Jackie and Lee's past resurfaced at this time to their embarrassment.

For years, Jackie and Lee's aunt, Edith Bouvier Beale and her once beautiful daughter—known in the family as "Big Edie" and "Little Edie"—had lived in a twenty-eight-room mansion on fashionable Lily Pond Lane in East Hampton called Grey Gardens. Big Edie had been something of a bohemian all her life and had once wanted to have a singing career. That was considered no life for a Bouvier, and she was forbidden to do so. She married and divorced a wealthy attorney, Phelan Beale, and became a patron of an assortment of avant-garde artists and writers. Her lifestyle and her wild weekend parties at Grey Gardens were a public scandal and a family embarrassment. The two women continued to live at Grey Gardens, but they were virtually destitute, and the mansion was in a sad state of disrepair.

Windows that had been broken had been boarded up rather than replaced. The women had always kept cats, but their population had grown unchecked, and now scores of cats wandered around the entire house and grounds. Several were sick, and at least one was dead, still lying untouched in the house. Adding to the unsanitary conditions, there were gaping holes in the roof where rain poured in, leaving the whole house damp and invaded by mold and fungi. Raccoons roamed at will. The plumbing had failed. There was no heat. There was trash everywhere. Like the untouched wedding feast that lay beneath a blanket of dust and mold for years in Dickens's *Great Expectations,* decades of Christmas and birthday cards from Bouviers and Beales and Auchinclosses and Kennedys lined the walls and mantelpieces, a poignant reminder of things past. The two women had become eccentric, and the elder was barely capable of looking after herself.

The cats and the unsanitary conditions began to affect neighbors' homes, and they pressured the local authorities to do something. Suffolk County Department of Health personnel literally raided the house and condemned it, ordering the eviction of the two women. The elderly Mrs. Beale believed it was all a conspiracy by East Hampton's Republican elite to punish her for her liberal ideals and to embarrass her niece Jackie.

When the story surfaced, it did come as an acute embarrassment to

Jackie. After all, here was a former First Lady, the wife of one of the richest men on the planet, a woman who at that time spent more on clothes in a month than most people earned in five years, and here were her father's sister and her cousin living in what could only be described as abominable squalor. Jackie was quick to help, but it is amazing that it took headlines to prod her into action.

The help, although it came in the person of Jackie and Lee, was actually provided by Aristotle Onassis. Big Edie had been the only member of Jackie's family to write to Onassis to congratulate him on their unlikely and almost universally derided union. When he visited New York, she called him and sang him a song over the phone. He sang her one in return. He had had no idea she lived under such circumstances and now offered financial help.

However Lee and Jackie's intervention was also controversial. Big Edie's son, Bouvier Beale, had been trying to get his mother and sister to leave Grey Gardens for years and live somewhere more suitable where they could be cared for. He had offered to buy them a home in Florida, but the old lady had refused to move. As sad as the situation was, the order to evict, in his eyes, was the best thing that could have happened to them.

After bitter fights between Jackie and Lee on one side and Bouvier Beale on the other, Jackie appointed an attorney to supervise the renovations and negotiate with Suffolk County. Lee handled the interior decoration and was overseer to the contractors. More than a thousand bags of detritus were removed, the house-cat population was brought under control, a new roof was erected, and the house fumigated and redecorated; the bills were sent to Onassis.

Jackie and Lee did provide emotional help for her aunt and cousin. They visited for hours at a time, to listen to the Beales' endless reminiscences. They brought their children, and John Jr., still accompanied by a Secret Service agent, spent hours exploring the attic, where decades of family memorabilia were stored. He removed odd items of interest, including, incongruously, old skates.

Beard accompanied Lee on several of her visits to Grey Gardens, and it became for him a focal point of the project he was planning with Lee. He saw the decline of the house into ruin and the eccentric life of the two women as a microcosm of the changes in life in the Hamptons. This motif began to become the theme of the documentary rather than the original subject, Lee and Jackie's childhood, although clearly there was a considerable overlap.

The documentary was not intended to be an art film or a long-form documentary for an intellectual elite. Lee and Beard hoped Jackie's name would generate a network's big-dollar interest. While Lee networked the networks, Beard and director Jonas Mekas, with whom he had worked on an earlier project, began shooting some preliminary footage that could be shown to TV executives. Soon another venerable Hamptons figure had become involved. Truman Capote, who was a friend of Lee's, lived in Sagaponack, and he agreed to do voiceovers. The involvement of three giant marquee names—Truman Capote, Jackie Onassis, and Lee Radziwill—appeared irresistible, at least on paper, and it wasn't long before network executives were swimming around and about to bite.

However, when they saw the few minutes of film that had been cut together by Mekas, they found it too dense for a mass audience and rejected the project, telling Beard that no network would air it. Beard called in two other filmmakers, the brothers Albert and David Maysles, who had made *Gimme Shelter,* the classic documentary about the Rolling Stones. They began shooting based on a list of fifty or so people and places that were relevant in Lee and Jackie's lives, including the two Edies. But as shooting progressed without a backer, money inevitably ran out, and Peter Beard, who had sunk twenty thousand dollars into the project, and Lee began to argue over the costs.

With the film on the back burner, Lee focused on her book on her and Jackie's childhood—and on her relationship with Beard. When in New York City, the two would stay at Lee's palatial apartment on Fifth Avenue; in the Hamptons, at the Church estate. She despised Beard's cottage, although Beard loved it. It came with six acres and was a short distance away. He planned to ship in a huge old windmill he had found and convert it into a home. Lee tried to persuade him instead to buy a mansion in Southampton, although that would not have been in character for him. Because they had very different personalities with very different tastes and values, it was inevitable that conflicts would arise to challenge their love, which was founded on what friends say was a remarkable sexual compatibility.

Lee and Jay Mellon, one of the heirs to the Andrew Mellon millions and a longtime friend of Beard's, dropped by Beard's cottage unannounced one fateful day to say goodbye because Mellon was driving Lee back to Manhattan. Mellon strode into Beard's bedroom and found him entwined in the arms and legs of an exotic-looking young Bermudan model. Both were naked and fast asleep—sated, it appeared from the state of the room, after a ferociously passionate night of lovemaking.

Mellon did what he could to protect his friend from the wrath of Lee Radziwill. Beard was asleep, he told her, and perhaps they should just be on their way. But something in his manner alerted Lee, and she strode into the bedroom. There was a painful scene as Lee alternated between a towering rage and self-pitying distress. Beard, as was his way, appeared indifferent.

That was not the end of the affair, however. Lee continued to see him, but she found she had another rival. Beard had agreed to be interviewed for Warhol's magazine, *Interview,* and found himself bombarded by questions about Lee by Rosemary Kent, the magazine's editor-in-chief. Kent then sent Barbara Allen, a beautiful former model and photographer who was married to one of the magazine's partners, Joe Allen, to photograph Beard at his Montauk retreat. Bob Colacello, one of the magazine's mainstays, recounts in his Warhol memoir, *Holy Terror,* that Beard and Allen began a passionate Hamptons affair, the explicit details of which soon got back to Warhol. Warhol was horrified that his financing for *Interview* and his intimate weekends with Lee and Jackie—not to mention the rent—would go down the drain if Barbara Allen left her husband for Beard. Lee was equally dismayed and reportedly began harassing Beard and Barbara Allen about their relationship, culminating in a furious confrontation with both of them in which Lee is said to have insisted to Barbara that Beard was "hers."

However, rather than ending suddenly or violently or even irrevocably, the affair between Lee and Beard staggered on intermittently and then petered out. Lee moved out of Warhol's estate and rented a beachfront home on fashionable Gin Lane in Southampton. It was not a mansion by any means, but it was a beautiful home and came with a pool, three acres of woods, and a little under a hundred yards of private beach. She ultimately bought the property for what just a few years later was a fraction of its value, $330,000.

Lee's divorce settlement from Prince Radziwill gave her the proceeds of the sale of their marital home, a fabulous estate outside London, and outright ownership of their New York apartment—a settlement worth about three million dollars. Stas was to live only two more years, dying in 1976. Financially, she got out just in time because when Stas Radziwill died just two years later, he was beyond bankrupt. His estate owed $15 million, and there was nothing at all for his children. Ultimately Jackie had to establish trust funds for them.

In her new home in Southampton, and away from Peter Beard and other distractions, she returned to the project of her childhood memoirs. She now had an added incentive. Truman Capote had helped her to get a lucrative publishing contract.

She was given a $30,000 advance by Delacorte Press with another $215,000 to come in increments as the work was completed. Such largesse in an industry not noted for charity to first-time authors, even of the stature of Lee Radziwill, can only be explained by a misplaced optimism that the final product would be a warts-and-all recounting of what had, after all, been a tempestuous and in many ways tragic childhood.

Lee, now forty-three, intended the work to be more whimsical than tell-all. Jackie came out to Southampton to help with the research, and together they toured some of their old East Hampton and Southampton haunts, jogging each other's memories about the past and taking copious notes. They uncovered treasure troves of old documents, letters, and Bouvier memorabilia in the Hamptons, in Newport, and the Auchincloss estate at Hammersmith Farm. Even Janet Auchincloss, their mother, helped, although she was probably motivated by a desire to influence the tone of the final product.

During their researches, Lee and Jackie came across their old journals of their trip to Europe in 1951. Rather than make hers part of her book, Lee saw a way to make even more money. She would have it published as a separate work. Delacorte Press, already committed to spending nearly a quarter of a million dollars for her reminiscences, paid her another $100,000. The journal was rushed into print—a hundred thousand copies of it—as *One Special Summer* with high hopes that it would become an instantaneous bestseller. It turned out to be a publishing disaster.

Undeterred, Lee pressed on with her other book in Southampton, setting up a writing nook on the windswept beach. Her method was to free-associate on paper, and her approach was undisciplined. When inspiration deserted her she would drive out to places she knew, get out of the car, and allow her senses to take over, taking notes describing a feeling or a recollection here or a smell or taste there. Sometimes she dreamed of some past event and got up and worked until she could see the sunlight penetrating the darkness on the far horizon. It was a slow, tedious, and somewhat untidy process, and while it might have worked for some writers, the result in Lee's case was, in the view of her editor, incoherent.

Lee's editor, Eleanor Friede, who had her own imprint at Delacorte, had a lot riding on the success of the book after the failure of *One*

Special Summer. She saw some of the early chapters and rewrote them and sent them back to Lee. Lee rewrote them back to essentially the way they had been originally composed. Friede asked Lee to let her give the chapters to another writer to put into shape, but she refused.

Friede made long visits to Southampton to help shape the book. While the writing style was one problem, a bigger problem was the content. Lee wanted to leave out many of the negative aspects of her childhood and produce a *Ladies' Home Journal* version of how wonderful it had all been. Friede wanted something more revealing about the conflicts and tragedies that childhood had entailed, although even she did not know just how much that was.

In the background, Lee was being pressured by Jackie Onassis and her mother not to embarrass the family. Not that she needed much pressuring. She was as reluctant to write about those aspects of their lives as they were for her to write about them. After a year, half the manuscript had been completed to Lee's satisfaction, if not Friede's, and a large payment on the remaining $215,000 was due. The chairman of Delacorte, Helen Meyer, told Lee that the book was dead.

Lee turned her attention to television. William S. Paley, the legendary founder of CBS, had a Southampton estate, and Paley, his wife, Truman Capote, and Lee Radziwill were friends. Lee pitched directly to Paley an idea for a sort of elitist talk show in which Lee would convince people who wouldn't be seen dead on, say, *The Tonight Show,* to be interviewed by her.

Paley liked the idea, and his word opened all doors at CBS. Within weeks a pilot was being shot. She recruited several friends: the ballet dancer Rudolf Nureyev, with whom she had a brief but vigorously muscular affair in England years before; the feminist Gloria Steinem; the fashion designer Halston, whom she knew from Hamptons social gatherings and from her extravagant purchases of his expensive clothes; and the economist John Kenneth Galbraith.

Today the show would probably have been a smash hit on PBS or A&E, but network talk shows of the time were shallow, more candied than candid. The interviews were heavily cut and distributed to CBS stations for inclusion in thirty-minute local evening news broadcasts.

At a Southampton luncheon party she met the man who was to be her next great romance, Peter Tufo, a Manhattan attorney who ran a successful law firm and was chairman of the New York City Board of Correction, which administers jails. He was socially well connected and had married into one of the Hamptons' most prominent families, the

Gardiners of Gardiners Island. When he met Lee, he was divorced from Alexandra Gardiner Creel.

Tufo cut an impressive figure in Southampton society. He had dated Bill Paley's daughter and other Hamptons socialites. For Lee, it was not an immediate, explosive attraction as with Peter Beard. After lunch they went for a long walk on the beach. Lee wore his jacket against the sea wind. Later Tufo drove her back to her home. They met several times after that, and it was some time before they became lovers. They would spend weekends together at Southampton, and sometimes he would fly out from New York in midweek just to spend one night with her.

He encouraged Lee in her next career—her most successful. She had a brilliant eye for interior design and had done all the interiors in her English country home with Prince Radziwill, his London house, and her New York City apartment. She now resolved to make interior design her profession.

She had already conducted something of a feud with the legendary designer Billy Baldwin. The story goes that Baldwin was working on a memoir called *Billy Baldwin Remembers*. Baldwin chose to fire some shots at people he didn't like, and one of them was Lee Radziwill. In a draft of the book, he reportedly wrote about a woman who had to all intents and purposes ripped off his ideas and sources. He did not name Lee Radziwill but mentioned "an American woman who married a Polish prince" and other obvious details that left no doubt as to her identity.

He claimed that she came to him as a putative client and together they talked about his concepts and went around to see the contractors and wholesale suppliers and craftsmen that he would use. Then, instead of hiring him, she independently negotiated with the same people he had introduced her to and produced the designs herself. Baldwin portrayed her as cheap and conniving—cutting him out, she avoided his fees and massive markups for material—and the topper was the title of her chapter: "La Princesse Manqué" (The Failed Princess).

Lee heard about the chapter and was furious. She felt that being thought cheap was one of the the worst things that could happen, much worse than anything that might have been said about her sexual adventures. She mounted a campaign to have the chapter excised from the final manuscript, at one point reportedly confronting the book's publisher at a Hamptons dinner party and threatening "to sue the shit out of that little fag." Baldwin withdrew it.

With few credentials other than the homes she had already decorated for herself, which had been featured in magazines such as *Architectural Digest,* and with the helpful advice of a designer friend who also lived in Southampton, she began stumping for commissions. Her decorating advice wasn't cheap. She charged five hundred dollars a day and twenty-five thousand dollars a room.

The new business quickly took off. She was very good at what she did, and being a celebrity with at least a claim to the title of princess certainly helped. What wealthy homemaker could resist having at least part of her family's Hamptons retreat decorated by Princess Radziwill?

Her decorating business led to a romance with one of her wealthy clients, Newton Cope, a San Francisco millionaire, who had asked her to redecorate part of a hotel he owned. Her relationship with Tufo had been declining, and there had been several public spats. Cope and Lee planned to be married in the spring of 1979, and Lee arranged to abandon her Hamptons roots for a second time. But an hour before the wedding, the ceremony was called off. Cope refused to sign a prenuptial financial settlement that Jackie had encouraged her sister to seek.

Lee soon found herself in the middle of a public feud with an old friend, Truman Capote. Capote had often been a guest at Lee's Southampton home and she at his in Sagaponack. But in the mid-seventies she had quietly dropped him, partly because she found his self-destructive alcoholism and drug abuse hard to witness, and partly because she was vaguely aware that his vicious tongue, so amusing when he talked to Lee and someone else was the target, was probably turned on her when she was not present.

For years, Capote had been in a vicious legal brawl with Gore Vidal. Vidal was suing Capote for some remarks he had made in an interview with *Playboy* magazine suggesting Vidal had been physically ejected from a party at the White House back in 1961 for some allegedly drunken and boorish behavior. Capote, foolishly, was fighting the lawsuit all the way. He claimed that Lee, who was guest of honor at the party, had been his original source for the story, and he wanted her to be a witness. Vidal was a member of her extended family, and Lee did not want to be a party to what seemed to be Capote's grandstanding.

Capote tried to get Hamptons social contacts who were friends of Lee's to intercede for him and badger her into giving evidence. When she refused, he started to badmouth her at parties, dinners, and other gatherings from Montauk to Madison Avenue. The feud was the talk of the Hamptons, and everybody seemed to be taking sides. To Capote's chagrin, they were mostly on Lee's.

Then it all got really nasty. Capote appeared on a TV talk show and began sounding off about his old friend. He revealed intimate details that he claimed she had told him about her relationship with Tufo and Cope. Capote claimed that she had tried to seduce William F. Buckley and called him "a queer" when he turned her down.

After the show he expanded on his remarks to reporters, who found much of what he said unprintable. However, the little that was, along with his remarks on the show, became headlines. Truman was ecstatic at the response. He called Andy Warhol, certain that the conversation would be recited back to Lee, complaining that the newspapers in New York were not playing the story as big as those in California and Washington and saying that he'd had calls from people supporting him against Lee. "It was the best live television assassination since Ruby shot Oswald," he gloated.

Most of Jackie and Lee's and Capote's circle were appalled, and some who had supported Capote switched sides. The bad blood continued even after the legal battle, which Vidal won. Capote, working in his Sagaponack house, created an erotic, some would say pornographic, object of which Lee was undoubtedly the subject. It was a three-dimensional collage of photographs cut from magazines and pasted on a small box. Capote made dozens of such pieces and sealed each in a plexiglas box with a title and signature. The one featuring Lee was called *Principessa en Vacances* (the Princess Takes a Vacation). It showed a woman in the Grand Canyon in the act of sexual intercourse, her face hidden by that of a snake. It was later sold for two thousand dollars.

Lee's next battle was more private but also more painful. For years she had had a well-disguised drinking problem. Alcoholism is at least in part hereditary, and her father, Black Jack, had undoubtedly been an alcoholic. Lee could go for long periods without a drink, then she would fall into a period of persistent drunkenness. She would have blackouts when she could barely remember what she had said in her cups, only the vague feeling that she had embarrassed herself and whomever she was with. Alcohol certainly played a role in many of her romantic adventures, and sometimes it interfered with her business and family life.

By the early eighties, when she was approaching fifty, her drinking had begun to get the better of her. She needed Valium to recover from bouts of heavy boozing, and she had to hide her alcoholic breath during business meetings. Sometimes she would be noticed in Southampton wandering apparently aimlessly. She once overheard a stranger remark that she looked "so sick" when what she really was was in alcoholic withdrawal. Each new broken relationship, each new disappointment or reversal would push her to drink. Sometimes her children had to physically assist her because she was so drunk.

In 1980 Jackie intervened. For years their relationship had swung from close sisterly affection through understandable sibling rivalry to outright feuding to silent indifference, then back to affection, where the pendulum would start swinging again. Jackie was always able to outdo her financially, romantically, and in terms of celebrity and public affection. It was the other rivalries that got to Lee. At any party, when Jackie was there, she became the focus of attention and Lee felt abandoned. When Jackie started her career in publishing (with Viking, later moving to Doubleday), Lee was insanely jealous, for she was having trouble starting her own career and Jackie didn't even need one.

She was relieved when Jackie decided to make her country base Martha's Vineyard rather than the Hamptons. She did not want to play second fiddle to Jackie on the Hamptons social scene. Jackie did, in fact, look at several estates in Southampton and East Hampton. She opted not to stay where her childhood roots were for precisely the reason Lee was drawn back to the Hamptons. Jackie did not want to be constantly reminded of this memory or that place or that sound or this smell. Lee needed those feelings as part of her security. The other reason was more practical: the Secret Service felt Martha's Vineyard was infinitely safer.

But Jackie did not need to live in the Hamptons to know how Lee was, even in periods when they were not talking. Both of Lee's children spent extended periods on Jackie's Vineyard estate and kept her informed of Lee's decline. Although Jackie's attitude to her sister has been widely criticized, she probably saved her life when, in the summer of 1981, she took her for help, not to an expensive rehab clinic but to the most obvious place imaginable: a local Hamptons meetings of Alcoholics Anonymous. Jackie strode in with her little sister, who looked, as most first-timers do, something of a wet rag. Once she was seated, a coffee in hand, and the meeting had begun, Jackie strode out again, waiting in the car outside for the hour or so until the meeting was finished.

It was the beginning of a long climb back for Lee, one with many setbacks, but one that ultimately proved successful. In her sobriety, she was better equipped to handle aspects of her life than she had been when drinking. Her relationship with her children improved, her business thrived, and she ultimately found love and financial security, but in 1987

Gossip Queens Liz Smith and Claudia Cohen dish at a Hamptons party.

(All photos in this section courtesy of Joan Jedell)

Supermodel Christie Brinkley at the Hamptons Classic equestrian event

(*Below*) Alec Baldwin at bat in a Writers and Artists softball game

Bianca Jagger at a Hamptons garden party

Steven Spielberg out for a stroll in East Hampton. Spielberg-spotting is a Hamptons sport.

(*Above*) Martha Stewart, look-ing most unlike a domestic god-dess, shops at Jerry's Market.

(*Left*) Calvin Klein and Bridghampton Polo President Neil Hirsch gladhand *après* polo.

A much more common sighting: Calvin Klein's ex-wife Kelly

(*Below*) Peter Brant, Stephanie Seymour and son Harry

Kathleen Turner and husband Jay Weiss at a Hamptons fundraiser

(*Below*) Tom Wolfe wearing the right stuff at a Hamptons gathering.

Chevy Chase and his wife Jayne at the Hamptons film festival. Chase resents his link to the Hamptons "Malibu East" image, because his family has been prominent in the Hamptons for generations.

Lee was once again in financial difficulties. She had to sell her home in Southampton. She received $3.5 million, ten times what she had paid for it, from Frances Lear, ex-wife of the television sitcom producer Norman Lear. A few months later that year, in Los Angeles, she met the man who was to be the solution to most if not all of her problems: Herbert Ross.

Ross, who was sixty-two when he met the fifty-four-year-old Lee, was a former dancer and choreographer who had turned to directing on Broadway and later directing and producing movies. His credits included *The Turning Point, Nijinsky,* and *The Seven-Per-Cent Solution.* He was brought to a party at the home of a prominent California art collector by producer Aaron Spelling. Lee was there. They were immediately enthralled with each other, and a romance was triggered. When he was in his twenties, Ross had reportedly lived in an openly gay relationship. He had put that aspect of his sexual identity behind him and married the ballerina Nora Kaye, who died the year before he met Lee.

The romance moved ahead at lightning speed and within a few months they had decided to marry. If Ross was discouraged by Lee's lavish spending, he did not show it. They were married at Lee's New York apartment, and Jackie gave a reception for her at her own, more spacious, Fifth Avenue home. They set up housekeeping on a magnificent ranch in the Santa Ynez Valley in California. It was a working ranch with livestock and a vineyard close to Michael Jackson's Neverland estate. But Lee was not to be kept from the Hamptons for very long.

They spent the following summer in the Hamptons, renting two homes—one on Further Lane in East Hampton from a Hamptons socialite, and a second for the following month a short distance away. They immediately became the center of Hamptons social life: Ross attracted figures from the movie colony and the entertainment industry; Lee, from the social set and her New York City culture crowd.

It was the beginning of a campaign by Lee to get Ross to buy a property in the Hamptons, and he finally did so, reluctantly selling his beloved ranch in California and another property in Provence. The new residence was a superb $5.5 million gabled mansion on the ocean and close to East Hampton's Maidstone Club, in the very neighborhood where Lee's traumatic childhood had been lived out.

It was here that Lee made a wedding for her son, Anthony. A producer with the ABC news show *Prime Time Live,* he married another ABC producer, Carol Ann DiFalco, whom he had met covering the celebrated trial of Erik and Lyle Menendez for the network. John F. Kennedy Jr. was his best man, and Caroline Kennedy Schlossberg her matron of honor, at the wedding ceremony at Church of the Most Holy Trinity.

The ceremony and reception were given added poignancy because of one who was not there. Jackie had died in her New York apartment just a few weeks before, and the day was dedicated to her memory. Jackie's life had ended. Lee's life had come full circle.

CHAPTER **8**

Cocaine Cowboy

IT WAS CALLED Ocean Castle. The house that bore that pretentious but not entirely inappropriate name was a sprawling turreted mansion off Dune Road in Southampton. Its facade was modeled on châteaux in France's famed Loire Valley. It had seventy-two rooms, including a library with wood panels that had been imported from a Scottish castle, a large wine cellar stocked primarily with hard liquor and expensive champagne, two large kitchens, and several vast bedrooms, some with two en suite bathrooms and arrays of walk-in closets. There was a spa with a sauna and a Jacuzzi.

The house was a maze of corridors and large open spaces that had no definable purpose. There were numerous outbuildings, including a stable, garages, workshops, and a gazebo. As the name suggests, Ocean Castle was on a grassy ridge above the Atlantic Ocean. The rear of the house looked more like a turn-of-the-century boardinghouse than a French château. It had a confusing array of covered verandas and porches and a large split-level deck, the upper one for dining, the lower one forming a wide walkway across a steep dune to a broad, sandy private beach.

The master of Ocean Castle did not expect the editors of *Architectural Digest* or *House Beautiful* to call asking to feature his home in their glossy pages, however. Parts of it were dark and poorly ventilated, giving it a slightly dank, musty atmosphere that suggested

123

poor maintenance. It was pragmatically furnished, and the various rooms had been given names as pretentious as the mansion itself. The media room, for example, was a sparsely furnished space that looked like a meeting room in a Howard Johnson's, with a somewhat battered large-screen television at one end. The games room held a ping-pong table and a small pool table, and little else.

The master of Ocean Castle was almost unique among the wealthy residents of the Hamptons. He was a local Long Island boy who had made good in his early twenties and could afford to move into one of the mansions he had gazed at as a child, awestruck by the wealth and status they suggested. His father was Alexander Radin, known as "Broadway Al," who had owned speakeasies in the twenties and nightclubs in the thirties and forties. He had abandoned his first wife for a beautiful, raven-haired stripper named Renee. They had one son together, Roy Alexander Radin.

Broadway Al retired from the Manhattan nightclub scene and opened a bar in Bay Shore, Long Island. He and his son spent many afternoons together in Southampton and East Hampton; Broadway Al telling Roy exciting stories, featuring Runyon-esque characters, about his days as a big-city nightclub owner. Roy listened, but as he did so he looked at the conspicuous wealth around him: the beautiful young women in skin-tight jodhpurs with their horses; the tanned, athletic, well-groomed young men in their immaculate tennis outfits; the huge chrome-and-pastel cars gliding into the driveways of magnificent homes. His father's life, as much as he loved and admired him, had brought him only to Cooper's Hotel in Bay Shore. For himself, he wanted much, much more.

Broadway Al had amassed a wide and colorful circle of friends in his career. They ranged from mobsters to movie stars, and many of them owed Al. Orson Welles was a close friend; so was Walter Winchell. So were a number of reputed members of the Genovese crime family. Between those two extremes were a coterie of show business veterans: talent agents, press agents, personal managers, club owners, stage performers, and musicians.

One reputed Genovese soldier, Johnny Stoppelli, and Broadway Al were so close that he stood as godfather to Roy Radin. (Al was Jewish, but Roy was brought up Catholic, his mother's faith.) Stoppelli took his responsibilities as godfather very seriously and remained an avuncular figure, in the background, throughout Roy Radin's life.

Broadway Al died when Roy Radin was still in his teens. His father's surviving friends, the notorious and the celebrated, helped give Roy his start in show business. He became a small-time agent and road manager for rock-and-roll bands, using his father's contacts to get them suburban bookings. He even tried his hand at performing himself. But his fortune was built in the early seventies on what seemed a ridiculously unlikely ambition: to bring back vaudeville.

Radin believed, correctly as it turned out, that there was still a market for a traveling vaudeville-style show featuring performers who had once been successful but who were having problems getting solo bookings. He rounded up a bunch of characters who might have been represented, years later, by the Woody Allen character Broadway Danny Rose. They were animal acts, magicians, ventriloquists, jugglers, sword swallowers, fire eaters, lounge singers, and club comics, a mix of nobodies and onetime headliners. Red Buttons, Eddie Fisher, Tiny Tim, Tessie O'Shea, George Jessel, Joey Bishop, the Shirelles, and Jan Murray all performed at various times in Radin's "Tribute to Vaudeville" road shows.

In a brilliant stroke, Radin approached small-town police departments around the nation offering to perform a benefit show. The deal gave the police benevolent associations a cut of the receipts. Radin and his associates then sold advertisements in a program to local businesses. Most businesses were only too willing to advertise to guarantee their relationships with the local police, but occasionally Radin's men had to twist a few arms.

Sometimes the arms that were twisted were those of his performers. A famous comedian who worked in one of Radin's road shows threatened not to go onstage one night because of some dispute. Radin couldn't have the star beaten up, so he had the man's manager worked over instead. The comedian went on.

Radin was amused to think that here was a promoter with mob ties running benefits for police departments. It was a surprisingly lucrative enterprise, and it was supplemented by others. He ran a small talent agency, which often booked performers into his own productions. He also had a small management business, and among his clients was the actor Demond Wilson. Wilson had become a star in *Sanford and Son,* a hit sitcom Norman Lear produced for NBC and one of the top shows of the 1970s, although later his career nosedived.

Radin's shows were so apparently profitable that it has long been suspected that he also dealt in drugs and used his vaudeville shows as a cover. This has never been proved, and even if it was true, there is no evidence to suggest that any employee of Roy Radin knew what was going on. By the mid-seventies, Roy Radin Enterprises was grossing over five million dollars a year. He married his high school sweetheart and bought Ocean Castle.

Together, Roy and Loretta Radin adopted two children, but the marriage did not last, primarily because Loretta found Radin's lifestyle too wild and daily life at Ocean Castle inappropriate for raising children. Radin used large quantities of cocaine, amphetamines, and other drugs. He insisted that employees of his road show live in the house, where he worked from a circular office in a turret. Whether as an affectation or because he had reason to, Radin slept with a pistol under his pillow. He was unfaithful, often with showgirls, strippers, or models sent out from New York by agents and photographers and friends who told them Radin could help their careers.

Radin's personality was much more suited to being single. He hung out in the legendary Manhattan disco Studio 54, where he snorted long, thick lines of cocaine in a private room and hobnobbed with celebrities. He staged wild weekend parties throughout every summer when he wasn't on the road.

The house always had several permanent residents and numerous guests. Radin and his cronies patrolled the Hamptons beaches and bars, inviting the most attractive women to Ocean Castle. Word of his weekly bacchanals, featuring flowing champagne, a seemingly limitless supply of cocaine, and orgiastic sex, spread across the Hamptons. Models, wannabe actresses, and weekenders just out for a good time came out in droves.

To add spice and to encourage the other women guests, Radin often hired call girls from a Manhattan escort agency to join the fun and service him and his friends. The video industry was still in its infancy, but Radin bought a video camera and a videocassette recorder and mounted the camera on a tripod over his bed so that he could videotape himself having sex. He talked of making Ocean Castle a movie set for pornographic videos, but he was afraid that they would adversely affect his vaudeville business and his relations with the police.

To Radin, this was Gatsby-esque splendor: a Hamptons estate; compliant women whose names he couldn't remember wandering everywhere; the sounds of partying and lovemaking echoing around the house. It was the lifestyle he had promised himself when he was a child listening to his father's clubland and vaudeville adventures.

By 1980, however, Radin's business was faltering. Despite his expertise and dynamism as a promoter and huckster, the demand for his menagerie of off-the-wall acts was drying up, and there had been a number of investigations of his business methods, effectively barring him from working in some states. His accounting methods were erratic, to say the least, and he barely kept any records of his expenditures, which were considerable.

His health was deteriorating too. At thirty-two, he was overweight and looked ten years older. Cocaine had played havoc with his sinuses, and he was prone to epic nosebleeds. Amphetamine abuse and his weight were placing an increasing strain on his heart.

Then one fateful weekend, his business, his reputation, his whole life went into a tailspin, one that would lead to his violent, horrifying death. It was the weekend that Ocean Castle entertained a beautiful young houseguest named Melonie Haller.

Haller was a stunning actress and model with a classically beautiful oval face, a long mane of luminous blond hair, and a splendidly generous figure. Her two biggest claims to fame were a spectacular nude spread in *Playboy* magazine and a regular role as Angie Globagoski, one of the sweathogs of *Welcome Back, Kotter*, the TV series that helped launch John Travolta to stardom. She and a friend, Robert McKeage, a New Jersey business executive, arranged to spend a weekend at Ocean Castle through a rather sleazy photographer and small-time drug dealer named Ronald Sisman, a mutual friend of Haller's and Radin's who was a regular guest at Radin's estate.

It was April 11, 1980. The Hamptons season wasn't yet under way, and Radin was expecting what for him was a quiet weekend. His partying had diminished in recent weeks because he now had a regular girlfriend, a tall, flapper-thin brunette named Toni Fillet, whom he would briefly marry.

McKeage and Haller joined Radin and some cronies for dinner. Also among the guests were two Rhode Island narcotics detectives who were discussing plans for one of Radin's benefits.

The police officers left after dinner. At some point, McKeage tried to lure Melonie Haller, who had had several drinks, and another woman into his bed with a wide range of drugs, from Quaaludes to mescaline. Later, both Robert McKeage and Haller appeared in Radin's bedroom and presented a bizarre sadomasochistic display. Both were wearing revealing leather outfits, dog collars, and chains, and they reportedly whipped or feigned whipping each other for Radin's enjoyment. The following day, Melonie and Radin were alone in his bedroom, and she showed him her portfolio of modeling assignments and her *Playboy* magazine spread. Whatever happened in the room, she was later taken back to her own room, where a loud and violent fight erupted with McKeage. Melonie returned to Radin's room, where there was another violent confrontation, in the course of which Radin's video camera, pointed at the bed, was smashed.

Most of Saturday passed peacefully, with Ocean Castle's several residents and houseguests sleeping off the previous night's alcohol and drug intake in their rooms or trying to clear their heads on the windswept beach.

That night, chaos returned when one of Radin's full-time residents, Mickey De Vinko, overdosed on barbiturates. De Vinko, a former bandleader and nightclub owner, had been married to Judy Garland under the name Mickey Deans and was now working for Radin's shows.

De Vinko was rushed to the emergency room of Southampton Hospital, and Radin stayed at his bedside until he was out of danger. He didn't get back to Ocean Castle until the sun was coming up and when he walked in he found more trouble.

Melonie Haller was screaming hysterically and running round the house half naked. She appeared disoriented and frightened, as if she were having a bad drug trip. She was bruised and was bleeding from a cut to the head. Radin ordered her and McKeage out of the house. When one of Radin's employees fetched McKeage, he allegedly attacked Melonie, pummeling and kicking her and at one point attempting to hit her with a statuette. After the two were separated, Haller was driven to the Long Island Railroad station and put on a train. A conductor found the beautiful young woman slumped in a seat and semiconscious, clearly bruised, an eye closed and blackened, a lip swollen and cut, with blood on a fresh head wound, and with her clothes in disarray. Fearing she had been raped on the train, he called police, and she was taken to Southampton Hospital, where Mickey De Vinko was still recovering from his overdose.

Suffolk County detectives interviewed Melonie Haller at the hospital as soon as she was able to talk. By then, she had called a family member, who had complained to the *New York Daily News* that Melonie had been beaten up at some rich man's mansion in the Hamptons. The police were getting calls from reporters before they themselves knew what had happened. Their reluctance to answer questions made it look like they were covering up for some wealthy, powerful Hamptonite.

Melonie said she had been beaten by McKeage, that she had been forced to take drugs, and that she had been stripped and repeatedly raped while Roy Radin's video camera was rolling. She said that after a night of terror, sexual humiliation, and physical abuse she had been dumped on the train for New York like so much baggage. The mansion where all this happened, she said, was owned by a producer named Rabin.

"Rabin?" said one of the detectives. He had never heard of him. Then it dawned. "You mean Radin. Roy Radin?" The detective knew him. The whole department had heard of him. "Yes," said Melonie. "That's the one."

Police raided Ocean Castle on the evening of the following day. Stories had already appeared in the *Daily News* and *New York Post* saying that a *Playboy* model had been drugged and brutalized at a Southampton mansion.

The reports, and a tip from a police contact of Radin's that a search warrant had been issued, gave Radin and his associates time to clean house. The pistol, which had belonged to a Louisiana detective, was hidden; quantities of drugs and pills were sluiced into oblivion down the toilets. Sheets were stripped and laundered, the carpets were vacuumed, and anything else that might have produced evidence of the events of that weekend was cleaned or removed.

Nearly fifty police officers executed the warrant. As they systematically searched each room in the mansion, they were harangued by Radin, Toni Fillet, and two senior Suffolk County officials who telephoned to try to get the search called off. During the search, in which the police carted away numerous items, ranging from pillowcases and sheets to videotapes, a police officer came across Radin's gun, hidden in a closet. It was unlicensed, and Radin was handcuffed and charged with illegal possession.

Melonie Haller's allegations of rape and brutality at a Hamptons mansion produced big headlines. Ocean Castle was referred to as Radin's "Sin Palace." Radin's vaudeville productions were likened to the wild, raunchy *Gong Show,* which had ceased production a couple of years earlier. Radin was portrayed as a sleazy, fat impresario with a casting couch.

Radin's embarrassment soon became depression. Although he had not been charged with assaulting Melonie Haller and had not even been at home when that incident happened, he believed the Haller affair was the death blow to his vaudeville business. It had been promoted as clean, family entertainment, but now police departments all over America could no longer claim ignorance of his shady reputation. He blamed Haller, who had brought the allegations, and he blamed McKeage, who eventually served thirty days in prison for assaulting her (Haller refused to cooperate with prosecutors over her original allegations of rape). Most of all, however, he blamed someone who had not been present at the weekend, Ronald Sisman. Sisman had arranged for Robert McKeage and Melonie Haller's visit to the Radin estate.

Sisman, who had often brought attractive young women to Ocean Castle with him on summer weekends and shared them with Radin, made a living as a commercial photographer. He also took portraits and portfolio fillers for aspiring young models who had nothing else to show agencies. Many photographers charged high prices for this service, but Sisman would do it in exchange for a night of sex. He was also a small-time cocaine dealer, at the time the drug of choice in the smart set and almost ubiquitous on the New York club and the Hamptons party circuit.

Several months after the Haller incident, Sisman was at his apartment on 22nd Street in Manhattan with an attractive twenty-year-old Smith College student. Sisman let someone, possibly two men, into his home. They proceeded to strip both of them, beat them, then forced them to the floor and dispatched each of them with a single shot to the back of the head. Their murders were never solved. Sisman's connection to Radin was well known, but police never discovered whether Sisman had been killed because of his link with the Haller incident, because of some drug deal that went sour, or for some other reason. One thing was clear: it was a very professional hit. When reporters suggested to Radin, who by that time was choking on Sisman's name, that he had arranged the hit, he just laughed.

Radin was right about his vaudeville business. It never recovered from the bad publicity generated by the Melonie Haller affair. Over the next two years, several tours had to be canceled. Police departments he had once worked with successfully no longer wanted to know Radin, and those that did, understanding Radin was in a hole, wanted a bigger slice of the proceeds for themselves. His last show closed in 1982, but by then Radin's ambition, fueled by increasing amounts of cocaine, on which he was then spending between fifteen hundred and two thousand dollars a week, was directed at Hollywood. In the meantime, his relationship with Toni Fillet, who had become the second Mrs. Radin, had ended.

In a short, tempestuous marriage, Radin had had numerous furious fights with her. She had left on a number of occasions, and Radin had barred the door to her on others. She believed he had tapped her phone calls in an attempt to confirm his fears that she was having an affair.

Playing the role of a wealthy Hamptons hostess and socialite, she had run the domestic side of Ocean Castle with an iron hand, going through a succession of household staff, some of whom stayed, according to one account, only a day. Some of her enemies in the Ocean Castle ménage convinced Radin that she was not only having an affair but having an affair with one of his employees. He had her followed, and at one point Radin even interrogated her secretary in his car, a gun sitting threateningly on the dashboard, about his wife's relationships.

Radin had long wanted to produce movies. He was even describing himself as a Hollywood producer when he was still hauling his vaudeville acts around the country, although his closest association with a movie had been buying a ticket. In September 1982, Radin and a close associate headed for Los Angeles to lay the groundwork for what Radin hoped would be a spectacular revival of his fortunes.

Although he was almost broke, Radin knew that he had to spend money to be taken seriously in Hollywood. He took two suites at the Regency Hotel on Hollywood Boulevard and rented a Mercedes convertible. His financial straits didn't worry him because there had been a phenomenal real estate boom in the Hamptons and Ocean Castle, which he had bought for three hundred thousand dollars, was now worth several million. Either as a sale or as a mortgage, the house would provide his seed money for his foray into Hollywood.

He had some projects in mind because over the years he had acquired several scripts, outlines, and proposals. The one he liked best, because it harked back to his father's colorful tales of New York nightlife, told the story of a legendary Harlem nightspot, the Cotton Club.

Radin had some Hollywood contacts, but he needed more. He got himself invited to a party at the home of a retiring movie company executive, expecting to work the room. He didn't make any useful connections in the movie industry, but he did make a connection of another kind. She was a tall, attractive, self-possessed blonde in her mid-thirties with a sing-song Southern-belle accent.

The woman was Karen Delayne Jacobs, who had become one of the few women to break into the shadowy, volatile, violent world of big-time cocaine dealing—handling not small amounts of the fashionable drug but significant consignments that could run into hundreds of thousands of dollars. She always carried uncut high-quality samples for her own and her friends' consumption. Radin and Karen Jacobs—everybody knew her as Laney—ended the night alone in the bedroom of her new house in Sherman Oaks, bingeing on her cocaine. Radin had found a soulmate; she was like him in many ways, charming with a broad streak of ruthlessness, ambitious, full of ideas and with the personal drive and energy to bring them about. Like Radin, she was a great salesperson and self-promoter.

Laney Jacobs had been raised in modest circumstances in Alabama and Georgia. Her parents divorced when she was five years old, and she was bounced around between her two parents and her maternal grandparents. She became an expert manipulator, playing each parent off against the other, and both against her grandparents. By her late twenties she had been married and divorced twice, and she had failed to take a single step toward her goal of a life of riches and luxury.

In the mid-1970s she moved to Miami, then one of the fastest-growing cities in America. There was a thriving drug scene, and Laney mixed easily in it. She had a succession of boyfriends who were small-time dealers, then fell in with a Cuban marijuana dealer who showed her the ropes of the drug trade. She was soon in business for herself, and thriving.

The drug business was exploding in Florida, primarily because of the comparative ease with which marijuana and cocaine could be brought into the state by boat and by air. Cuban immigrants acted as importers and distributors doing business with Colombians who exported the drug. It was a business conducted mainly on a consignment basis. Losses had to be made good by whoever had possessed the drug last. This system, plus a crowded field of competing dealers and the immense profits to be made on the street, produced complex disputes, which inevitably were settled violently. Colombian drug dealers, toting Uzi submachine guns, won a reputation for being unusually cruel and conspicuously brutal. It was a reputation they wanted, because it meant people would fear to cross them.

Laney developed Colombian contacts and dealt frankly and straightforwardly with them. She appeared fearless, kept detailed records, and always made good. She also proved she was willing to hire the muscle to enforce her will when anyone was foolish enough to believe that because she was a woman she was weak. Her reputation spread to the epicenters of the drug trade, Medellín and Cali, Colombia.

By 1982, she had made several million dollars for herself. Miami had become hot for dealers. It wasn't just the violence. There was a backlash by the authorities, and Laney knew plenty of trader who had found themselves in prison forfeiting all of their property, the sleek boats and the private aircraft, the sprawling estates and the fast cars. She set her sights, like Roy Radin, on the movie business. It was a potential method of laundering her drug money and an eventual route out of the drug trade. She moved to Los Angeles to help set up a West Coast operation for a powerful Florida dealer.

Laney had been in Los Angeles a short time, but she had made a very interesting contact. After knowing Radin a few more weeks—and after selling him some of her personal supply of cocaine—she offered to introduce Radin to her new friend. His name was Robert Evans.

Evans's family had built one fortune already in the New York rag trade with the Evan-Picone company. He had become a small-time actor, but his talents as a salesman and deal maker had made him a legend in the movie industry. He had risen to executive vice president of Paramount Pictures in his thirties and produced a number of hit movies, including *Rosemary's Baby, Love Story,* and *The Godfather.* He had become an independent with less success but added *Chinatown* to his credits along with a series of unsuccessful ventures. A highly publicized drug conviction had left his career in ruins. But someone at the top of his game wouldn't have done business with Radin. Evans had all the connections but was regarded as a has-been. He was exactly what Radin was looking for.

Laney Jacobs made good on her promise to put Evans and Radin together. They met for lunch in Beverly Hills, and the two men hit it off. Radin pitched Evans an idea for a movie about the Cotton Club; in Radin's eyes it was to be a musical. Evans had had a similar idea for a movie about the legendary club, but he had been unable to raise financing for it. He wanted to make it more like *The Godfather* and use members of the *Godfather* team, particularly director Francis Ford Coppola. Radin started referring to it as "*The Godfather* with music" and "*Godfather III.*"

After Radin returned to Ocean Castle to try to organize one last vaudeville tour, this time with Milton Berle as the headliner, he received a disturbing phone call from Laney. Evans was not the only person she had introduced him to. Another was Tally Rogers, one of her drug couriers, and Radin and Rogers had begun to spend a lot of time together. After Rogers delivered a very large consignment of cocaine to Laney—worth somewhere in the region of a million dollars—that consignment had been stolen from her house. She was convinced that Rogers had ripped her off and that Radin had put him up to it, and she angrily told him so. Radin said he didn't know what she was talking about and hung up on her.

The rules of the drug trade were that Laney still had to pay for the
lost cocaine and that it was up to her to deal with Rogers. If she failed to
pay she could be hit. She hired several bodyguards to protect her and a
private detective to search for Rogers. Radin, meanwhile, continued to
develop his relationship with Evans. He was at a disadvantage, however,
because he was unaware that Evans and Laney had become lovers. He
was also unaware that Evans and Laney had traveled to Miami together
and talked to potential investors. Evans claims he did not know Laney's
and her associates' money came from narcotics.

Evans and Radin talked about forming a company to produce *The
Cotton Club,* and several other movies. Evans lined up director Francis
Ford Coppola and *Godfather* author Mario Puzo. Radin brought in a
Puerto Rican banker who could broker the participation of the Puerto
Rican government to the tune of thirty-five million dollars. But the
negotiations, in numerous meetings over several weeks in New York and
Los Angeles, stalled over Laney Jacobs's participation. Evans insisted she
be given a stake in the company. Radin believed she deserved, at the
most, a finder's fee. Laney Jacobs pressed her case hard, backed by
Evans, but Radin wouldn't budge. There was an impasse for a time. It
was a delicate situation: none of the putative partners could now
proceed without the others, because they would be risking a lawsuit that
would cripple the project. At one point Evans proposed giving Radin $2
million to withdraw from the field, leaving Laney Jacobs and Evans to
form the company. Radin rejected the offer.

Radin's godfather, Johnny Stoppelli, who had invested a fortune in
Radin's shows, was brought in to eyeball Laney Jacobs and some of
some of her cronies. Whether by knowledge or instinct, he recognized
Laney Jacobs for what she was, a well-connected cocaine dealer. He
advised Radin as forcefully as he could to have nothing more to do with
her.

Some days after a particularly acrimonious meeting, Laney surprised
Radin by calling and suggesting dinner to iron out their differences.
Radin was suspicious, and some of his associates advised him not to go.
Radin shrugged off their fears, but took the precaution of asking
Demond Wilson to be his bodyguard. Since the cancelation of *Sanford
and Son,* Wilson had starred in an ill-fated sitcom, *Baby, I'm Back,* and
was currently appearing in an all-black version of *The Odd Couple* on
ABC. He was given a pistol and told to follow Radin in a car, run into
him in the restaurant as if by accident, and drive him back to his hotel
after the meal.

Laney Jacobs picked Radin up at the Regency in a limo, but Wilson lost them almost immediately. He drove straight to La Scala, the restaurant where Laney and Radin had planned to meet, but they never arrived.

The limo had pulled over on Sunset Boulevard, Laney got out, and two other men, who had been following in a car behind, got in.

Radin's body was found a month later, badly decomposed, in a remote canyon outside Los Angeles. He had been shot several times in the head from close range. One of the people Laney Jacobs called in the hours after the murder was Bob Evans. It was to tell him, she said later, that she and Radin had had a fight. Once the body had been found, Laney left town, abandoning her cocaine business and the movie deal.

Radin's funeral was a modest affair, contrasting sharply with his flamboyant life. With dozens of reporters around, few show business friends wanted to admit knowing him, and still less did his underworld contacts want to appear in public. Red Buttons gave the eulogy, saying of Radin, "He had an angel on one shoulder and the devil on another, and it was a perpetual tug-of-war." He was buried in Southampton, a short distance from Ocean Castle.

The Cotton Club was made without Laney Jacobs's money. The murder of Roy Radin contributed to the preproduction hype and remained a shadow over the movie, which was dogged by troubles throughout its production, notably a feud between Evans and Coppola that had to be settled by the courts. The movie went grossly over budget and was panned by critics. The circumstances of the case threw suspicion on Evans, and Radin's slaying became known as "the *Cotton Club* Murder." However, Evans has always maintained that the murder had everything to do with drugs and nothing to do with the movie, or with him.

It was to be over four years before anyone was arrested for the murder of Roy Radin. Piecing together the puzzle was a gradual, painstaking process, but the two hitman had boasted of their hit, and their boasts made their way back to police. In July 1991, after a nine-month trial, Bill Mentzer, whom Laney Jacobs had hired as a bodyguard, and Alex Marti, who had been hired by Mentzer, were both found guilty of first-degree murder and kidnapping. Robert Lowe, who had been the limo driver, was found guilty of second-degree murder. Laney Jacobs, who successfully managed a multimillion-dollar cocaine business, tried to portray herself in court as a weak and easily manipulated woman who was a bystander to the events that led to Radin's murder, but the jury didn't buy that. She was found guilty of second-degree murder too. All received life sentences without possibility of parole.

Roy Radin's mother died before her son's killers were brought to trial. She had a host of medical problems, but her surviving relatives claim it was her broken heart over the death of Radin that really killed her. Ocean Castle was sold to a Manhattan real estate developer, Barry Trupin, then to another realtor, Jason Carter. A saga that had begun with a wild weekend in the Hamptons a decade earlier was finally over.

CHAPTER 9

Take My Wife—Please!

SHE WAS SLENDER, auburn-haired, and attractive, if a little shopworn. Years of seasonal outdoor activities—tennis at the country club in the spring, sailing off Long Island and Massachusetts in the summer, and skiing in Colorado and New York in the winter—had ruddied and dried her complexion. But these activities and a childhood pursuit of an Olympic dream had left her with a taut, athletic, youthful body. She was in her mid-forties, and a woman more vain than she might have had a cosmetic surgeon fix her slightly drooping eyelids.

She affected a patrician hauteur that belied her humbler origins in Asbury Park, New Jersey. She dressed in country-manor chic—tweeds set off by an Hermès scarf, or a Burberry trenchcoat with the belt knotted jauntily. Her stylish dress and bubbly, energetic personality succeeded in making her look almost glamorous.

Yet here she was, a wealthy Southampton socialite, the wife of one prominent, well-connected Hamptons millionaire and the widow of another, cruising the campus of a state university looking for athletic lovers among men less than half her age. What her Hamptons friends and neighbors would have found even more fantastic was that she was looking for sexual partners who would make frenetic love to her while her husband stood in full view and watched.

Her name was Nancy Wood. Her husband, Rodney Thorp Wood, was a haughty, snobbish, British-born doctor who had been educated at

Oxford and immigrated to the United States in 1953. He had established
a thriving practice for himself in the Hamptons and now, at sixty, was
chief of anesthesiology at Southampton Hospital. This was the third
marriage for both. Nancy Wood, born Nancy Steffen, became a child
figure-skating star, narrowly missing out on an Olympic place. When
her figure-skating days were over she went to Southampton College and
married a Hampton Bays pharmacist and volunteer fireman, known to
just about everyone as "Suds," and had two children with him. She kept
up with her sport and became a prominent judge on the figure-skating
circuit, one of the anonymous experts who decide the complex decimal
scores for competitive figure-skating routines.

After her first marriage ended, in 1974, she began dating an eccentric
Hamptons figure, Thomas Clyde, a wealthy but dissolute stock analyst
whose family was listed in the Hamptons' "Blue Book"—the social
register of wealthy Southampton and East Hampton families. When
they were married after a five-year affair, he was sixty-seven and
seriously ill. She was an athletic thirty-four.

He had had a heart attack a few weeks prior to the wedding and suffered from hemophilia, which left his joints painfully swollen and gave
him spontaneous and copious nosebleeds. He bruised easily and had to
have regular transfusions of plasma and blood products. A skin disease,
pemphigus, left him with blister-like skin lesions and required extensive
doses of cortisone—so extensive that he ultimately became addicted and
had to be hospitalized for withdrawal. He had fractured his skull in an
accident and survived with a metal plate in his head.

Clyde's alcohol consumption can only be described as gargantuan.
According to court papers filed by Nancy during a court battle over his
estate, it was Clyde's habit to start drinking hard liquor at 7 A.M.,
consuming increasing quantities throughout the day. He would down a
full bottle of wine at dinner and finish his evening at 11 P.M. with a
nightcap of a six-pack of beer and cognac. Little wonder, then, that
along with his other health problems he suffered from cirrhosis of the
liver, which almost certainly left him impotent. One of Nancy's
intimates described him as "the archetypal rich old man with a cough."

Nancy was his nurse as much as his wife. Clyde set up a house in
Hampton Bays for her first husband and their children, and she moved
into Clyde's rambling, leaking mansion on Captain's Neck Lane in
Southampton. Clyde's hemophilia meant he was incapable of any
sporting activity beyond lifting a glass, so Nancy looked for other

partners at Southampton's exclusive Meadow Club. Among those she became close to was Rodney Wood.

Wood was a brilliant, silver-haired physician who carried himself with an arrogance and grandeur that a minor aristocrat might have affected in Wood's native England. He had settled in the United States as part of Britain's postwar "brain drain," which saw thousands of well-trained doctors, scientists, and researchers, whose education had been largely paid for by British taxpayers, emigrating in search of higher salaries. Although he had lived in the United States for thirty-six years, most of his adult life, he had still not lost a trace of his upper-class British accent and diction.

Wood might have earned a knighthood had he stayed in Britain and risen to head a department at a large hospital, but his remuneration would have been much reduced. As it was he had to make do with his post of chief of anesthesiology, an annual income of several hundred thousand dollars, a prominent place in Southampton society, a forty-foot yacht, and multimillion-dollar homes on South Main Street and Terry Court.

He had been married twice and had five children when he met Nancy. His first wife, Gael, whom he divorced the same year Nancy met Clyde, produced three children, Sean, Ian, and Jennifer. His second wife, Sharon, had been a nursing assistant at Southampton Hospital. Her stunning beauty, it is said, had overcome his renowned snobbery. That marriage produced two children, Melody and Nicholas.

Wood divorced Sharon six years after his divorce from Gael. It became a joke at dinner tables and cocktail parties in Southampton that Wood's divorces were more protracted than his marriages. It was a joke Wood himself found funny. He delighted in forcing his former spouses to spend the money they squeezed out of him on their legal fees rather than on themselves or their children, and both ex-wives were routinely in court. Wood was involved in fourteen separate lawsuits with his first wife and a similar number with his second, most of which he initiated. The litigation, between Wood and Sharon particularly, became proverbial among lawyers in Suffolk County courtrooms for its bitterness and intensity.

The most optimistic prognosis for Thomas Clyde, given his overwhelming health problems and his elephantine appetite for alcohol, was that he would be fortunate to celebrate his seventieth birthday. He defied the doctors' forecasts, however, almost succeeding in making it to his seventy-second. Whether Clyde believed that Nancy and Dr. Wood were having an affair, or whether he was simply dissatisfied with her nursing, he changed his will late in 1984. A few weeks later, in February 1985, he slipped into a coma brought on by liver failure. His will left Nancy "such part of my estate as she would be have been entitled to receive had I made no provision for her"—or the New York State legal minimum of one third of the net. An earlier will had left her the bulk of the fortune.

However, by that time Nancy had taken management of Clyde's finances into her own hands. She had allegedly transferred most of his assets—about four million dollars—to a private corporation that she controlled. After his death, his estate, in the person of his executor, sued Nancy claiming "intentional, malicious, fraudulent and deceitful conduct" in transferring her husband's assets out of his hands and challenged the authenticity of his signatures on documents affecting the transfer.

The legal action dragged on for a year until Nancy struck a deal. She returned the disputed properties and over three hundred thousand dollars in cash. In exchange, she was allowed to inherit two-fifths of the estate rather than one third. She came away with a little short of $1.4 million.

RodneyWood and Nancy were married later that same year, and Nancy moved into the white-shingled Terry Court mansion. It was an idyllic lifestyle, fueled by their combined wealth: winters skiing in Aspen and upstate New York or following the sun to Palm Beach, where they kept a condominium; tennis at the Meadow Club from spring through fall; leisurely weekends on Dr. Wood's oceangoing yacht; and every other day the health club, the country club, and the Hamptons' au courant restaurants. Nancy also joined in another of Wood's favorite pastimes: bringing legal actions against his ex-wives. When Sharon Wood took some bedding from her ex-husband's property on South Main Street, the house they had shared during their marriage, Nancy filed a complaint charging her with burglary.

Any couple who have four ex-spouses between them in a community as incestuous as the Hamptons is sure to be gossiped about—and the Woods were the subject of some ferocious gossip. But nothing prepared Southampton society for the bombshell that was to drop about two of its most active members.

In September 1989, Rodney and Nancy Wood flew to Vancouver, British Columbia, for what was to be something of a working vacation. They checked into a downtown hotel, and Nancy headed to a college campus where students were assembling for the start of the academic year. She handed out a number of leaflets to several of the more athletic-looking students, one of whom was a strapping college hockey player.

"Meet Nancy S," the leaflet began. "I am one of a small group of volunteers engaged in a research project evaluating the sexual potential of the mature female. This project is to determine the response in the human female to intercourse with one or more male partners as evaluated by the number of orgasms that the male or female are able to attain in a two-hour period. The male subjects are limited to from five to ten for each female researcher to be chosen by her, to be between the ages of 18 and 23, physically active and unknown to the subject. A stipend to the male volunteer of $10 U.S. for each orgasm achieved by either party will be paid at the end of each session. Each male candidate in the study will be known by his first name and last initial. He will be questioned and examined by a physician to ensure that he is not a carrier of any sexually transmissible diseases and his physical parameters will be recorded.

"The physician will be present throughout the encounter and will determine the number and quality of the orgasm by each individual involved, and at his discretion, photographs and audio recordings will be made. Every effort will be made to maintain anonymity. If you wish to be considered as a candidate for the project, please call Nancy S."

At least two young men called a telephone number on the leaflet—Nancy Wood's hotel—later that day. Each made an appointment to meet her in her hotel room, where they were introduced to her husband. Tape measure in hand and a 35mm still camera around his neck, he proceeded to "record their physical parameters" as the flyer had promised.

In each case, Nancy Wood indicated that she was willing for the "research" to proceed. One of the young men, the hockey player, more than fulfilled the promise of his hard-body physique. Throwing himself into the project with remarkable enthusiasm, he proceeded to have a loud and earthy series of sexual encounters with Nancy Wood for the next hour. He earned seventy dollars at ten dollars per orgasm—three his, four hers. He also received a twenty-dollar tip on the nod from a thoroughly impressed and undoubtedly sated Nancy Wood.

Throughout the lovemaking session, the sixty-year-old anesthesiologist hopped around taking photographs and, according to one report, videotaping the encounter. Although no videotapes have ever surfaced, Wood's photographs, notes on yellow legal pads, and graphic audiotapes leave no doubt as to what occurred. Another research partner was of more modest talents. He left the Woods' hotel room after a somewhat less exhaustive research session with thirty dollars in his pocket—twenty dollars for his, ten dollars for hers.

After a satisfying sojourn in British Columbia, the Woods headed south in a rental car and stayed in Seattle. Whether or not they conducted further sexual research there is not known. Their next stop was in Eugene, Oregon, home of the University of Oregon campus. Having checked into the city's Hilton Hotel, Nancy once again headed for the university campus. Dressed conservatively in a tweed skirt and maroon V-neck pullover, she began handing out flyers to male students who caught her eye as potential sex partners. One student who met her said later it seemed like an unlikely invitation from an even less likely source.

"She looked like one of the freshmen's moms," said one student. "I'm reading this leaflet which more or less said, 'Take me I'm yours' and halfway through reading it I started looking for Allen Funt from *Candid Camera.*"

One of the students she approached was Jeffrey Lee Bevier. "There sure are a lot of nice-looking girls around here," she said, smiling. Bevier happily agreed. Nancy Wood then asked about the male-to-female student ratio on campus. There was some polite, flirtatious banter for a few minutes, then Nancy Wood handed Bevier her flyer, "Meet Nancy S."

Another student who received a flyer was Scott Kent Hughes, a nineteen-year-old freshman. He was attracted by the prospect of what seemed to him to be an X-rated movie fantasy come to life. A few hours after his chance meeting with Nancy Wood on campus, he phoned her at the Hilton and made a date.

That evening he appeared at the Woods' hotel room to be greeted by Rodney Wood, legal pad and tape measure in hand. Draped on the bed was Nancy Wood, wearing only a pink Ralph Lauren button-down Oxford shirt. After the mundane preliminaries, Hughes stripped and sat on the edge of the bed as Nancy unbuttoned her shirt, placed his hands on her breasts, and knelt before him. She performed oral sex, according to a police report, while Rodney Wood recorded her efforts with his camera.

She climbed up on the bed with her young partner and stripped off the shirt, and the two had sexual intercourse. After some twenty minutes, the romp for science was over. Hughes left with thirty dollars—twenty dollars for his orgasms and ten dollars for hers, according to Rodney Wood's notes and audiotape recordings.

"I was vaguely aware that the doctor was taking photographs, but I was not paying too much attention. I was concentrating on performing," Hughes told police later.

But the evening's research was not complete. After Hughes left, Nancy showered, then returned a call from another willing subject. Nancy believed this call was from Jeff Lee Bevier, the young man with whom she had talked earlier in the day. But Bevier had taken the flyer to the University of Oregon campus police department, and Rodney and Nancy Wood were now the subject of a sting operation. On the other end of the line was not Jeffrey Lee Bevier but a Eugene police officer, running a tape recorder of his own.

After some good-natured banter on the telephone, Nancy suggested they get together. "Would you like to meet the doctor and maybe enjoy a little time together?" she said. "It could be fun."

"Sure would," came the reply. "I'm looking forward to meeting you again."

An undercover police officer arrived at the hotel at nine o'clock that night. As Scott Hughes had been, he was greeted by Rodney Wood, who had a camera and a flashgun hanging around his neck. Nancy was recovering from her earlier exertions on the bed, once again dressed in the pink shirt.

"I'm Jeff. Are you the couple I spoke to earlier, the couple doing the sex project?" said the police officer.

"Yes," said Rodney Wood.

Almost immediately, three more police officers pushed into the room and identified themselves. Within seconds, Rodney Wood's hands were behind his back and he was being cuffed.

The police officers' routine recital of the Miranda rights was almost drowned by Nancy's screams and Rodney Wood's outraged shouts. The respected anesthesiologist reacted bitterly when he heard the word "prostitution" fall from the arresting officer's lips.

"I am a doctor and this is my wife," he protested. "We are conducting academic research."

When the police indicated they were dubious, Dr. Wood, disregarding the Miranda warning that he need say nothing, showed the officers his notes and let them know he had watched while a number of young men had sex with his wife. He showed them his "performance evaluations" of her sexual partners. "By tape-recording and photographing my wife while she is engaged in intercourse with young fit males, I can determine the intensity of her orgasms," he continued. The police officers remained unimpressed.

They confiscated the camera, rolls of film, notes, a file with the heading "Orgasm in the Mature Female," which contained his notes and "evaluations," and packets of condoms. Despite the promiscuous nature of the encounters with total strangers, the men had not used any protection.

Rodney and Nancy Wood soon discovered they had chosen the wrong state in which to conduct their research. Not only is Oregon one of the few states where all parties to a sexual transaction for money are guilty of prostitution, it is also one of the few jurisdictions where a liaison of the kind the Woods indulged in is likely to be prosecuted. Nancy Wood was charged with prostitution and her husband with promoting prostitution—a far more serious crime, carrying a hundred-thousand-dollar fine and up to five years in prison. For good measure—and doubtless to secure his testimony against the Woods—Scott Hughes was also charged.

The Woods were released on their own recognizance and allowed to return to Southampton, where the story soon broke in New York newspapers under headlines like DOC PAID TO WATCH WIFE HAVE SEX, DR. SEX! and TAKE MY WIFE—PLEASE!

Nancy tried to prevent the story from being published in the local newspaper, the *Southampton Press,* by calling on the editor and demanding that the newspaper remain silent. Naturally, it had the opposite effect, and photographers were waiting for Nancy as she left the offices.

Little credibility was given to the Woods' story that they had been selflessly conducting scientific research. Neither of them had any qualifications to conduct such research—at least no academic qualifications. One sex researcher quoted in news stories was Bill Young, then deputy director of the Masters and Johnson Institute. "Bona fide sex research is never done in a hotel room. It is at best spurious," he said.

The Woods stuck by the story, however, despite being unable to name any academic journal where their research was likely to be published. The Woods' New York attorney, Harry Issler, even announced that they had wanted to persuade other doctors to take notes while their wives had sex with men half their age too. "It was never their intention to do this on their own. They wanted to get a number of medical couples, doctors and their wives, to do the same research nationwide and to collate that study and then to have the results published," Issler said.

A man describing himself as one of Nancy's Vancouver partners came forward to detail their encounter to tabloid reporters: "It was like a fantasy come true—going to bed with your girlfriend's mother or your high school history teacher.

"When you see her face now she looks haggard by what has happened. But when I was with her she had a lovely smile and a beautiful body. She was athletic and experienced and uninhibited and enthusiastic. We had sex almost every way you can. She was loving and affectionate and I think she was really into it.

"The fact that someone—her husband—was watching and skipping about taking pictures kind of put an edge on it. It felt wrong and that made it more enjoyable."

Rodney decided to ride out the storm. "He strutted about the hospital like absolutely nothing was wrong," said a colleague at Southampton Hospital. "I suppose that's what the British would say is a stiff upper lip, but it came across as just arrogant. He had an arrogant demeanor to begin with, but this sure didn't do anything to make him more humble. At least not then." Wood also sent a three-page memo to colleagues at the hospital portraying himself as a victim rather than a perpetrator and blaming the Eugene prosecutor and the New York media for his troubles. Southampton Hospital suspended Wood "in the best interest of patient care," and Wood vowed to contest both the criminal charges and the suspension.

Legally, however, the Woods were in a very difficult position. The media circus likely to be generated by a trial would be catastrophic regardless of the outcome. Photographs of a naked Nancy in orgasmic ecstasy would be shown to the jury, and although these could not be published even in the brashest of tabloids, they would be public documents; some would doubtless find their way into print in such magazines as *Hustler* and *Screw*. Audiotapes of the sexual encounters would be played in court and transcripts published in every newspaper. Even respected newspapers, including the *New York Times, Los Angeles Times*, and *Washington Post*, had begun reporting the story.

Publicly, the Woods' Oregon attorney, Richard Urrutia, kept up a brave front and predicted an acquittal, saying that there was clearly no intent to commit a crime and that sex experts would vindicate the Woods' activities. But even if it was possible to convince a jury in conservative Eugene, Oregon, that the Woods were conducting legitimate sexual research, nothing could alter the fact that money had changed hands for sex. On the other hand, pleading guilty could put Rodney Wood's position at Southampton Hospital—and perhaps even his medical license—in jeopardy.

After consulting with their lawyers, the Woods agreed to make a plea bargain with prosecutors in Eugene and concentrate their efforts on saving his license to practice medicine. So, some six weeks after their arrest at the Eugene Hilton, Rodney and Nancy Wood returned to Oregon to face justice. They entered the Lane County Courthouse and sat in court number one holding hands. Prosecutor Sean Hoar read the charges, and the Woods each pleaded guilty to prostitution. Hoar outlined the events leading to their arrest and added that there was clear evidence that, had they not been stopped by their arrest, the Woods had intended to continue their activities in other locations on the West Coast.

Judge Jack Matthison accepted the plea bargain and sentenced the Woods to pay a fine of twenty-five hundred dollars each. There was to be no jail time, no probation, and no community service. Their attorneys claimed that they stood by their account but had pleaded guilty only to bring about a swift resolution. The conviction triggered an automatic review of Wood's medical license.

Back in Southampton, some of the friends who had once defended the Woods now cold-shouldered them. It was made clear by the attitude of their fellow members that they were no longer welcome at the Meadow Club, although there was no attempt to remove them from the rolls. There was even a gossip item in *Newsday* that club members were "panic stricken" at the thought that the Woods might turn up at the annual indoor tennis tournament at the club that November.

The Woods decided to head for Palm Beach, where they were less well known. They put their Southampton home up for sale, preparing for the possibility that Wood might lose his licence to practice medicine. Nancy Wood seemed to be facing up to the future more confidently than her husband, making constant plans for investments that would allow him to retire. A friend in Florida suggested they buy a bottled-water distributorship. They paid twenty-five thousand dollars for a franchise and began training.

It must have been during a training session that the full force of what had happened in a few short weeks finally struck Rodney Wood. In September he had been rich, respected in the community he had tried so hard to impress, and anonymous outside it. Now, in November, he was known from coast to coast as THE SEX CASE DOC. He was losing his job, his friends, his home—and now he was going to spend his twilight years as a spectacularly well educated bottled-water distributor.

He found he was unable to concentrate on the simplest elements of his training program. He became restless and irritable. He was so despondent that Nancy Wood took him to see a therapist in Boca Raton. He took sedatives to sleep and antidepressants to get through the day. Then the gossip and cold-shouldering followed them to their new home. They were made to feel personae non grata at the tony Everglades Club.

Rodney Wood wanted to go home to Southampton. Apart from being depressed by the prospect of having to become a bottled-water distributor, he was worried that his ex-wives would attack his assets if they got wind of his plans to start a new life somewhere else. He wanted everything to appear normal while he converted the assets to cash. The Woods put their franchise plans on hold and drove back to New York. It was an exhausting journey, and they arrived in Southampton on December 6 after more than twenty-four hours on the road.

The irrepressible Nancy left the following day for Washington, D.C., where she consulted a Virginia attorney, Mark Sandground, about strategy for protecting her husband's key assets. Rodney Wood was too depressed to accompany her and stayed at home, sedated. She called him that afternoon, but there was no answer from the Southampton mansion.

The endlessly ringing phone worried Nancy. She phoned a friend who was also an Episcopalian minister, Rev. Peter Larsen, and asked him to drop by the house and see that nothing was amiss. When he did so, he found there was no answer at the door. He retrieved a key from a realtor who had been showing the house, then, fearing that something was amiss, he asked a police officer to return to the house with him.

Peter Larsen and the police officer entered the house and looked around. Everything seemed in its place inside the beautifully kept mansion. Then, in a second-floor bedroom, the two made a gruesome discovery: a body barely recognizable as that of Rodney Wood lay on the bed, a red halo of blood on the wall and headboard behind him. He had put a twelve-gauge double-barreled shotgun in his mouth and pulled the trigger with his thumb.

Rodney Wood's ex-wives, who had little cause to be sentimental about their former spouse, knew that he had put one house up for sale, and they had started to search for his other assets—just in case he had begun a process of hiding them before his death. They were uneasy in case they were about to be excluded from any claims on his estate. Gael Wood had filed a lawsuit attempting to ensure that any proceeds from the sale of the house would be placed in escrow until a settlement with her and her children. She also made a startling discovery.

"It looked to me like they were planning to sell up and leave, and so I had a title search done on his property in Southampton and in Florida," she said. "Rodney had transferred them from single ownership to joint name in December 1986. The homes would become hers if he died, and there could be no claim on that part of his estate. My blood ran cold. Rodney never, ever gave anything away, and after his messy divorce from Sharon he would have been too afraid to put anything in his wife's name."

Other elements of the suicide appeared suspicious. A shotgun blast in the head seemed a quick but messy way for an anesthesiologist to kill himself. Rodney Wood, who had spent a lifetime gently lulling people into a painless twilight, surely had less violent means of suicide at his disposal. This anomaly, and the transfer of property, which mirrored the transfer of her previous husband's property prior to his death, raised all kinds of suspicions in the minds of people who were predisposed to think evil of Nancy Wood. There were even rumors that Rodney Wood had played a role in the onset of Thomas Clyde's coma.

In fact, there was never any evidence that Rodney Wood's death had been anything but suicide or that Thomas Clyde's last illness had been anything other than a hepatic coma. The medical examiner who performed an autopsy on Rodney Wood, Sigmund Menchel, found nothing untoward. There were no indications that Wood had not fired the shotgun himself.

Nevertheless, Gael Wood hired a private investigator to look into the suicide, and her lawyers got to work. They filed a suit on behalf of Ian Wood, Gael's sixteen-year-old son with Rodney Wood, to prevent Nancy from having the body cremated and another suit demanding the body be handed over to the children for burial rather than to Nancy.

The body lay unburied for two weeks while the dispute went on. A memorial service was held at St. John's Episcopal Church in Southampton, with Gael, Sharon, and their children entering through the front door while Nancy was led in a side door by Rev. Larsen. About a hundred people were there, including many of Dr. Wood's former colleagues. Two nurses from Southampton Hospital who had worked closely with him read passages from the Gospel According to St. John and the Book of Romans. At the end they all said the Lord's Prayer— "forgive us our trespasses as we forgive those who trespass against us"— but there was little of that spirit present in the ice-cool atmosphere between Nancy and the rest of the Woods.

Eventually lawyers for both sides hammered out an agreement

allowing Rodney Wood to be buried under a flat headstone in a funeral to cost no more than four thousand dollars. A bizarre ceremony took place shortly before Christmas. All three Mrs. Woods stood by the graveside and watched as the taupe coffin containing the remains of Rodney Wood was lowered into the ground, a crowd of reporters and photographers standing a prearranged 25 yards away. Once more, Rev. Larsen said a few words. Gael and Sharon shivered on one side of the coffin, and Nancy stood impassively on the other.

A flurry of litigation lay ahead over the Wood estate. The lion's share, about $3.5 million in real estate, had been transferred to Nancy's name, leaving only seven hundred thousand dollars to fight over. The mundane details of that battle only occasionally surfaced in the newspapers, but the question remained: why had a respected doctor risked so much—including his life—on such a sordid escapade?

Nancy Wood has said little about the affair since her husband's death. A Southampton socialite who remained a stalwart friend throughout the crisis says she questioned Nancy but got few satisfactory answers: "I said, 'Nancy, you know, how could you? Apart from anything else you could have gotten a disease.' She just said it had been her husband's idea and she loved him and she was just so desperate for the marriage to work."

Gael and Sharon Wood have always maintained that Rodney Wood had never betrayed the slightest hint of any comparable peccadillo during the time they were married to him. The newspaper 7 Days and Cosmopolitan magazine quoted Gael as saying that the research project amounted to "goodies for Nancy."

An ex-girlfriend of Rodney Wood did provide a clue to the mystery. Lisa Allen, now a real estate broker living in Connecticut, says that when she dated Wood in the Hamptons he evinced a morbid curiosity about her sexual history.

"He wanted to hear stories about my past, the more lurid and more detailed the better," Allen says. "He pestered me to the point where I made things up—ludicrous things—me with two strange men in a hotel bar and things like that. There was something very voyeuristic about it. It was as if he were watching me with another man. It really turned him on. I think perhaps that as he got older he needed more of that sort of thing and in the end curiosity got the better of him. He certainly paid one hell of a price."

PART THREE

The Hamptons at War

Introduction

On August 26, 1939, a week before Germany invaded Poland, German Admiral Karl Doenitz sent the first U-boat patrols into the Atlantic to prepare for what was to become one of the crucial struggles of the war—the Battle of the Atlantic. Transatlantic shipping was to be Britain's lifeline, and it was the U-boats' job to cut that lifeline by sinking British, American, and other ships bringing essential supplies from U.S. ports to Britain. It was a war of stealth. The U-boats tracked their quarry unseen, struck quickly and lethally, and disappeared.

Even before the United States joined the war in December 1941, the Battle of the Atlantic had brought the war home to the Hamptons and other parts of Long Island. The U-boats lurked just a few miles offshore, and oil, debris, and bodies from torpedoed merchant ships occasionally washed up on Hamptons beaches. Fishing boats from Greenport and Montauk sometimes went out on freelance submarine patrol and sighted U-boats lying in wait. Some fishing vessels are said to have traded with U-boat commanders, who were invariably short of fresh food.

After Pearl Harbor and the U.S. entry into the war, Long Island became a literal front line. No longer deterred by U.S. neutrality, the U-boats patrolled closer to shore and could sometimes be heard from the beaches. One even sailed within sight of the lights of lower Manhattan.

There were other signs of the war in the Hamptons. Antiaircraft batteries were placed throughout the East End to protect aircraft factories farther west on Long Island. Volunteers who manned them were taught to recognize German bombers—although none were ever seen. No German bomber had anything like the range necessary for a transatlantic raid, and the Germans had no aircraft carriers. Westhampton airport became a military base for the U.S. Army Air Corps. The Montauk Manor Hotel was commandeered by the navy and used to house sailors testing torpedoes at a base in Fort Pond Bay. Long-range artillery was placed at Camp Hero in Montauk. Some wealthy New Yorkers allowed their homes in East Hampton and Southampton to be used to house children from English cities who had endured heavy bombing, although the journey across the Atlantic was at least as dangerous as staying home.

In 1942, private sailing vessels, most of them racing yachts, were manned by men who were unfit for military service and were recruited to form the Picket Patrol, which also became known as the Hooligans' Navy. Officially a special detachment of the Coast Guard, the Picket Patrol was a fleet of seventy yawls, ketches, sloops, and schooners whose mission was to patrol the entire East Coast from Maine to Key West looking for U-boats. Sailboats were chosen because they were fast, low-maintenance vessels, could stay at sea for long periods and were most likely to be ignored by U-boat commanders who sighted them.

The idea of using civilian vessels had come from Britain's success at Dunkirk in 1940, when the defeated British army had been evacuated from French beaches by an odd fleet of small craft, including fishing boats, tugboats, ferries, and sports craft. One of the Picket Patrol's bases was Greenport on the North Fork, and many of the Picket Patrol's crews were Hamptonites.

The Picket Patrol vessel with a special claim to fame is the *Zaida*, a fifty-eight-foot yawl commandeered into the Coast Guard as the more prosaic CGR 3070. The skipper was Curtis Arnall, a thirty-four-year-old yachtsman who had been the radio voice of Buck Rogers before the war. The crew included Joe Choate, the scion of a New York banking family, Ward Weimar, a twenty-one-year-old pre-med student who had dropped out of Dartmouth College to join up, and Ted Carlson, a Brooklyn taxi driver.

In November 1942, the *Zaida* was sent out to patrol a fifteen-square-mile area about fifty miles off Montauk. At the end of an otherwise uneventful week's duty, the *Zaida* was caught in a violent storm with winds of up to fifty miles per hour. The mizzenmast was blown off, sails were ripped apart, and the ship's only source of heat, a pot-bellied stove, was lost. The radio was drenched, and the sea took the lifeboat, a row-boat, and essential supplies.

For the next three weeks the *Zaida* was taken on a nightmarish journey. The crew had to place their tongues on the mainmast to catch fresh rain water dripping down it. They had to bail seawater from the cabin for hours at a time. They were battered by mountainous seas, exhausted by lack of sleep, and weak from hunger.

They encountered several ships, but the bad weather prevented any rescue. At one point a British destroyer took them under tow, but the line broke in bad weather and they were alone once more. Eventually, on Christmas Eve 1942, they were found drifting into a minefield off Cape Hatteras and rescued. Few people heard their story of courage and endurance.

The men who crewed the *Zaida* are dead today, but the *Zaida*, now in private hands again, is still sailing. She returned to Greenport in 1997 when the East End Seaport Museum staged an exhibit on the little-known Picket Patrol. There is also another *Zaida*. Chuck and Ward Weimar Jr., sons of the Ward Weimar who served in the Picket Patrol, are now Montauk fishermen and operate a fishing boat under that name as a tribute to their father.

The Picket Patrol's job was to observe and report, not attack, submarines. There were too few vessels patrolling too large an area for them to make a serious impact on the Battle of the Atlantic. And one of the most daring U-boat operations against the United States easily evaded the yachts of the Picket Patrol. It was a German attempt to insert teams of saboteurs into the country, called Operation Pastorius after the leader of the first German immigrants to the United States. One of the targets of that operation was the Hamptons.

CHAPTER 10

The Nazis Have Landed

IN THE EARLY HOURS of June 13, 1942, the dark shape of a submarine conning tower broke the surface of the churning waters of the Atlantic two miles off the Hamptons village of Amagansett. It was the beginning of Operation Pastorius, one of the most bizarre episodes of World War II, an episode whose details and importance remained secret for decades after the end of the war.

The twenty-eight-year-old captain of U-202, Hans Heinz Lindner, was a veteran of the Atlantic U-boat war and had sunk several freighters off Newfoundland and Cape Hatteras, North Carolina. He had also been one of several U-boat commanders who tried but failed to force their way through the Straits of Gibraltar and into the Mediterranean to prey on Allied shipping supplying troops in North Africa.

But the purpose of this mission was not to attack convoys on the Atlantic shipping lanes. His orders were to drop a group of agents from the German military counterintelligence agency, the Abwehr, on the Long Island coast. At the moment U-202 emerged from the Atlantic, a second U-boat, U-584, commanded by an old friend of Lindner's, Joachim Deecke, was heading southwest to Florida on a similar mission: to land German agents on a beach near Jacksonville.

Lindner inched the U-202 toward a sandy spit off the Amagansett beach and into dangerously shallow waters. He ordered a landing crew up top and told the leader of the Abwehr group he was cleared to take

156

his men and supplies ashore. The four agents and two submariners loaded four crates of explosives and other supplies into a dinghy tethered by a line to the U-boat. The seamen climbed into the rubber craft and let it drift to shore while the other members of the crew played out the line. When the seamen unloaded the crates, they pulled hard on the rope and the deckhands hauled the dinghy and its two-man crew back to the submarine. The four Abwehr agents then went ashore in the rubber dinghy in the same manner.

The operation had taken longer than expected, and the entire time, Lindner was being drawn closer and closer to the beach. By the time the rubber dinghy was recovered and they were ready to push off, the U-202 was caught fast on a sandbar. Lindner repeatedly ordered the engines full ahead and then astern to try to free her, but it was futile. She was aground, and every time he started her engines he risked being heard by Coast Guard patrols.

The four men that Lindner had risked his ship and the lives of his men to place on American soil seem unlikely choices for the mission they had been given. They had only one attribute in common. They were Germans who had lived in the United States for years. They spoke almost accentless English and could pass for American citizens, if not for native Americans. They were led by a thirty-nine-year-old former member of the U.S. Air Corps named George Dasch. Dasch had first come to the United States in 1922 as a teenaged stowaway aboard a Swedish freighter. He served on several ships plying transatlantic routes and also worked as a waiter in hotels in New York and San Francisco. Between jobs he earned money as a professional gambler. He spent one year in the American military and married an American woman nicknamed "Snooks" who ran a beauty parlor in the Bronx. In 1926 he had been arrested for running a Long Island brothel and selling illegal liquor but never prosecuted.

In 1941, afraid that German nationals would be interned if the United States entered the war, he applied for U.S. citizenship, but before his case could be heard he changed his mind and returned to Germany. Crossing the Atlantic was dangerous because of German U-boats, so he took a longer and tortuous route. He traveled from San Francisco aboard a Japanese passenger liner, the *Tatuta Maru,* to Yokohama.

From there he traveled to Vladivostock and across the Soviet Union to Moscow and on to Berlin, just managing to reach Germany before the Nazi invasion of Russia. In Berlin he was recruited to monitor British and American radio broadcasts. Once he was settled he sent for Snooks, his American wife. She tried to fly to Portugal via Bermuda and was interned there by the British.

In November 1941, just days before the Japanese attacked Pearl Harbor, Dasch was summoned by Walter Kappe, a lieutenant in the Abwehr who directed foreign covert operations. Kappe was looking for loyal Germans who could pass as Americans, and Dasch had come to his attention because of his military experience in America and his firsthand and encyclopedic knowledge of American life.

Kappe wanted to send a small group of saboteurs into the United States to blow up railroads, factories, and other installations. It was to be called Operation Pastorius, after Franz Pastorius, the first German immigrant to the New World. The Germans had gone to a considerable effort to build rings of spies and would-be saboteurs in the United States in the 1930s, but those networks had been uncovered by the FBI early in 1941, when dozens of German agents were interned or deported. The Abwehr feared that those who escaped the roundups had probably been compromised by those who had not. In any case, they could not take that risk. Under pressure to rebuild the networks fast, Kappe was forced to turn to people with Nazi loyalties and strong ties to America but who were otherwise amateurs.

At first Dasch was confused by Kappe's approach. The United States was at that time at least nominally neutral. Kappe assured him that America would soon be in the war. Together they studied records of Germans who had returned to the United States and were likely candidates for the operation, as well as dossiers on Germans still in America whose loyalty was with the Reich. Within a few weeks they had assembled a strike team that would pose an unprecedented threat to American life.

The next to join the saboteurs was Ernst Peter Burger. Burger was one of the original members of the Nazi party and had taken part in Adolf Hitler's attempted Beer Hall Putsch in Munich in 1923. After Hitler went to prison for his part in the uprising, Burger fled to the United States. He served in the National Guard in Michigan and Wisconsin and held laboring jobs in Detroit, Milwaukee, and Chicago. He became an American citizen in 1933, just days after Hitler came to power in Germany. When he found himself unemployed that summer, he returned to Germany and rejoined the party. His record from the early days of the party stood him in good stead, and he quickly became an aide to Ernst Rohm, the head of Hitler's SA or Brownshirts. When Hitler turned on Rohm and had some of the heirarchy of the Brownshirts executed,

Burger survived, but he was later jailed for criticizing the Gestapo. When he was released after eighteen months, he was drafted into the army and was soon back behind bars, this time as a guard at a prisoner of war camp outside Berlin. Despite his questionable background, he became second in command of Operation Pastorius.

Dasch and Burger recruited Richard Quirin, a locksmith who had immigrated to America in 1927 but returned on the outbreak of war. Next to join the group was Edward Kerling. Kerling had lived in New York from 1928 to 1939, when he took part in a bizarre attempt to return to Germany. He and a group of other Germans bought a small yacht, which they tried to sail across the Atlantic from Florida. At that time the Coast Guard was secretly helping the British navy blockade vessels heading for Germany, and the boat was turned back a few miles from shore and impounded. When he ultimately returned to Germany via Spain, he became a producer of shows designed to entertain German troops.

Another of the men who had tried to slip out of the United States with Kerling was Herman Neubauer. The thirty-one-year-old chef had worked at the Century of Progress exhibit in Chicago, settled in the city, and married a local German woman, Alma Wolf. Like Kerling, he refused to give up trying to return home, and he eventually joined a German panzer division. He was wounded in the first few days of the invasion of Russia.

Werner Thiel had come to the United States in 1927 on vacation and decided to stay. He had organized a chapter of a pro-Nazi organization in Illinois, and in 1941 he returned to Germany via Japan, coincidentally leaving San Francisco on the same ship as George Dasch, though the two did not meet.

Heinrich Heinck, thirty-five, was a merchant seaman who had jumped ship in New York in 1926. He had been an active member of the German-American Bund, a pro-Nazi group, and had extensive contacts among Germans in the United States who remained loyal to the Nazis. He also had another skill considered vital to the success of the mission: having worked in arms plants, he knew enough about their operations to help target their most vulnerable points for the saboteurs.

The youngest member of the group was Herbert Haupt. He spoke English more fluently than he spoke German and knew American life better than life in Germany. He had been brought to the United States at the age of five and became a citizen at twelve when his father changed his citizenship. He was working at a Chicago company that manufactured bombsights when he got a girl pregnant and decided to make himself scarce. He abruptly quit his job and disappeared without telling his parents where he was going. He traveled to Mexico, obtained a German passport, and shipped out to Japan, where he joined a German naval ship that ran a British blockade to occupied France.

Like the others, he had a colorful story to tell about his return home, which he no doubt embellished. In fact, Kappe, with little else to go on, chose as his recruits Germans who had endured hardships to get back to Germany as evidence of patriotism, daring, and enterprise, attributes he believed necessary for the Pastorius mission. However, none of them had the specialized training or experience or the particular kind of courage necessary for operating undercover.

The eight men were taken to an estate in eastern Prussia that had been confiscated from a wealthy Jewish shoe manufacturer and converted into a secret military school. There they underwent just a few weeks of training and briefings. They spoke only English and brushed up on their slang. They studied American magazines and newspapers with particular emphasis on the sports sections. They sang songs together— even practicing "The Star-Spangled Banner." They watched the latest Hollywood movies and listened to recordings of CBS radio programs and dance records sent from Berlin. Joseph Goebbels, the German minister of propaganda and one of the most powerful Nazis after Hitler, had personal knowledge of the operation and arranged for the films and recordings to be supplied to the saboteurs. Meanwhile Dasch and Kappe worked out their list of targets to be bombed.

The targets were ambitious. They included the Brooklyn Bridge, which was to be bombed along with other bridges in Manhattan, Aluminum Company of America (Alcoa) plants in New York, Tennessee, and Illinois and the Cryolite Co. aluminum plant in Philadelphia—aluminum was a strategic material—the New York City water system, locks along the Ohio and Mississipi rivers, the Niagara Falls hydroelectric plant, railroad stations, including Penn Station in New York, and bridges and track along the Chesapeake and Ohio railroad. In addition to these industrial targets, they were also to plant time bombs in public places such as department stores and movie theaters to create public panic and lower civilian morale.

To bring off these feats, the eight-man team split into two groups. Dasch, Burger, Quirin, and Heinck were to be put ashore on Long Island and the other four on the Florida coast. They were given $180,000, mostly in hundred-dollar bills, most of which Dasch kept in a money belt strapped to his waist. They had dozens of detonators hidden in cigarette lighters and fountain pens, bombs disguised as lumps of coal, incendiary devices made to look like packs of cigarettes, commercial explosives, and recipes for making explosives from chemicals that could be easily purchased. They planned to meet up in Cincinnati, make contact with Nazi sympathizers in Chicago, St. Louis, and New York, establish a network of supporters, and begin their campaign of terrorism.

The eight were sent to Paris, where they spent a weekend's leave in Parisian cafes and brothels before setting off for Lorient, one of five German U-boat bases established on the Atlantic coast of France. There they boarded U-202 and U-584 to start their mission. Three other U-boats set off with them. They were on separate special missions to mine New York harbor, Cape May, and Boston harbor.

Thus did their separate fates bring the four saboteurs to the beach at Amagansett. They buried their crates of explosives and equipment, then listened as the U-boat struggled to free itself from the sandbar just a short distance away in the darkness. They could even smell the diesel exhaust hanging in the still air. The four stripped off their German naval uniforms and changed into civilian clothes. With the submarine engines still laboring in the distance, Dasch saw a flashlight in the darkness, and a voice shouted, "Who's there?"

It was a one-man Coast Guard patrol. Long Islander John Cullen had joined the Coast Guard soon after Pearl Harbor, expecting a posting on a ship. Instead he had been given a six-mile stretch of beach in the Hamptons to patrol at night by himself armed only with a flare gun. He was fighting, he thought, the loneliest and dullest war imaginable. He had spotted what he thought might be fishermen on the beach. Fishing was forbidden in wartime before dawn, and Cullen strolled over to investigate. He could hear what sounded like a boat's engines out at sea. One of the group became tense at the sight of the Coast Guard and lapsed into German. Dasch told him to shut up, but Cullen had heard him.

"What are you men doing?" Cullen asked.

"We're just bringing some clams in," Dasch told him.

The answer only made Cullen more suspicious. Clams are found only in the bay, not out in the surf. As Cullen got closer he saw one of the men dragging a large canvas bag. It contained the four German uniforms.

"What's in the bag? Clams?" Cullen asked, pretending he believed their story.

Dasch was now face to face with him. "How old are you?" he asked Cullen.

"Twenty-one."

"You don't know anything about this," Cullen told him. "You have a mother and father? You want to see them again? You never saw us. Understand?"

Dasch then pulled out some money—a little under three hundred dollars—and gave it to Cullen. "Here, take this," he said. "Forget you ever saw us. Maybe I'll see you in Southampton sometime. Will you recognize me?"

"No," Cullen said, and started to back away.

He kept backing away until the figures were swallowed by the darkness, expecting at every moment to be shot. The bullet never came. When the men were out of sight he started running to the nearest Coast Guard station, which was three miles away. On the beach, Dasch and the other three saboteurs hurriedly buried their uniforms and began to walk toward the Long Island Railroad. When they reached the track, however, they began following it in the wrong direction—east toward Montauk instead of west.

Cullen raised the alarm, but his claim that Germans had landed at Amagansett was treated with skepticism. Then a number of others reported hearing powerful engines roaring a short disatance offshore. Cullens's commander, Captain J. S. Bayliss, ordered a search, but there was nothing to see until first light.

As the Coast Guard patrol, with Cullen leading the way, arrived on the beach at dawn, the U-202 was still stuck on the sandbar but shrouded from view by the morning fog. Captain Lindner ordered the engines cut. He and other crew members could hear voices on the beach. Unable to scuttle the submarine, he considered surrendering his vessel. He even gave orders for the sub's codebooks, encoding machines, and other secret material to be destroyed.

Then a miracle happened. The tide lifted her off the sandbar. The engines were gunned into life again, and U-202 headed for the open sea. Minutes later she slipped beneath the waves and set a course to Cape Hatteras to prey on Allied shipping. An opportunity of incalculable value had been lost.

On shore, the search party heard Lindner's engines fire up and fade away. It did not take long to find the place on Amagansett Beach where Cullen had confronted the strangers. In just a few minutes he discovered an empty pack of German cigarettes. Now, finally, his superiors believed him. Nearby was a trail where it appeared something heavy had been dragged through the sand. One member of the Coast Guard patrol poked a probe beneath the sand where the trail ended and hit something solid. Buried just beneath the surface was a canvas bag with German uniforms inside.

At that moment, the four saboteurs were on board a Long Island Railroad train, the 6:50 from Amagansett headed for New York City. They had walked nearly six miles before they had discovered their mistake and doubled back to find the railroad station. They were the only passengers on the early train, and the stationmaster, Ira Baker, engaged them in conversation. They told him they had come out for some fishing, ran aground in the fog, and decided to return to the city ahead of schedule.

When they reached Jamaica, Queens, they split up and continued to Manhattan separately, agreeing to meet again later in the day at Columbus Circle. Dasch and Burger registered at the Governor Clinton Hotel in midtown Manhattan; Heinck and Quirin took rooms at the Hotel Martinique nearby.

Continuing their search on Amagansett Beach, the Coast Guard patrol discovered the four crates that had been brought ashore by the submarine crew and the saboteurs the previous night. They took the crates back to the Coast Guard station to open them and found hundreds of pounds of explosives, detonators, and other devices, including bombs disguised as rocks, coal, logs, and cigar tins. Cullen had stumbled onto one of the most audacious undercover operations of the war.

Yet it only brought him under suspicion. When FBI agents were summoned, they could not understand why the Germans had let him go. They believed he was hiding something and wasted valuable time trying to break his story. Finally, taking Dasch's reference to Southampton as a clue the Germans might still be in the area, they took Cullen home to change into civilian clothes so he and other Coast Guard personnel could cruise bars, restaurants, and hotels in the Hamptons looking for Dasch.

Soldiers in plain clothes staked out the beach waiting for the Germans to retrieve the explosives. Roadblocks were set up to stop every car leaving Suffolk County. Trains were searched—but the saboteurs had already slipped through the net.

Four days later, unaware that Operation Pastorius had been fatally compromised, the U-584, commanded by Joachim Deecke, broke the surface off Ponte Vedra Beach, Florida, between Jacksonville and St.

Augustine. The other four saboteurs—Kerling, Haupt, Thiel, and Neubauer—came ashore.

It was a much less eventful landing than the one at Amagansett. They clambered into two inflatable rafts with their boxes of equipment and rowed stealthily ashore. The four buried their uniforms and equipment between two palm trees on the beach under cover of darkness and walked three miles into town. Kerling asked the local postmistress, Alice Landrum, about bus schedules, then all four took the next bus to Jacksonville. Once there, this group also split up. The plan called for Haupt to go to Chicago to make contact with sympathizers in the sizable German community there and to try to get his old job back at the optical company where parts for bombsights were made. The others made their way to Cincinnati.

In New York, Dasch had come to a momentous yet inexplicable decision: he was going to turn the whole group in to the FBI. He had become friends with Burger, and over dinner at their hotel he told him what he intended to do. He offered Burger the chance to throw in his lot with him. Burger, unlike Dasch, was an ardent Nazi, but he broke down in tears and said he had no stomach for the mission. That same night, Dasch called the FBI office in New York and told Special Agent Steve McWhorter he had come ashore from a submarine at Amagansett. He told them he was going to Washington, D.C., and would contact the FBI again under the code name Pastorius. He said he wanted to surrender only to J. Edgar Hoover himself. A couple of days later Dasch did go to Washington. He ate an expensive meal, then called the FBI from Room 351 in the Mayflower Hotel. Investigators led by Agent Duane Traynor descended on his room to interrogate him. He handed them a handkerchief, saying it was covered in handwriting in invisible ink. When it was coated in ammonia, it revealed lists of names and addresses of potential and active Nazi sympathizers, targets, and other information. Then Dasch stunned the agents by telling them there was to be a second landing at Ponte Vedra.

Agents alerted the Miami bureau, but it was too late. Agents there questioned Alice Landrum, whose husband was a sheriff's deputy, and she remembered the four strangers who had appeared in town the previous day asking directions to Jacksonville. She had believed they were construction workers. The FBI agents realized the landing had already taken place.

Using Dasch's information, FBI agents began rounding up the other saboteurs, starting with Burger, who was arrested at the Governor Clinton Hotel. He confirmed every detail of Dasch's story. Heinck and Quirin had spent most of the previous night in a brothel and found FBI agents waiting for them at the Hotel Martinique the next morning. Three days later, Kerling and Thiel, who had traveled on to New York to meet the others, were arrested at the Commodore Hotel in Manhattan.

Haupt and Neubauer were at large for another week. Haupt had turned up in Chicago at the home of his uncle, Walter Froehling, a known Nazi sympathizer, and confided the entire scheme to him. Froehling told him the draft board had alerted the federal authorities after his disappearance the previous year. Haupt borrowed his uncle's car and went to the FBI office voluntarily to report that he had been traveling and had not been trying to evade the draft.

The FBI agents looking for Haupt couldn't believe their luck. They let Haupt go and began following him, hoping he would lead them to Neubauer. When he did not do so, his car was pulled over and he was arrested. He gave them Neubauer's address, and the last of the saboteurs was captured.

Dasch and Burger also gave the FBI interrogators the names of more people in the German community who had been expected to help them. Several were rounded up and interned.

J. Edgar Hoover reported personally on the affair to President Roosevelt. They decided that the arrests should be made public but that the trials should be swift—and secret. Hoover announced that eight saboteurs and several other conspirators had been arrested, but he left out Dasch's role, making it appear that United States counterintelligence methods were more efficient than they actually were. This may have been motivated partly by Hoover's well-known penchant for public self-aggrandisement, but it was primarily aimed at discouraging other similar missions.

None of the eight had done anything under criminal law that deserved the death penalty, but Roosevelt believed it was important to set an example and execute them. Fearing that a federal court might give them relatively light sentences, he had all eight turned over to the military authorities for court-martial. As commander-in-chief he would have the final say on their fate. They had only a few days to prepare a defense before going on trial in a room on the fifth floor of the Justice Department Building before seven senior army officers. The last of the saboteurs had been arrested on June 27, and the court-martial convened just eleven days later. Dasch and Burger both gave evidence. So did Cullen, who identified Dasch as the man who had spoken to him on the beach at Amagansett.

The court-martial sentenced Dasch to thirty years in prison and Burger to life. The other six all received the death penalty. The sentences were carried out with surprising speed. It took less than a month to complete the appeals process, such as it was, ending with a review by Roosevelt, who had his mind made up at the outset. The president ordered that the six be given the electric chair rather than a soldier's death by firing squad.

On August 12, 1942, less than two months after the Amagansett landing, the six condemned men were executed in the District of Columbia jail. The first to be led to his death was Haupt, the youngest, who had tried to cheat the executioner by sticking two wet fingers into a light socket during the tense days of waiting on Death Row. The execution had been scheduled for noon, at which time an air raid siren sounded in the street.

"As though this was the appointed signal, as the siren's wail thrust itself into the death house, the switch was thrown," wrote a witness. "Two thousand volts of electricity struck the spy in the chair. Under the tearing impact the German surged foward, his chest swelling and the cords of his arms knotted. As the air raid warning died down to a thin wail, the spy slumped, unconscious, his head sagging. Then five hundred volts, with more amperage. Then nearly two thousand volts again—and the invader was dead." It took a little over an hour to execute all six in the jail's one electric chair. All died quietly. None made any outbursts nor even any final statements. They were buried in secret in numbered graves in a potter's field at Blue Plains outside Washington. In 1962 their remains were quietly returned to their next of kin for reburial in Germany.

Dasch was sent to a federal prison in Connecticut to serve his sentence and was later transferred to Leavenworth. Burger was sent to a federal prison in Atlanta. They served only six years; in 1948 President Harry Truman reviewed the case and had both released and deported. Burger returned to his trade in Augsburg, Germany, and lived in obscurity.

Dasch had more difficulty settling down. The story of his role in turning in his comrades emerged, and he had to move several times because of the hostility of his neighbors. In time, however, he prospered as a commodities broker in the new Germany. In the 1960s Dasch petitioned the United States government for permission to return to America. He was turned down.

Dasch's motives in betraying his comrades will probably never be known. He may have realized after the confrontation with Cullen that he was not up to killing people at close quarters. He may have believed that they would all be inevitably caught and shot. And he may have thought he could keep the $180,000 he had been given to finance the mission.

Interestingly, the FBI agents who interviewed dozens of people who had known Dasch in his years in the United States came to the conclusion that, far from being a Nazi, he was in fact a Communist. He had been fired from one of his jobs for pro-Communist union agitation, and before he left the United States he told a number of people he was going to Russia to study Communism.

This has given rise to some speculation that Dasch was a Russian agent who helped set up and then blow Operation Pastorius to encourage America to focus on the war in Europe at the expense of the war in the Pacific. Russia desperately needed the Western allies to establish a second front in Europe. More likely Dasch had become convinced Germany could not win the war once the United States and Russia were both involved, and he believed Operation Pastorius was his ticket back to the United States.

John Cullen, the tall, strapping youth whose alertness and courage probably prevented many deaths, never got the action he was hoping for when he joined the Coast Guard. After the discovery of the scope of the operation he had obstructed, he was hailed as a hero and sent to bond rallies and fund-raising banquets to make morale-building speeches and personal appearances. He kept applying for postings on ships and kept getting turned down. Meanwhile, by the end of the war, he gained forty pounds eating at banquets. Decades later, the lifelong Long Islander often strolled along the beach at Amagansett, thinking about that fateful night, his confrontation with Dasch, and what might have happened if the Germans had been able to complete their mission.

PART FOUR

Low Life

PART FOUR

Introduction

THE EARLY SETTLERS in the Hamptons were tough on crime—but their definition of criminal behavior was somewhat different from our own. Take, for example, the experience of Goody, or Mrs. Edwards, who was an outspoken and quick-tempered woman but whose sense of social rivalry in the 1650s can be well appreciated by residents of the Hamptons today. She boasted of owning some expensive English petticoats, but when she was challenged to produce them, she could not. Humiliated, she flew into a rage in which she slandered her own husband and the entire colony. She was sentenced to pay a fine of three pounds—which she could not afford—or to stand for an hour with her tongue in a cleft stick. When the East Hampton town constable arrived to impose her punishment, she attacked him, kicking him in the shins.

The following year, 1654, several young men were found masturbating and placed in a pillory and publicly whipped. The punishment doesn't seem to have had much effect on one of the youths, Daniel Fairfield. In 1655, he was hauled before the community leaders, known as townsmen, accused of having had sex with a preacher's maid and of attempting to seduce the preacher's daughter.

Major crime was rare, but the whole colony was transfixed by one scandalous accusation in 1657. The fifteen-year-old daughter of Lion Gardiner, Elizabeth Howell, who was married to an East Hampton merchant, died after giving birth. Hallucinating on her deathbed, she claimed to have been bewitched by Goody Garlick, the wife of a carpenter named Joshua Garlick. Goody Garlick had worked as a servant on Gardiner's Island and had wet-nursed several children, some of whom had died. The true cause of Elizabeth's death was probably a postpartum infection known as puerperal fever, and at least one of the

171

children who had died had been starved by its own mother, who had wet-nursed another's child for money.

The facts did not get in the way of a good scandal even then. Several of the accused woman's enemies came forward as witnesses to her witchcraft, claiming that she had caused the death of several cattle with spells. She was sent to Connecticut to be tried as a witch, but, thanks to the intervention of Lion Gardiner, who was more enlightened than his neighbors, she was acquitted.

Piracy was common—the coastline dotted with coves and inlets made it a smugglers' paradise—so the Hamptons served as a haven for numerous pirates and privateers. The pirate Captain Kidd is said to have buried treasure on Gardiner's Island. Nearly three centuries later, the Hamptons was a venue for piracy of a different sort. During Prohibition, the Hamptons became a strategic hub for bootleggers, who brought in three thousand cases of liquor per week.

Bootleggers' ships carrying commercial alcohol from Canada, the Caribbean, and Europe would anchor in international waters off Montauk, safe from the Coast Guard. Small, fast vessels from shore would rush out to meet the bootleggers, then try to run a Coast Guard blockade and get back to shore. The bootleggers' boats were often much more powerful than the Coast Guard's vessels and usually outstripped them. As well as numerous small-time entrepreneurs, there were several major rival bootlegging operations being run in this way, and ship-to-ship gun battles were common. Among those who were involved in bootlegging operations off the Hamptons was Joseph P. Kennedy, whose vessels came from Canada to Montauk, where their cargo was unloaded onto a flotilla of small craft, then driven in trucks to New York City.

Getting the alcohol to shore was only half the problem. Trucks carrying the alcohol from the Hamptons to New York were vulnerable to hijackers and had to have convoys of gunmen to protect them. This made the convoys stand out, so local police had to be paid off to ignore obvious large shipments of alcohol. Many convoys were attacked by rival groups, and there were numerous gun battles. The Rev. George Brown of Patchogue Methodist Church claimed that the East End of Long Island was "the wettest place in the country."

The *East Hampton Star* reported during the last week of 1923 that from one to five truckloads of liquor passed through East Hampton per night and that twenty ships unloaded liquor offshore during one week. In one incident, twenty-five gunmen fanned out through East Hampton searching for two hijackers who had stolen liquor from a secret warehouse. They were rounded up by the local police chief, who persuaded them to leave town.

Not all the liquor reached New York. East Hampton residents—rich and poor—were excellent customers for illegal liquor. Some Southampton mansions were reputed to have tunnels leading to coves where everything from Canadian whiskey to Jamaica rum to the finest French champagnes was taken directly into cavernous cellars. Several rum-running ships ran aground or were wrecked in storms off the Hamptons, and local baymen spent days stripping them of their cargoes.

Today, the illicit traffic is from the other direction. Drugs are brought to the Hamptons every weekend in significant quantities. One reputed Hamptons drug dealer who lives in a two-million-dollar beachfront house pays a posse of New York City models and escort girls to bring cocaine and other drugs by road to the Hamptons, where they are distributed at house parties from Quogue to Montauk. He calls the models "snow-cats."

The assassination of the Italian designer Gianni Versace in July 1997 sent a chill through the Hamptons because the assassin, Andrew Cunanan, was known in the gay community there. He had spent part of the previous summer as a houseguest of a prominent Hamptons summer citizen. He was then using the name Andrew Phillip DeSilva. His host, who requested anonymity when he talked about Cunanan to the *East Hampton Star*, said Cunanan and a friend had just returned to the United States from a month-long vacation in France. The host had several other houseguests and paid little attention to the chic young Filipino-American who had come to stay.

Cunanan had claimed to be an Israeli who had attended the best Connecticut prep schools, he said. "There seemed nothing very unusual about him. It was clear he didn't do anything, meaning gainful employment. He was a good guest—well mannered, literate, and articulate."

Cunanan was a gay gigolo and sometime drug dealer who was adept at insinuating himself into monied circles to be supported by wealthy gay men. During his stay in the Hamptons he cruised beaches and managed to get himself invited to several house parties and private dinners. His host says he would have been unremarkable but for what happened next.

In April 1997, Cunanan dined lavishly with several friends and told them he was going to San Francisco to start a new life. He handed out several prized possessions, including expensive clothes and jewelry, as farewell gifts. He then embarked on a cross-country killing spree, eliminating a former lover, naval engineer Jeffrey Trail, architect David Madson, Chicago real estate agent Lee Miglin, New Jersey cemetery worker William Reese, and finally Versace, before committing suicide on a Miami houseboat. Only one murder had an apparent motive: William Reese was killed for his truck as Cunanan continued his flight. Stories that Cunanan was HIV positive proved to be baseless.

There was panic in the Hamptons even before the Versace murder. The murder of Reese in New Jersey, following the murders in Minneapolis and Chicago, showed that Cunanan was heading east, and the Hamptons seemed a likely destination. The resident who had played host to Cunanan was warned by friends in San Diego that Cunanan might be heading to East Hampton, and everyone who had met Cunanan was contacted. Every Southampton and East Hampton police patrol car carried posters of Cunanan, and the FBI followed up numerous unconfirmed sightings. The FBI is reported to have talked to sixteen people who may have known Cunanan in the Hamptons.

Following the murder of Gianni Versace, there was further concern that Cunanan might try to return to the Hamptons to attack another high-profile target. Several rich gays hired bodyguards to patrol their Hamptons property. A Cunanan task force was ordered to work with private security personnel hired for "Take-Off '97" an East Hampton fund-raiser for the Long Island Association for AIDS Care. At one point, according to FBI sources, Calvin Klein was on a list of possible Cunanan targets in the Hamptons.

"When Cunanan was found dead you could almost hear the sighs of relief on the East End," said a Suffolk County detective. "The bodyguards were sent home, and everyone got back to their summers. People come out here to get away from crime, not to worry about it."

Yet the Hamptons has had more than its share of high-profile crimes.

CHAPTER 11

Victim or Killer?

THE PORTERS OF GEORGIA and the Johnsons of Tennessee had been rich familics and owned plantations and slaves, but after the Civil War they fell on hard times. Their descendants eked out livings as little more than sharecroppers. In 1929, James Clard Porter found his way to Rossville, Georgia, but discovered life was not much better there than back home in Tennessee. He did, however, find a wife, Esther Johnson, and together they had a daughter, Arlene. Arlene grew up in poverty, her mind filled with half-truths about her ancestors' vast wealth; the family lore was reinforced by the release of the movie *Gone With The Wind*. Arlene imagined that she was destined to restore the family's wealth, much as Scarlett O'Hara had, by marrying a rich man. Those horizons narrowed as she got older. She just wanted someone who would take her away from Rossville.

She found him in Tommy Kirby, who came from the same dirt-poor background but who had joined the navy and was serving at a naval base near Seattle, Washington. She was eighteen when they were married by a naval chaplain in 1946. The first years were difficult. Handsome Tommy Kirby was routinely unfaithful and equally routinely indiscreet, leaving evidence of his betrayals in their car for Arlene to find.

He was posted back east to Norfolk in 1948. Tommy and Arlene had two children in quick succession, Belynda and Joel. When the Korean War began, Tommy was shipped out to active duty in the Pacific. Arlene, incapable of looking after both children alone, found herself back where she started, in Rossville. She abandoned the children to their grandparents, rented a room for herself, and took a job in a local factory. Arlene had an affair with a former high school classmate and became pregnant.

She hurried to rejoin Tommy Kirby, now stationed in San Diego, and convinced him the child was his. It was a deception that did not last long; Wade Kirby did not look like the other two Kirby children. Tommy moved the family to New York City in an attempt at a fresh start, but the family remained intact for only two years more. Tommy Kirby erupted periodically at the realization that he was being forced to raise another man's child. He beat his wife, he abused the child, and he eventually tried to choke Arlene to death in her sleep, before abandoning them all.

Arlene was left to raise three children. She moved east to Riverhead, Long Island, and took a night-shift job with an air cargo company based at Kennedy Airport, then known as Idlewild. Belynda, aged seven, was responsible for feeding the other children and putting them to bed at night while Arlene worked, then giving them breakfast and seeing Joel off to school in the morning while her mother slept.

Arlene created a new persona for herself away from home: she was a Southern belle from a genteel, impoverished Georgia family. She cultivated what she supposed to be Southern graces and manners. At home, she became a tyrant, mercilessly beating the children when they stepped out of line, abuse that continued unabated for years.

When Belynda was twelve, Arlene was seriously injured in an accident at work and the children were placed in foster homes. Just as Arlene was coping with a fresh setback, she struck gold. In 1961, recovered from her accident but not yet reunited with the children, she met Robert Lotz at a single-parents' event in the Hamptons. She was thirty-three, he was fifty-six. Lotz was a successful businessman with a boat, a country club membership, and a large Long Island home. Robert Lotz already had two unsuccessful marriages behind him and was not interested in a third. He was even less interested in Arlene's three children. She spent weekends on his boat while Belynda was left to care for the other children. After a year, Arlene announced she was pregnant with Lotz's child, and she gave birth to a daughter, Rosalind, in July 1963. The relationship with Lotz declined after Rosalind's birth and ended about a year later.

In the mid-1960s, Arlene became involved with Frank McDonald, the owner of a small trucking firm, Five Star Trucking, and they worked together to build up the business. Frank was president, and Arlene had a vice president's title. Arlene and the children moved into his home in Commack, Long Island, and her son Joel, now in his teens, began driving for the company. After a year or two, Wade moved down to Georgia. Joel, caught stealing from the trucking company, joined the military, and Belynda, desperate to escape Arlene, married and moved first to Louisiana, then to Florida. Only Rosalind was left at home. Then, without warning, Arlene moved out. This time she had struck gold for real. She had met Bob Caris.

Caris was from a prominent Pennsylvania family. His father, Ivan Caris, had been a top executive with a New York insurance company. Robert Caris worked as a pilot for Pan American, then took his wife Sally and their adopted daughter, Sharon, to Dhahran, Saudi Arabia, where he worked for Aramco, the international oil conglomerate. Aramco employees and executives enjoyed enviable benefits. They were able to employ Palestinian and Lebanese servants in homes in a luxurious expatriates' compound populated by Americans. They were paid well, and their income was free of U.S. or Saudi taxes. They had few living expenses and little opportunity for extravagance. Each year the company gave employees a three-month vacation anywhere in the world.

Sharon was sent to private schools in Beirut, Lebanon, then a thriving Middle Eastern cultural center, and to an expensive school in Switzerland. She went on to Whittier College in California and married shortly after graduation. By the mid-sixties, her mother's health was failing, and Robert Caris decided to retire to the United States. Money was not a problem. He considered a beachfront home in Florida, but Sally Caris said she had seen enough sand to last her a lifetime and needed a more temperate climate.

They chose the Hamptons and bought a $350,000 Cape Cod home, smaller than he could have afforded, in an upscale neighborhood of saltboxes and mansions in Southampton, at 40 Adams Lane. Robert and Sally Caris spent the idyllic early months of their retirement exploring the Hamptons—it had been years since they had seen the seasons change—and rummaging through antique stores. But Sally's health deteriorated quickly. Robert spent much of his time caring for her, and she died in 1969.

Arlene met Caris a year later. In an effort to keep busy and meet people, Caris took a part-time job as a coastal radio operator with ITT.

He had long been an amateur radio "ham" and had a state-of-the-art radio installation in his home. One of his coworkers knew Arlene from a single-parents' organization and arranged a date. Caris never realized his attractive new girlfriend was already living with another man.

That summer, 1970, Wade Kirby, Arlene's younger son, was arrested in Tennessee; while visiting a relative in Chattanooga, he had killed the sixty-one-year-old owner of a boardinghouse. He later pleaded guilty to involuntary manslaughter and served only two years in prison.

Arlene, forty-three, and Robert Caris, fifty-five, were married in June 1971, and Arlene and eight-year-old Rosalind moved into the Adams Lane house. Overnight, Arlene finally had a taste of the champagne life she had dreamed of since her childhood in a Georgia shack. She spent her new husband's money freely, going to beauty salons, buying jewelry and furs, and exploring boutiques on Southampton's famed Jobs Lane.

Rosalind was assigned the task of intercepting bills and phone calls from stores. The phone ringer was turned off and a red light was installed in the kitchen so that Rosalind and Arlene could see when there was a call without Bob Caris hearing the phone ring. Bob Caris, in any case, appeared oblivious to his wife's spending and machinations. It was a short step from secret purchases to outright embezzlement. According to Rosalind, Arlene Caris intercepted a $250,000 check that had been part of a Caris family inheritance.

Bob Caris appeared to dote on his wife. In contrast to Sally, who had been an invalid in the last years of their marriage, Arlene had a powerful physique and superassertive personality. She seemed afraid of nothing. On a trip to New York City, she found someone trying to break into their car and beat him up while Bob Caris watched. Caris called her "Wonder Woman."

They settled into a life that, to their Adams Lane neighbors and friends of Bob Caris at ITT, seemed one of quiet contentment. Robert Caris doted on his stepdaughter and retreated from all conflicts with his domineering wife to his amateur radio rig in the basement.

However, as the years passed, some of the seeds sown by Arlene's ferocious, violent, dysfunctional parenting bore tragic fruit. After his release from prison, Wade Kirby embarked on a career of serious but unprofitable crimes. He was prosecuted for burglary, drug possession, auto theft, assaults, and carrying a concealed weapon. To Southampton Town he was a drug dealer who sold marijuana to Hamptons weekenders, who knew him as "Sundance" and "Tex." He was in and out of prison throughout the seventies.

In 1981, Wade Kirby was released after serving a prison sentence for a botched burglary and moved into a Suffolk County halfway house. He was straight for a time; then, out late one night, he met an attractive young woman and took her to a bar for drinks. High on speed, he raped her in the back of a car. He fled to New Orleans, where he was eventually arrested for drug and arms possession. After being extradited to New York to face rape charges, he was sentenced to fifteen years to life.

Joel, Arlene's elder son, was injured in a car accident, and routine X-rays revealed that he had an illness far more serious than his injuries: Hodgkin's disease, a cancer of the lymph nodes. It was treatable, but because he had no symptoms, Joel refused to accept that he was sick until it was too late. By the time pain and fatigue drove him to seek help, the disease had advanced too far. Eventually, the disease spread to his liver, lungs, and kidneys, and he was taking massive doses of morphine. He died in June 1978, aged twenty-seven. He was cremated, and his ashes lay in a cardboard box at the funeral home, unclaimed, for seven years. Arlene told people she and Bob Caris had taken a boat out into Long Island Sound and scattered Joel's remains at sea in compliance with his last wish.

Arlene's youngest daughter, Rosalind, also had problems. She drank heavily from the age of fifteen and quickly graduated to marijuana and barbiturates. When she was sixteen her mother gave her sixteen thousand dollars, and she bought a Ford Mustang convertible, which she drove at high speed around the Hamptons. Almost inevitably, she totaled the car and was taken to the hospital, where doctors uncovered a secret Rosalind had been keeping from her mother. She was nearly seven months pregnant.

Rosalind gave birth to a daughter, Danielle. Although she had no blood relationship to Bob Caris, he treated her like his own daughter, feeding her, changing her, and playing with her constantly. Rosalind had hoped to use the birth of her child as an escape from Adams Lane, but the teenager who had fathered the child refused to leave home to live with Rosalind.

With a child to care for, Rosalind felt more trapped than ever. For a teenager with a child, boyfriends were hard to come by, and she despaired of ever getting away from Arlene. Wade, whom she adored, was in prison, Joel was dead, and her relationship with Belynda had soured years before. Belynda had by now divorced her first husband, moved to Southampton, and married an aircraft engineer named Fred Sabloski. She had three children, one with each of her husbands and another, Lori, from a relationship Arlene had encouraged with a married man.

Life at Adams Lane grew increasingly bizarre. Rosalind started to suspect that Arlene was trying to kill Bob Caris. She was taking laundry down to the basement one day and found the light was out on the stairs. Negotiating the steep steps in the darkness, she tripped over a fishing line that had been strung across the top of the staircase. Arlene claimed the booby trap had been aimed at her and had been set by Bob Caris. If they genuinely thought that was the case, neither of them apparently confronted him.

Another time, Arlene told Rosalind to take Danielle out of the house while they were having dinner. Bob Caris was used to eating with Danielle on his knee, letting her pick at his plate. As Arlene made this unusual request of Rosalind, Bob Caris came in, drawn to the kitchen by the smell of food cooking.

As he entered, Rosalind noticed Arlene hurriedly concealing something that appeared to be a medicine bottle. She scurried out with the child. When she confronted her mother later, she says, Arlene admitted she was lacing her husband's food with a powerful drug. She had tried giving it to him in his coffee, but he complained about the taste, so she had started putting it into his meals. Because Danielle picked off his plate, she needed her out of the way. Not long after, Bob Caris's health began to deteriorate. His skin became pale, he felt tired all the time, and he inexplicably started to lose weight.

Rosalind, by now willing to try almost any escape route, became involved with an inmate at Riverhead County Jail. A friend had a boyfriend in the jail and set up a first "date" behind bars. They liked each other, and Rosalind began visiting regularly, often with Danielle, even after he was transferred to a distant prison upstate. His name was Tony Campanella. They were allowed only the briefest physical contact. Arlene objected to the relationship, but Rosalind silenced her by pointing out that she was busy trying to kill her own husband.

Tony Campanella's prison counselor had a frank talk with her about his history of mental problems and his dependence on powerful mood-altering prescription drugs. She told him her entire family was crazy. After six months of prison visiting, Rosalind married Tony Campanella in the chapel at the maximum security prison at Danemora. Then she returned to Adams Lane to wait for him to be paroled.

In April 1985, neighbors and friends of Bob Caris noticed he wasn't around any more. They didn't see him in his immaculately kept garden, strolling by the impressive estates and mansions that Adams Lane bordered. His amateur radio contacts around the world stopped hearing from his call sign. His adopted daughter, Sharon, who for years had kept in touch by mail and phone from her home in California, suspected Arlene was stalling her, but she could not begin to understand why. Her father was out, and she had just missed him, Arlene would say. She sympathetically expressed surprise to Sharon that he hadn't called her yet.

After some weeks passed, Arlene told people Bob had gone to Saudi Arabia for a visit to his old haunts or on a round-the-world trip without her. Arlene even convinced her daughter Belynda, and as weeks became months with still no sign of Bob Caris, she elaborated on the story. He had had a heart attack in Saudi Arabia and stayed there to recuperate. Then he was in California visiting Sharon.

Arlene even said she had flown out to California to see him but came home earlier than expected because she didn't get along with his daughter. Later she claimed he had resumed his trip abroad. It made no sense to Belynda, but she had no information other than Arlene's fragmentary accounts, and Rosalind confirmed her story.

Belynda rarely visited Adams Lane, but that summer the house was damaged by Hurricane Gloria, which swept across central Long Island after threatening to make landfall on Manhattan. Arlene had to have the shingles replaced, and Belynda dropped by when the work was finished. She noticed a foul, indefinable odor in the house. Arlene told her she thought perhaps a raccoon had gotten into the wall cavity and died and the workmean had inadvertently shingled over it. Belynda recommended an exterminator.

Tony Campanella was released from prison in August and came to 40 Adams Lane to live. He and Arlene did not get on well, and within days he and Rosalind were at odds too.

He would disappear for days at a time, and there were unwelcome visitors to the house—girlfriends who thought Rosalind was his sister, men demanding money they said was owed them for drugs, and the enraged fathers of seduced daughters. Most serious of all, he had stopped taking his medication, and his counselors at the prison had warned Rosalind he was a paranoid schizophrenic. Rosalind suspected that she had been set up, that Tony had married her because he would be more likely to get parole if he had what appeared to be a stable home. However, she was reluctant to go too far in her arguments with Tony Campanella. She had confided to him what had really happened to Bob Caris.

Labor Day 1985 came, and the familiar summer rituals of the

Hamptons ended. The homes that had been occupied all summer by New York City professionals were shuttered and closed; the expensive cars that had clogged Main Street and Jobs Lane disappeared; the beaches, which had been so crowded since May, became suddenly deserted. That week also brought bad news: Arlene announced that she had learned Bob Caris was dead.

She met Belynda for lunch and broke the news, but there were no outward signs that her husband's death troubled her. She went to the hairdresser and shopped for clothes with Belynda as if the deceased had been a distant relative with whom she had had no contact for years. Belynda told her husband that night that Arlene's stories and behavior made no sense. She knew her mother was capable of weaving any web of lies to suit her purposes, but as Belynda told her fears to her husband, Arlene's most complex web was about to unravel.

Rosalind awoke the next morning to hear arguing in the kitchen. It was Arlene and Tony, who had been out all night again. As she entered the kitchen she heard her husband say, "If I don't get what I want, the cops are going to find out about your little secret upstairs." Reacting to Arlene's stunned expression, he went on, "You think I don't know there's a dead body in this house? You think I believe that shit about dead animals in the attic? You better come up with some heavy cash!"

In the face of Tony's apparent blackmail, Rosalind countered that she had information too: information that could have his parole officer recommend a long stay back in Danemora. Tony's eyes narrowed, and he stormed out. Arlene followed him, ready to make a deal.

Rosalind had finally reached the breaking point. She realized that she, as well as her mother, could be going to prison. She would talk to Belynda. Belynda and Fred were already on their way to Adams Lane, determined to get some answers about Bob Caris's long absence and mysterious death. They arrived just as Tony was leaving, followed by Arlene. Inside the house, they asked Rosalind what was going on.

The smell Belynda had noticed weeks before was now overpowering. It permeated the entire house and the furniture, carpets, and drapes. Garbage was piled high in the kitchen, but that could not explain the nauseating stench. Belynda noticed air fresheners on the walls, on the stairs, on window ledges, everywhere. They did little to disguise the smell, only made it slightly sweeter and somehow more sickening.

Rosalind told Belynda she wanted to talk and asked her to go upstairs. In her room Rosalind looked Belynda squarely in the eye and said, "Mom killed Bob. He's in the attic. He's been there six months."

Belynda flew down the stairs and told her husband, but he refused to believe her. Nor did he believe Rosalind when she repeated what she had said. "Okay," she said. "Come on. I'll show you."

When Arlene returned to 40 Adams Lane, the Suffolk County police were already there. A police officer summoned by Fred Sabloski had gone up the open staircase to the attic. There was a trunk blocking a door that led into a crawl space. Behind it was a large bundle wrapped in tin insulating foil. Beneath the foil was a layer of heavy-duty plastic, and beneath that a tightly folded mattress cinched with rope. There was no need to open the bundle entirely to know what was inside. That, in any case, would have to be done by experts. For now, the hundreds of air fresheners stuck on the walls of the crawl space and the putrid, uniquely pungent smell of death spoke for themselves.

Downstairs, Arlene hyperventilated as she told her story to detectives. She admitted killing her husband by shooting him in the head. She told the detectives she just could not stand any longer the years of constant abuse at his hands. "I reached a breaking point," she said, "and I just couldn't take it any more."

She was taken to Riverhead and booked for murder while Detective Donald Delaney of the New York State Police talked further with Belynda, who had never seen any abuse. Rosalind, on the other hand, knew the whole story. She said she had found her mother one morning in late March badly bruised after a fight with Caris. Her mother admitted immediately that she had killed him in his sleep to prevent any further beatings.

Belynda visited Arlene in the county jail hoping she could get the story out of her mother. Arlene was more interested in persuading Belynda to do her a favor. There was a brown bottle of a powerful sedative drug in the bathroom. She had stolen it from a clinic. The police, she told her daughter, might not understand why it was there, so she wanted Belynda to get rid of it. Not in her own garbage, she said, "but far, far away, in the sewer or the town dump." It was the medication Rosalind had seen Arlene put in her husband's food. Belynda immediately realized the significance of her mother's request. After all the years of physical and emotional abuse by her mother, after all the years of lies and deceit and dysfunction, the truth about her mother dawned. "I understood right then what kind of monster my mother really was," Belynda said later.

Belynda told Detective Delaney, who was also busy persuading Tony Campanella to cooperate. There is no law in New York State specifically compelling citizens to report a crime, but Campanella's ignorance of that fact was a bargaining chip. In return for his cooperation now, Delaney offered to keep the courts from revoking his parole.

Tony Campanella admitted he had known about the body even before he was released from prison. Rosalind had told him, but Arlene didn't realize he was her silent partner. Rosalind had also told him how she and her mother laboriously heaved the heavily shrouded body into the attic.

Arlene herself had told him about the existence of bank accounts under false or previous names, such as Lotz, Kirby, and Potter. Digging deeper, police found accounts in banks all over the Hamptons in a variety of names, all traced back to Arlene. She had two separate Social Security numbers and identities. She had not only been taking money from Bob Caris while he was alive and salting it away in a dizzying web of accounts he knew nothing about, she had been cashing his pension and investment checks since his death.

Detective Delaney believed he had built a good case for second-degree murder. He didn't buy the wife-beating story, and there was precious little evidence to support it. There had been domestic dispute calls to the Adams Lane house, but they had involved Wade Kirby. He believed that Arlene had executed Bob Caris while he slept—possibly because he had discovered some of her embezzlements and high spending, possibly because her attempts to stage a fatal accident had failed. Either way, he believed, the motive was greed and money—her greed and his money.

However, prosecutor William Ferris had to see it the way a defense attorney would, and to a defense attorney there were numerous options open. One was to stand by the claim of self-defense and spousal abuse. The self-defense argument was weak, because Bob Caris was asleep when he was shot with his own .22 Mossberg rifle, but spousal abuse and domestic violence were powerful issues. There were a number of instances of judges showing leniency to battered wives who saw no other way out of their dilemma but homicide. Even if Arlene didn't fit the pattern, she seemed an accomplished liar, and there was a good chance the jury might acquit her.

There was another even more sinister possibility. Arlene might try to point the finger at Rosalind, who admitted she knew of the murder from the beginning and was facing jail for hindering a prosecution. Without any evidence to support Rosalind's responsibility for the murder itself, Arlene's defense attorney, William DeVore, could, in cross-examining Rosalind, paint a dark portrait of her troubled youth, heavy drinking, and drug abuse.

(*Above*) Joe Pikul with his attorney,
Ronald Jay Bekoff (*The New York Post*)

(*Right*) Diane Pikul (*The New
York Post*)

Martha Stewart at home in East Hampton
(*Eyemark Entertainment*)

(*Opposite*) Martha Stewart's East Hampton house
(*The New York Post*)

(*Above*) Serial killer Joel Rifkin in custody (*The New York Post*)

(*Left*) Steve Ross and Courtney Sale Ross (*The New York Post*)

Steven Spielberg was encouraged to move to the Hamptons by Steve Ross.
(*The New York Post*)

Saul and Gayfryd Steinberg (*The New York Post*)

Kim Basinger and Alec Baldwin are married on the beachfront estate of fashion designer Josephine Chaus in East Hampton. (*The New York Post*)

(*Right*) Another view of the Basinger-Baldwin wedding day (*The New York Post*)

Barry Trupin's Dragon's Head mansion in Southampton (*The New York Post*)

Marriage to a mentally disturbed, violent, and persistent offender was hardly an advertisement for family values. To plant a seed of reasonable doubt, he would only have to suggest to the jury that Rosalind might have been responsible for the murder and that Arlene's initial confession had been a maternal attempt to protect her. There was even a chance, Ferris reasoned, that Arlene could convince Rosalind to go along with such a defense, knowing the likelihood of her being prosecuted for the killing was slim indeed.

When DeVore proposed a plea bargain, Ferris was prepared to listen. He offered to plead to manslaughter, which carried eight and a half to twenty-five years in prison as opposed to the twenty-five years to life she could get if the state proved premeditated murder. Ferris accepted; assured that Arlene would be in prison for a significant period, he was content to save the state the expense and risk of a trial.

Sentencing was set for April 10, 1986, just over a year after the shooting. The judge, Thomas Mallon, did little to disguise his distaste for the plea bargain arrangement and referred to the suspicion of two other murder attempts—the fishing line on the stairs and Arlene's alleged lacing of her husband's food.

"I've got to admit that I'm not fully convinced," Judge Mallon told her of her explanation for the killing. "You knew fully well what you were doing, what you intended to do, and what you would accomplish by doing it." Nevertheless, he upheld the state's bargain. Arlene Caris was taken away to begin her sentence in Bedford Hills Correctional Center. Rosalind was given five years' probation for her role in helping conceal the body.

Bedford Hills had another celebrated inmate, Jean Harris, who had shot her lover, Dr. Herman Tarnower, to death and later claimed he had emotionally abused her. She was serving fifteen years to life. Harris was eventually freed after serving twelve years, and Arlene, comparing their cases, campaigned for her own release. She claimed that she had feared for the lives of Rosalind and Danielle as well as her own, that Caris was capable of murdering all of them and committing suicide. In a plea to Governor Mario Cuomo in 1992, she detailed her account of the killing for the first time.

According to Arlene, she had endured years of verbal, emotional, and physical abuse from Caris, who had been critical and unbending from the first weeks of their marriage. He had accused her son Joel, who was dying of cancer, of feigning his illness; he punched her in her sleep and deliberately drove his car off the road with her and her granddaughter in it. She claimed she told no one of this abuse because she was ashamed at having made a third bad marriage. She also said she was afraid of trying to support herself again if she divorced him.

On the night of the shooting, she said, she had endured a tirade of vile accusations and name-calling that went on from morning until evening. She had already missed a night's sleep and was exhausted. She was afraid to go to her daughter Rosalind's room, which was in a section of the house that could be locked off, because she was afraid she would be trapped there with her daughter and granddaughter if Caris burned down the house.

Desperate, she packed a bag to go to a motel to get some rest. Caris was incensed by her intended departure, she claimed; he beat her, knocked her forcefully against a wall, and threw her across the bed, where she struck her head on the headboard. She said she could not remember actually shooting Caris, but when she came out of a blackout, he had been shot in the head and she was holding a rifle they had bought in fear of burglars.

There was not one shred of evidence that Caris was ever abusive to Arlene other than her own statements, and Governor Cuomo rejected her petition. But in 1995, after serving nine years, Arlene was paroled and eventually returned to Southampton to live. So ended one of the most bizarre homicide cases in Hamptons history. A woman from the wrong side of the tracks had fought and worked and lied her way into relative wealth and security, only to find a prison gate shut behind her and see her wealth evaporate.

Was she a victim or a conniving killer? One person who has no doubt is her daughter Belynda. She claims that while in prison, Arlene threatened to get even with her for calling the police and helping them build a case against her. It was a threat Belynda took seriously. Before her mother's release from Bedford Hills, Belynda moved away from Southampton; she is now living under an assumed name.

The house, 40 Adams Lane, that under two mistresses, Sally Caris and Arlene Caris, had known so much happiness and so much pain, so much love and so many lies, could not be sold. It had gained too much notoriety, and even after a thorough fumigation the overpowering smell of putrefaction still clung tenaciously to the walls. It was eventually demolished in the hope that the memory of the terrible events that had happened there might one day be expunged from the neighborhood's memory.

CHAPTER 12

The War of the Roses

NBC CALLED IT "Black Monday." On October 19, 1987, the Dow plunged more than five hundred points. It was the worst single day in Wall Street history since the crash of 1929. The market had been dipping since the summer, and by mid-October it was like a mountainside loaded with wet, unstable snow, needing just one big shout to start the avalanche. When the shout came and the avalanche started, no one was safe. It destroyed fortunes, wounded careers, and sent a chill through every boardroom and executive suite in America. Real estate values plummeted almost immediately. It would ripple on, affecting entertainment conglomerates down to mom-and-pop businesses.

Wall Street's front line was the youngest in history—men and women in their twenties who had never known tough times. The Wall Street they knew was a global casino where you almost always won if you stayed for the next roll, the next spin, the next hand. Many of those young gods and goddesses of greed were now facing financial disaster and reacting with panic. The same week the market crashed so spectacularly, one of the men who had made a fortune during Wall Street's fat years pondered the fix he was in. Like almost everyone else he knew, he had just taken a serious beating in the market.

He owed forty thousand dollars in alimony to his first wife. His second marriage was in the process of breaking up. He faced a long, costly, and potentially bitter custody battle over access to his two young children, daughter Claudia and son Blake. He was keeping two expensive Manhattan apartments—a three-thousand-dollar-a-month duplex in Greenwich Village for his wife and children, and a secret two-thousand-dollar-a-month pied-à-terre for himself in Battery Park City, a newly built yuppie enclave in lower Manhattan overlooking the harbor.

He had a house in the Hamptons he had bought for a modest quarter of a million dollars four years before. He and his wife had agreed to put it on the market to help smooth the start of their new lives apart, but he knew that inflated real estate prices would be in free-fall within days. Instead of doubling his investment, he would be lucky to get his money out. His wife held all the aces in any impending legal dispute. But all of this paled into insignificance against the other news he had had that week, news he had so far told no one.

That Thursday afternoon, Joseph Pikul took his first wife, Sandy, out to lunch. He paid her in cash for her traveling expenses to New York from Massachusetts and for a new dress to wear for the occasion. The lunch date was ostensibly to talk about the delinquent alimony payments, but they talked amiably about old times and Pikul's disintegrating marriage.

Late that afternoon, Pikul took his ex-wife to his second wife's duplex apartment on Sixth Avenue at 10th Street. He dismissed the babysitter, and he and Sandy took the children to Rumpelmayer's, a landmark ice cream parlor on Central Park South. When he arrived home with Claudia and Blake, his second wife, Diane, was waiting. She was furious because he had taken the children out without letting her know where they were going. She was also annoyed because he had dismissed her babysitter, who was supposed to cover for her while she went to a writing class. She didn't like the children tagging along on dates with his ex-wife.

Soon there was a loud and furious argument in front of the children that the neighbors could hear. Diane lunged at Joseph Pikul and tried to scratch him. He walked out of the apartment, and Diane followed, walking behind him down Sixth Avenue shouting insults. "You faggot!" she said as people stopped and stared and Joseph Pikul scurried on. "You motherfucker! You creep!"

Despite that argument Joseph and Diane Pikul agreed not to change their plans to spend the weekend at their summer house in Amagansett. They were hoping to divide some of their furniture and other belongings, and the argument only fueled their determination to put their failed marriage behind them.

So, less than twenty-four hours after the vicious public duel witnessed by dozens of strangers, Joseph and Diane Pikul were talking civilly to one another and making arrangements to drive out to the Hamptons. Diane hurried home from her job as assistant to the publisher at *Harper's,* got the children into their pajamas so they could sleep on the journey, and helped load them into Joseph Pikul's station wagon. It was the last time they would see her alive.

Diane Pikul was to follow later in her own car. Pikul stopped to pick up a few things at the Battery Park City apartment, then gunned the car toward Long Island. Diane went to dinner—with whom, if anyone, isn't known—and it was after 9 P.M. when she collected her car from her parking garage. She headed east on 14th Street, then north to the Midtown Tunnel for the long drive to Amagansett.

It was not the first time that Diane Pikul had had to dismantle the dilapidated structure of one life to rebuild another, one she hoped would stand on a stronger foundation. Each instance had been difficult, painful, even traumatic. But this time she felt more empowered than on the earlier occasions, more able to carry the burden, and now, she would have enough of her husband's money to cushion the problems ahead. About that she was determined.

Diane Whitmore was born in South Bend, Indiana, in 1943. She was an only child, and her family moved several times. She was raised in Indiana, Michigan, and New Jersey. An intelligent, creative youngster, she went to the all-girls Mt. Holyoke College, in Massachusetts. She established a wild reputation there, dating older men from Ivy League colleges, staying out all night, and spreading detailed stories of her colorful sexual escapades around the campus.

She wanted marriage more than she wanted a career, and by the time she was in her second year at college, she was engaged to a talented, Yale-educated surgeon with dazzling prospects. However, Diane's heavy drinking and casual infidelity fractured the relationship, and although they dated each other off and on for years, the marriage never happened. She held several entry-level jobs that ultimately led nowhere and had a series of casual affairs with men who shared a common trait: they were dangerous or in some way nefarious. Diane herself described most of her men as "strange but exciting." At least one was married; another a rock star; another a drug dealer. Most of the affairs were fueled by alcohol and, occasionally, drugs. Diane was searching for excitement and adventure.

In 1970, she met the man who was to become her first husband.

Ralph Schnackenberg was a photographer with something of a mysterious background. He saw the beautiful thirty-two-year-old Diane sitting alone on a train to Massachusetts and tried, successfully, to pick her up. From the start it was an intensely sexual relationship—and equally volatile out of bed. Despite frequent violent arguments and Diane's steady decline into alcoholism, they were married. Schnackenberg was absent for weeks at a time. Precisely why was never clear even to Diane and his closest friends. She told some people he was a CIA agent, something he has denied. Diane was convinced he was unfaithful and tried to monitor his mail and phone calls.

He was intermittently violent. When he wasn't around, she would go to a Manhattan bar, get drunk, and wake up in some stranger's bed. Their marriage quickly deteriorated into wretched, alcoholic combat. It lasted just a few weeks beyond their first anniversary.

By then, Diane was working as a secretary in the New York City Parks Department. Her drinking led to frequent absences, binges that lasted a week or more. But in December 1977, after she had been shaken by the breakup of her marriage and the sudden death of her mother, Diane walked into a small, ill-lit room in what had once been a storefront on Perry Street in Greenwich Village. It was a meeting of Alcoholics Anonymous.

Of all the three thousand or so meeting places where New York's alcoholics share their experience, strength, and hope and help each other recover from alcoholism, Diane had chosen Perry Street Workshop, an eclectic mix of artists, actors, writers, professionals, street people, and Greenwich Village characters. At her first meeting, she caught the eye of a tall man whose expensive wardrobe made him stand out from the other AA members even in this dim yellow light. He was dressed in a Brooks Brothers suit and a Burberry raincoat. His name was Joseph Pikul.

Joseph Pikul was nine years older than Diane. He was born in Ware, Massachusetts, the second child of working-class parents. His mother was illiterate; his father was a heavy drinker and sometimes violent. His parents were too poor to pay for his college tuition, so he worked two and three jobs at a time to raise enough money to put himself through college: in a textile mill, as a gravedigger, as a construction worker, in a deli.

He graduated from Northeastern University in Boston and in 1959 married Sandy Jarvinen, another Northeastern student. They moved to New York the following year. Joe Pikul worked at Standard & Poor's, then opened his own brokerage firm, Sage Associates, on Wall Street. Within a decade, he was so successful in what for most other money managers on Wall Street was a bad period that he was featured in the *New York Times* business section.

While Pikul was successful on Wall Street, his marriage was a battleground. He had a violent and unpredictable hair-trigger temper, and he beat his wife on numerous occasions. Once he battered her with a statuette of a nymph. Pikul may even have attempted to murder her. She was at the wheel of a brand-new car whose brakes failed mysteriously, causing a serious accident. She spent months in hospitals. Suspicious, she tried to get the car's brakes checked, but Joe Pikul had disposed of it. Despite suspicions, and the obvious danger she was in, she returned to him. When the beatings resumed with greater intensity, she finally summoned up the courage to leave him.

Alone, Pikul was even more prone to violence. He beat and threatened to kill a limo driver who had come to collect him, apparently convinced, in a paranoid, drunken state, that the limo driver was a hitman sent by his wife. He could have gone to prison, but after Pikul gave the driver some money, he refused to testify against him. It was after this incident that he sought help and found his way into Alcoholics Anonymous.

This, then, was the man whose path crossed Diane Whitmore's at the Perry Street Workshop. They were a couple made for each other: a classic abuser and a classic victim.

Recovering alcoholics in AA are advised against emotional involvements in their first year of sobriety. Nevertheless, Joseph and Diane struck up a friendship almost immediately and were dating within a few weeks. Six months later, Diane obtained an annulment, and they were married in July 1978. Diane was two months pregnant.

The quiet wedding in upstate New York was followed by a romantic Hamptons honeymoon. They borrowed a friend's house in Montauk and toured the Hamptons' most serene locations. Pikul took her to the best restaurants and lavished gifts on her. At last, she believed, she had found the man she had fantasized about since she was a child: a wealthy, powerful husband who would treat her like a queen. They so adored the Hamptons that it was easy for Diane to persuade Pikul to make Hamptons weekends part of their routine.

They moved into a Greenwich Village apartment, bought a four-poster waterbed fitted with mirrors in the canopy so they could watch themselves make love, and embarked on a lifestyle of conspicuous, trivial, self-indulgent consumption. The spending spree continued despite difficult times on Wall Street. Pikul had to close his brokerage with half a million dollars in debts, but he took a job at a prestigious firm, Arnhold & Bleichroeder, and was soon earning a million dollars or more a year in commissions.

Diane Pikul gave birth to a daughter, Claudia, in 1979. She was thirty-six. On the outside, Diana and Joseph's situation seemed idyllic. They had put their addictions behind them and maintained their sobriety. They had started new, successful lives enriched by a child. They rented a house in Windmill Lane in Amagansett and later bought it. It was not an impressive home by Hamptons standards. It had been a fisherman's shack and was dressed up with two large modern additions in matching styles. It did, however, come with a pool and an expansive, well-landscaped yard. Diane would live there all spring and summer, while Pikul came out at weekends. The Pikuls had several New York friends who were also summer Hamptonites, and Diane involved herself in local organizations that formed the fulcrum of middle-class social life there—and in Alcoholics Anonymous.

Joe Pikul's behavior did not endear him to his Hamptons neighbors. The house abutted the Stony Hill horse farm and riding school, and Pikul objected when the owner, Liz Hotchkiss, sought permission to build a windmill. The windmill was nearly two hundred yards away and would hardly have interfered with the Pikuls' enjoyment of their property. It was an important and practical, ecologically sound measure for the owner of the farm. Joe Pikul turned the issue into a cause célèbre and made so much trouble about the proposal that he was criticized by the local newspaper as an interfering weekender. The building of the windmill went ahead.

Other aspects of Pikul's behavior in the Hamptons also attracted attention. He bought a rifle and shot at rats and other pests from the window. There were noisy target practice sessions against target cards pinned to a fence post. He even interrupted one of Diane's dinner parties to shoot a rat. Diane tolerated Pikul's quick and violent temper and bizarre habits. Once a gardener removed an overgrown bush near the Pikul's Amagansett house. When Joe Pikul arrived for the weekend he was furious that the bush was missing. He gave Diane such a hard time that she went to the gardener in tears and begged him to find it at a local dump and replant it.

When the family traveled, Joe Pikul went first class while his wife and child sat in coach. When they went to dinner or the theater, Joe sat in a stretch limo while Diane followed behind in a yellow cab. Although he spent money freely, he was secretive about the family's finances and refused to allow Diane access to any information about them. She was forbidden even to handle his mail or to enter his office in their duplex.

When Diane was roused, however, she possessed a temper as vicious as her husband's. Friends and neighbors recalled frequent heated arguments, apparently erupting out of nowhere, in which the Pikuls traded the vilest insults. Despite the obvious fragility of their relationship, Diane became pregnant again. She told friends she couldn't bear the thought of Claudia being an only child. When she was seven months pregnant with her second child, Diane accompanied Joe on a business trip to California—flying at Joe's insistence, despite the obvious dangers that late in her pregnancy.

During that trip, after a business meeting near San Francisco, Joe was driving with Diane when one of their wildcat arguments broke out. Diane peppered her husband with a string of obscenities, and he pulled over and forced her out of the car in the pouring rain, at nighttime in a strange city. Diane retaliated by disappearing for days, but she ultimately returned to her husband and gave birth to her son, Blake, in December 1982. In the months that followed Blake's birth, their relationship nosedived further. Joe Pikul's interest in sex seemed to evaporate, and when Diane confronted him about it he accused her of turning him off. However, he didn't believe she turned other men off. He was constantly accusing her of having sex with numerous men when she was in the Hamptons without him.

Many of Diane's friends advised her to leave, but she was too enamored of the lifestyle that her husband's million-dollar-plus income allowed her. Joe would tell her during their fights that he would never allow her to take his money and that he would seek custody of the children. She believed that in any legal battle between herself and her husband, Joe's money gave him all the aces. So she stayed.

Then, in 1986, Diane made a discovery that turned the tables on Joe and left her holding the trump cards. Diane, who was secretly delving into the family's finances, found a check for four hundred dollars to Victoria's Secret. She had made no purchases there, so she began to suspect her husband was having an affair. After he returned from a business trip, she went through his suitcase while he was at the New York office. She found a collection of bras, panties, and hosiery. They were all in large sizes—much larger than would fit any woman she could imagine being attractive to Joe. She carefully replaced them, then drove out to Amagansett to search the house. She spent an entire day looking in every box, suitcase, and bag that belonged to Joe. She was amazed by what she found.

There were enough brassieres, panties, girdles and garter belts to stock a small store. There were vibrators and women's wigs and homosexual pornography. She did not need much imagination to understand the meaning of the find: there were Polaroid photographs of Joe dressed as a woman and videotapes that showed Joe dancing and mincing around masturbating.

Diane looked at the figure of Joe dressed in drag on the TV screen and recognized the setting. It was their own summer and weekend home—the house where he had stashed so much incriminating material. As she studied the video more carefully, she saw a room she did not recognize. It was fully furnished with a bed, a dresser, a desk, and cabinets. It must be a secret room in the house. She flew upstairs to find it in the attic space—an entire sex den for Joe's cross-dressing episodes—in an area of the house off limits to Diane because he kept business documents there.

Despite the icy wind and cold, stabbing rain, Diane walked along Amagansett Beach trying to figure out what she should do. In some ways, the discovery changed everything. Joe could not risk the embarrassing publicity of a divorce or custody fight in which the tapes and photographs figured prominently.

She did face one major problem. Although the tapes and photographs gave her leverage, during their arguments Joe had threatened to give up making money and live in some far-off resort in the Seychelles or Mexico or Costa Rica on what funds he had already squirreled away. He would go anywhere where Diane could not get at his money. He would leave them both penniless before he allowed her to take his money and his children. So Diane decided, shivering and wet on Amagansett Beach, to say nothing of her find. At least not yet. She packed up some of the tapes and the photographs and went through the house trying to make it look as if Joe's secrets had never been uncovered. She took the photographs and tapes she had set aside to a bank where she kept a safe deposit box and placed them there. When she finally got home, she pretended nothing had happened.

Before long, Joe discovered some photographs were missing and realized what must have happened. He guessed correctly that Diane would hide them in her safe deposit box and tried to bluff his way into examining the box at her bank. The bank clerks wouldn't let him have access to his wife's property, so he resorted to other means. Using some phone jacks and an answering machine hidden in an attic crawl space, Joe Pikul managed to bug the phone at the Amagansett house.

He soon had a collection of tapes of Diane discussing her discoveries with her girlfriends and a possible future divorce. Diane, in turn, discovered the bug. Rather than pull it out, she left it in place and tailored her phone calls for Joe's ears.

It was a destructive and emotionally exhausting game and could not go on forever. In the summer of 1986, Diane confronted Joe with her discovery. Realizing he could not afford either a divorce or the publicity that would ensue from a custody battle, he promised to change his ways. He convinced Diane not to leave him, sweetening his pleas with lavish gifts of furs and jewelry. She agreed, but the rapprochement lasted only a few months more.

Diane had consulted a high-profile divorce attorney, Raoul Felder, and although she gave him some of her cache of incriminating photographs of Joe, she was not willing to let him go ahead and file for divorce. However, she did appear to begin preparing for a new life without Joe. In February 1987, she got a job—her first in eight years— as assistant to the publisher of *Harper's* magazine. It paid very little— just a tiny fraction of Joe's income—but it was an impressive title for her resumé and it brought her into contact with, in Diane's eyes, some rich and powerful people.

That summer, Diane's job prevented her from going to the Hamptons during the work week. She had planned to keep the children in the city in the care of babysitters, but Joe insisted on taking them to the Hamptons house for most of June and July. This time Diane came out on the weekends. The decision was a source of further friction. There was a lot of action on Wall Street that summer, and Joe's absence from work was costing him hundreds of thousands of dollars. Worse, he kept telling Blake and Claudia that their mother didn't join them during the week because she didn't love them. The long vacation was over before she realized what Joe was really up to. He was laying groundwork for his custody battle. He wanted to be able to claim that he had sacrificed a small fortune to spend a few weeks with the children while Diane had stubbornly insisted on staying in New York without them.

It was not until late September 1987 that the warring spouses finally decided to get a divorce. The decision followed a weekend of brutal fighting at the Amagansett house, Diane reveling in her discoveries of his cross-dressing habits and Joe tormenting her with her small income, supposed affairs, and reliance on babysitters and other help. As she screamed obscenities at her husband in front of the children, Diane was unaware that he was recording their arguments with a microcassette recorder that he used for business meetings and memos.

Joe began to spend more time at the Battery Park apartment. Diane was unaware of its existence, and Joe took the precaution of blindfolding the children when he took them there so they would not be able to tell their mother the address. Diane finally wrote a five-page account of their marriage and her desire for a divorce to Raoul Felder. Meanwhile, Joe Pikul confided his plans for a custody battle to his ex-wife, Sandy.

Selling their Hamptons home was central to their plans. The money was to be used to finance their new lives apart. Then, just as Joe and Diane were planning to make a last trip to the Hamptons to split up their belongings and put the place up for sale, the market crashed.

Joe was already in financial trouble. He owed money to the IRS; he owed margin calls; he had tens of thousands of dollars in unpaid bills. The failure of the market and his other troubles combined to put Joe on a razor's edge emotionally.

So on the evening of Friday, October 23, 1987, Joe Pikul brought his car to a halt outside his Hamptons home. Blake, aged four, was already asleep, and Joe carried him inside and put him to bed. Eight-year-old Claudia was still awake. After he had put her to bed he made some coffee and waited for his wife to arrive. Later he claimed to have made a discovery that proved to him she was having an affair: an opened box of condoms beneath their bed.

It was late when she arrived—much later than he had expected—and by the time she pulled in behind Joe's car, Joe was convinced she had stopped at the home of a lover on the way. There was one final, furious, violent argument. Joe grabbed Diane by the throat and squeezed. She punched him in the mouth and broke a tooth. He beat her with some unknown object, possibly a hammer or a bat. Over and over he hit her, nine or ten times, on the head and in the face. He did horrifying damage to her beautiful face, and she might well have died of those injuries, but at last, Joe Pikul began strangling his wife. After less than a minute her body became limp and she died at his feet.

All of this was accomplished without waking the children. Joe Pikul now busied himself cleaning up the traces of blood. He wrapped his wife's body in a tarpaulin and closed the ends with rope, then carried her to his car and drove to a nearby field, leaving the children alone in the house. He couldn't find a convenient burial site, so he drove to a secluded spot overlooking Gardiner's Bay. He buried her beneath the sand, but her legs stuck out, so he unearthed her again and put her back in the station wagon. He then drove back to Windmill Lane and slumped, exhausted, on an armchair and slept.

The next morning he told the children that their mother had left early that morning and might not be back all weekend. He drove into Amagansett with the children and stopped at the hardware store to buy a dizzying list of items, from heavy-duty gloves and garbage bags to ice chests and a wheelbarrow. At the nearby deli he purchased twelve large bags of ice. On the way back to the Windmill Lane house, he stopped at the town dump and disposed of bags of Diane's belongings. He was now desperate to get rid of Diane's corpse and cover his tracks.

He took the children to a friend's house to play, then repacked the body in the tarpaulin with some ice to slow down decomposition. He called a dentist and left a message saying he had broken a tooth on some peanut brittle and needed an appointment to get it fixed, then called a cleaning service to ensure the house would be thoroughly cleaned on Monday.

He called an old friend who had been best man at his first wedding, a man he had not seen in years, and said he needed to visit him and bring the children. Henry Sawoska and his family lived in New Windsor, New York, near the Catskills, at least a four-hour drive from Amagansett. Sawoska and his wife agreed to the sudden, unexpected visit, and Joe and the children set out late that afternoon. It was after nine P.M. when they arrived. Joe Pikul then dropped another bombshell: he was going to leave the children with the Sawoskas and come back the next day. The Sawoskas were perplexed but, more for the children's sake than anything else, agreed. Joe set out again at 10:15 P.M.

He drove to the home of his ex-wife in Massachusetts, roused her from bed, and asked if he could bury something. At first she thought he meant legal documents or assets that he wanted to hide from his wife during their divorce, but it was not long before she realized he had killed Diane. She recommended a lawyer she knew, let her ex-husband rest for a while, then sent him on his way at first light.

He drove on to the Berkshires, where he used to rent a ski lodge, but he couldn't find anywhere to dump the body unseen. Afraid to linger, he continued driving, finally ending up back in New York at his Greenwich Village apartment. Diane's body was still in his car.

After a fitful few hours' sleep, he got back on the road. He was almost out of time. It was Monday morning. He had to pick up his children. He had to dump the body as best he could. The car was beginning to smell.

Just a few miles from the Sawoskas' home, he pulled off the New York State Thruway and dropped the tarp-covered body in a culvert. He collected the children, giving no rational explanation for his disappearance for over a day and a half, and drove away. On the way he stopped at a car wash, had the car cleaned inside and out, and threw out more bags of Diane's belongings, including her array of credit cards. These were found almost immediately by the car wash staff.

Back in New York, Diane's co-workers at *Harper's* were alarmed by her unexplained absence from work. Someone called the children's school and discovered they were absent too. Someone else called her father in Florida. He called the East Hampton police.

By the time Joe and the children reached New York City, police were already looking for Diane. Joe was alerted by a call from one of Diane's coworkers who demanded to know where she was and who revealed that all her friends and family already knew she was missing. Joe insisted Diane had simply left him, but to cover his tracks, he called the East Hampton police and reported her missing. Two East Hamptom detectives, with Joe's permission, went to the Windmill Lane house.

Although Joe had cleaned up after the murder and the house had been cleaned again by a service Monday morning, they found tiny blood spots in several places. They immediately sealed it as a crime scene. Meanwhile, the credit cards found by the car wash workers had been given to police upstate. Suspicious, but still not knowing of Diane's disappearance, state police searched the dumpster where they had been found. They discovered a host of personal belongings—notebooks, keys, apparently current address books, underwear, and other items—too many things to have been discarded by mistake and too new to be treated as garbage. One other thing puzzled them. Along with the regular-size bras and other clothing there were several extra-large bras. They were Joe's.

It was two more days before the body was found, by two state workers assigned to look for debris in drainage culverts off the Thruway after a night of heavy rain. After an unsuccessful attempt to hide out in a Manhattan hotel, Joe was arrested and confessed to killing Diane after a fight over her late arrival at the Hamptons. Although he gave varying accounts about his motive—no particular reason, Diane's alleged affairs, his fears of her using his cross-dressing activities as leverage in their divorce—the essential details never changed: he had beaten and choked her to death.

There was one more surprise awaiting detectives. After a strip search was ordered, Pikul reluctantly removed his shirt and jeans to reveal that he was wearing a bra, flowered panties, and pantyhose beneath them.

That would have been the end of a not very complex case. But as in a much more highly publicized case a decade later, the O.J. Simpson trial, it was not long before the wheels of justice began to go in reverse. In Simpson's case, that was primarily because he was famous. In Joe Pikul's case, it was because he was rich.

The children were taken to live with Joe Pikul's nephew, Edward Pawlowski, and his wife Lauren in Washington, D.C. Joe was in prison for less than two weeks before he made bail and almost immediately demanded to see his children. New York State made an attempt to have the children taken into state care but failed because there was no proof that Pikul had ever neglected or abused them.

A cousin of Diane's, Kathleen O'Guin and her husband Michael were recruited by Diane's father and friends to step in and challenge Pikul for custody. Felder, drawing on a retainer given him by Diane, agreed to represent them. It was an unaccustomed role for Felder, whose expertise and fame were as a divorce lawyer. Both sides settled down for a protracted legal battle. In the meantime, to the dismay of Diane's family, friends, and neighbors, the children returned to the Greenwich Village apartment to live with their father.

Life went on with surprising normality for the Pikul children. They continued to attend the fashionable Grace Church School in Greenwich Village and had play dates with the other children there. After one play date, the mother of classmate Jennifer Bain called Pikul to arrange to bring Claudia home. The woman who was to become Joe Pikul's third wife spoke to him for the first time.

Mary Bain worked in the fashion industry. She was in her mid-thirties and married to a pharmacist. They had one daughter together, and there was also a son by her husband's previous marriage. Mary Bain befriended Claudia and Blake, and through them, Joe Pikul. She plunged into the center of the family, at the expense of her own, her friends claim, even offering during the custody proceeding to adopt Blake, now five, and Claudia, nine, herself.

The custody hearings produced no evidence that Joe Pikul had ever abused Blake or Claudia, despite having murdered their mother and driven around with them while her corpse lay in the well of the station wagon. Justice Kristin Booth Glen ruled that Pikul could keep custody until his trial but that the O'Guins would assume custody during the trial itself and retain the children if he were convicted.

Pikul, flush with victory, now maneuvered to circumvent the ruling by convincing Mary Bain to marry him and become the children's legal guardian. In order to divorce her husband and marry Pikul quickly, she had to surrender custody of her own daughter. Mary Bain became Pikul's third wife at a ceremony in the upstate New York town of Lanesville, just eight months after the murders. Almost immediately she filed to have the judge's order changed so that she would get custody during and after the trial.

It appeared to be another easy victory for Joe, but in their first weeks of marriage Joe visited the same brutal abuse on his third wife that he had on his first two. He timed her absences, even to go shopping. He complained about business trips she had to make. In one incident, in front of the children, he cut her dress with a hunting knife because she returned to the apartment later than expected.

The abuse inside the Pikul household might have remained a secret, but Mary confided to a domestic abuse counselor at a county medical center. Worried about the safety of the children, the counselor passed what would otherwise have remained confidential information to a state agency, Special Services for Children, whose officers gave the information to the O'Guin attorneys.When the details of the abuse of Mary Bain Pikul were described in yet another custody hearing, Pikul's case collapsed. His attorney withdrew, custody was revoked, and the children were immediately taken to stay with the O'Guins.

The criminal case against Joe Pikul had become a sideshow as the seesawing custody battle was played out. Pikul's attorneys had won two significant victories. His confession to police after his arrest was ruled inadmissible; he had already been charged and was awaiting arraignment when he was questioned without his attorneys being present. The evidence of his cross-dressing was likewise ruled inadmissable as prejudicial. The trial opened in January 1989, more than fourteen months after the murder. In court, Pikul pleaded self-defense, claiming that in the course of a confrontation over Diane's late arrival and Pikul's discovery of condoms under their bed, Diane had rushed at him with a knife. He had grabbed her by the neck to protect himself, and moments later she was dead. The other injuries, he claimed, were postmortem, caused by his moving the body.

The jury did not believe his story. After two days of deliberations, Joe Pikul was found guilty of second-degree murder. Before he could be sentenced a month later, his attorneys moved for the verdict to be set aside because of newly discovered exculpatory evidence, a tape Pikul had made of the two of them arguing violently at the Amagansett house.

In the end he was never sentenced. Joe Pikul had two more surprises in store. The first was that he had AIDS, apparently contracted from a homosexual encounter some years earlier. Diane had long suspected that he was HIV positive, but she had been too afraid to get a test herself. Pikul had been told just a few days prior to the murder that he might have as little as a year to live. He had seemed in good health during his trial, but just days after the guilty verdict was read, his condition began to deteriorate. On June 2, 1989, with his appeal still pending, Pikul was transferred from prison to Arden Hill Hospital in upstate New York. Just a few hours later he was dead.

The final surprise came when his estate was examined. It had been assumed that Pikul had millions of dollars stashed in secret bank accounts, money that now belonged to Claudia and Blake. In fact, Pikul was broke. He had taken out insurance policies in his children's name but had failed to keep up payments after his arrest. He had several mortgages on the Amagansett house, and with the real estate market flat the market value of the house was significantly less than the outstanding loans. That was supposing anyone would buy a property where such a notorious murder had been carried out.

There were rumors of Mexican bank accounts, but they could not be found despite the best efforts of a battery of lawyers. One Swiss bank account was discovered, but it had less than a hundred thousand dollars left in it. Pikul had withdrawn a quarter million to pay his legal expenses.

There were also hundreds of thousands of dollars in debts, ranging from outstanding IRS claims and tens of thousands in back alimony due Pikul's first wife to thousands of dollars on each of the Pikuls' many credit cards. Pikul had earned millions of dollars in his career. It was either all gone or had been so expertly hidden that no one could find it.

Pikul was buried in a graveyard in Amagansett just a few yards from the house where he murdered his wife. Believing that gravesites would one day be at a premium, he had bought every remaining plot himself. There was one final twist. Under New York State law, if a convicted felon dies before an appeal can be heard, his conviction must be erased. Pikul's appeal on the new evidence, his tape of an argument with Diane, had never been heard. So, six months after his death, Joe Pikul was declared legally innocent of the murder.

CHAPTER 13

Murder by Stealth

HIDDEN HILL FARM, a 192-acre spread just outside Southampton, is one of the last large farms in the Hamptons. The land would be worth many millions of dollars for real estate development, but it is zoned for agriculture, so Hidden Hill Farm has trailers instead of palatial homes. Korean farmers live in the trailers and lease lots on the farm to grow produce that ends up in Korean markets in Brooklyn, Manhattan, and northern New Jersey. Several dogs roam the farm to keep campers, hunters, and other trespassers away.

On Mother's Day 1993—May 9—a group of Koreans in the Hamptons for the weekend trekked up an old gravel road and paid one of the farmers for permission to search for wild vegetables in woods near his lot. The Koreans spread out to conduct their search, and after half an hour or so, one of them noticed some wild edible ferns—plants a Westerner might have dismissed as weeds. He bent down and picked them, then noticed something else. Just below the surface of the soil there were five fingernails, with some scratched and worn red enamel still on them. He scraped away at the soil and found that the fingernails were attached to a skeletal hand.

Two hours later, Southampton Town police and Suffolk County detectives had removed from her shallow grave the body of a young woman in her twenties. The body was badly decomposed. It had obviously been in the ground for several weeks, possibly all winter. She was white, with dark brown, shoulder-length hair. She probably weighed about ninety pounds at her death and was very petite, under five feet tall. She had been wearing a long-sleeved white shirt with a Gap label and a blue sweater. Her other clothes were missing.

She had no identification with her. It was not even possible for the medical examiner to give a conclusive cause of death. Clearly, however, the missing clothes and the attempt to hide the body pointed to murder. There are relatively few murders on the books of the Southampton Town police. As a result, they have very limited resources to deal with those that do take place. There were no local reports of missing persons that matched the description of the body on the farm. Detectives concluded that she was most likely murdered somewhere else and driven out to the Hamptons for disposal.

The first step had to be to match a name—a person, a family, a history, and therefore a list of suspects—to what were little more than skeletal remains. The skull and other bones were carefully measured and photographed and sent to a special unit in Tennessee for a computer graphic to be made showing what she might have looked like in life. That process would take several weeks, and in the meantime there was little for investigators to usefully do. Those investigators had no way of knowing that they had uncovered just one victim of one of the most cunning, meticulous, and dangerous serial killers in history: one who for four years had been murdering women without police even realizing his existence. And he was using the Hamptons as a graveyard.

The body on the farm was Leah Evens. She was the daughter of a Manhattan judge, Lester Evens, and Susan Evens, a public relations executive. Her father was controversial because of two incidents in his courtroom. In one, he had invited a prostitute to sit with him on his bench while he conducted court business as she waited for someone to arrive to pay her fine. When nobody showed up, Evens decided that her afternoon with him was "time served" and let her go. The incident was picked up by the New York newspapers, and his fellow judges agreed the action was improper and censured him. On another occasion he was criticized for releasing a robbery suspect who had been jailed a number of times on only $250 bail when prosecutors had asked for twenty-five thousand dollars.

Leah Evens was a student at Sarah Lawrence college when the prostitute shared her father's bench. At the time there seemed no indication that she herself would one day drift into prostitution. She had had a privileged lifestyle—private schools, weekends in the Hamptons, where her parents rented homes each summer, and ambitions to forge a career as a lawyer.

Soon afterward, Lester and Susan Evens's marriage broke up. Susan Evens kept the family's Brooklyn townhouse, and Lester Evens moved into an apartment in Greenwich Village. Leah Evens remained close to both, living with her mother in Brooklyn when she was home from college and visiting her father often.

After Sarah Lawrence, Leah Evens had several low-paying jobs as a waitress and cook in Manhattan restaurants and diners. When she became pregnant, Leah and her boyfriend decided to have the child, whom she named Julian. The couple remained together, but unmarried, for several years and had a second child, Eve.

When they broke up Leah Evens was depressed. She despaired of making anything of a life that had once held so much promise. She had abused drugs for years; now her addiction deepened. She turned to cocaine and heroin. When she could not afford to buy drugs she would go to bars to find someone who could. It was a short step from exchanging sex for drugs to exchanging sex for money to buy drugs.

Leah Evens's family and friends deny that she was ever a prostitute, but that is almost certainly how she met the man who murdered her, drove her body to the Hamptons, and buried it in a shallow grave. On February 27, 1993, about ten weeks before her body was found, Leah Evens had been hanging around late at night on East 12th Street off Second Avenue in Manhattan's East Village looking to turn a trick so she could buy heroin from a street dealer two blocks away. At some point a gray, battered, 1984 Mazda pickup truck pulled over. The man inside was tentative and nervous. We know from his dealings with other prostitutes something of the conversation that probably took place. He had picked up other women on this same street and always asked the same question: "Have you been working a long time?"

The question often leaves prostitutes nonplussed. They want to give the customer the answer he wants to hear. Some johns want a hooker who is experienced, efficient at her work, and not tempted to rip a client off. Others want a less experienced partner: one unlikely to give them a disease and not jaded by her profession.

Some of the women who worked East 12th Street knew that this man sought a less experienced prostitute. Leah Evens was certainly that. They quickly agreed on a price: forty dollars. Leah climbed into the cab of the pickup. She must have noticed the trash covering the floor, including women's tights, panties, a pink sock, and a wood-handled steak knife.

She may have seen the Grateful Dead dashboard sticker and another that said: STICKS AND STONES MAY BREAK MY BONES BUT WHIPS AND CHAINS EXCITE ME.

It isn't known where they went to complete their sexual bargain. Probably, they drove to a quiet block off Manhattan's less-populated Houston Street or Avenue A. What is known is that while Leah got on with her work, the man groped and fumbled beneath her shirt and sweater. Then, as the act came to an end, his hands fumbled upward and found her throat. By the time Leah Evens realized what was happening to her—if she ever did realize it—it was too late to put up much of a struggle. The man tightened his grip on her throat and strangled her. He pushed her into the well in front of the passenger seat, covered her with a blanket, and drove uptown toward the Midtown Tunnel.

He headed toward his home in East Meadow, Long Island, but when he got to the exit he pressed on for another fifty miles until he reached the Hamptons. It was not yet dawn, and at that time of the year the roads and most of the houses he passed were deserted. He reached County Road 51, then after a few miles he turned up Old Riverhead Road, which is not much more than a gravel path. He pulled the pickup over and dragged Leah's body a hundred yards through the woods. As the sun came up, he finished digging a shallow grave. He rolled Leah's body into it and covered her with dirt. There it would lie for the next ten weeks.

Leah Evens wasn't his first victim, nor was she his last.

A few months earlier, Joel Rifkin had pulled over next to a pretty, dark-haired woman named Lauren Marquez, from Sunnyside in Queens, on the corner of Houston and Allen streets in lower Manhattan. Like Leah Evens, she was a mother of two. Also like Evens, she was a prostitute and drug addict, and her hurried and perfunctory sexual encounter with Joel Rifkin would be the final act of a painful and misdirected life. After he had strangled Lauren Marquez to death, Rifkin drove through what remained of the night to the Hamptons to bury her. The spot he had chosen was one he knew well. He had explored the Hamptons thoroughly as a teenager—on long lonely walks in woods and nature reserves and in equally lonely visits to beaches crowded with beautiful young women. Those women, with their fashionable clothes, scant bikinis, and tanned, oil-coated bodies, had ignored, rebuffed, and intimidated him. Now he was exacting a terrifying revenge.

As the new day dawned, Rifkin steered his pickup truck on to a Long Island Lighting Company access road near Suffolk County Airport in

Westhampton Beach. In a secluded, heavily wooded area he dug a shallow grave and buried Lauren Marquez. When he was done, he drove into Westhampton for breakfast and to sleep.

Joel Rifkin's killing spree had begun in 1989 when he picked up a prostitute on Manhattan's Lower East Side, paid her for sex, then strangled her. He drove her body to his home and dismembered her with a chainsaw before dumping the parts in a Hamptons nature reserve. She has never been identified. He committed a second murder several months later. In that case too, he dismembered the body and dumped the parts, this time in the Hudson River. Again, no trace was ever found.

Rifkin waited almost another year before striking again. Barbara Jacobs was a thirty-one-year-old prostitute he met on Allen Street on Manhattan's Lower East Side. Like the others, she was small, weighing less than a hundred pounds, and she was a drug addict. Her nude body was found in a plastic garbage bag inside a cardboard box floating in the Hudson River. For almost two years, she was wrongly listed as having died from a cocaine overdose. At the end of the summer of 1991, the body of a thirty-one-year-old Korean prostitute, Yun Lee, was found in a trunk in the East River near the 59th Street Bridge. Another body was found only eight days later, but as it was discovered in upstate New York, there was nothing to connect her to the others. Six murders of women by the same psychopathic killer had gone virtually unnoticed.

Joel Rifkin, the man behind this grim harvest, had grown up in East Meadow, Long Island. He was one of two children adopted by Ben Rifkin, a structural engineer, and his wife Jeanne. He had been born in 1959 to an unmarried college student and handed over to the Rifkins three weeks later. The Rifkins were caring and responsible parents. Ben Rifkin joined the local school board and was elected vice president, and he was a trustee of the local library.

Joel Rifkin was told he was adopted when he was six years old. The Rifkins tried to ensure that he understood that he was loved and very much wanted, but while he had a secure home life, he had a hard time fitting in at school. There was something odd about his appearance and temperament that the other students latched on to and exploited. He had a thin face with angular features, his eyes framed by wire-rimmed spectacles. He walked with a shuffling gait and stooped shoulders. His clothes were unfashionable. He habitually wore pants that were an inch or two too short, exposing light-colored socks. He was teased and bullied mercilessly.

Even when he managed to make the track team, the achievement gained him little acceptance. He was forced to train apart from the others. When he was fifteen, he attended a track and field training camp in Connecticut, but he was left stranded there by his teammates; his father had to make a three-hour trip to fetch him.

Joel Rifkin was often beaten and abused in the school locker rooms, and he was the victim of cruel practical jokes. He would find letters in his locker purporting to be from girls at the school who wanted to date him; when he pursued the invitations he would invariably find they were hoaxes. One night he was pelted with eggs as he left a part-time job. Another time his camera was stolen.

Unsurprisingly, his grades were mediocre and he only barely managed to get into the State University of New York at an upstate campus, Brockport. His performance there was poor, and he dropped out after a year and returned home to Long Island. For the next several years Rifkin alternated between low-paying jobs and desultory attempts to complete college courses.

Then, in 1986, Joel Rifkin's adoptive father was diagnosed with prostate cancer. For the next several months he endured the agonies and humiliations of both the disease and the treatment, until, in February 1987, he committed suicide with an overdose of painkillers. Joel Rifkin became even more withdrawn following his father's death. The two had made many trips to explore the Hamptons together on spring and summer weekends.

The younger Rifkin was an enthusiastic amateur photographer and took many photographs of homes and landscapes in East Hampton, Southampton, and Montauk. He also took his camera to the beaches to surreptitiously photograph bikini-clad weekenders—young women he was afraid to approach.

But there were other women he was not afraid of. Since the age of eighteen Rifkin had regularly patronized prostitutes. He would drive to Hempstead or New York City to seek a hurried sexual tryst in a car his parents had bought him. By coincidence, one young woman he actually dated turned out to be a prostitute. He shared her apartment for a few weeks, then she threw him out.

Rifkin paid prostitutes for sex because he never learned to relate to other women, but there was also another reason. He had come to believe, erroneously, that his own mother had been a prostitute and that she had put him up for adoption to return to the streets. He told at least one prostitute he knew that his biological mother had also been a prostitute and a drug addict.

Stephanie Roberts says she met Rifkin late one night as she waited to turn a trick on a corner of Allen Street on Manhattan's Lower East Side. They parked near the Manhattan Bridge, he handed over forty-five dollars, and they had sex. They met several more times after that. Roberts says she became wary about meeting him because he started to ask too many questions. She would lie about herself and then forget what lies she had told him. However, unlike most prostitutes, who keep their work and social life entirely separate, she agreed to meet him for other than professional reasons. They drove out to Long Island to some of Joel Rifkin's favorite haunts. They went to Jones Beach and, in the summer of 1987, visited the Hamptons twice.

"It was the middle of the week," she says. "I couldn't afford not to work on weekends. We strolled around East Hampton and went to the beach for an hour or two. We stayed at a motel somewhere near Hampton Bays. The next day we drove out to Montauk, and he took some photographs at the lighthouse. He told me he had a landscaping business and that he worked at some of the rich people's houses in the Hamptons. We went out there again a couple of weeks later. But I couldn't get my head together to have a boyfriend, and if I could have it wouldn't have been him."

The relationship ended when Stephanie Roberts switched to working on the West Side of Manhattan to avoid Rifkin. She says his attentions had become stifling. "He kept telling me that his real mother had been working the streets and was a drug addict. He told me I should quit. He kept asking me if I had any children and if I did would I put them up for adoption. Later, when his picture and his victims' pictures were on all the front pages, I kept thinking—that was going to be me. That would have been me."

What Rifkin told Stephanie Roberts about his landscaping business was true. He had taken courses in agriculture at the State University of New York at Farmingdale, Long Island and worked as an intern at Planting Fields Arboretum, a four-hundred-acre public garden on the North Shore. He never completed his college courses and his fellow interns at Planting Fields regarded him in much the same way as his fellow students had at East Meadow High, but he learned enough to start a landscaping business with his mother's gardening equipment and a 1978 Chevy pickup. He worked on the Long Island estate of former CIA director William Casey and at a number of small homes in East Meadow and picked up several short assignments replanting the gardens of summer rentals in Amagansett and East Hampton.

Like everything else he tried, Rifkin's landscaping business was a failure. He didn't always show up when he said he would. He failed to complete several jobs and found himself replaced by other landscapers. Within a few months he was in debt and work was drying up. Another interest had begun to consume him. He began collecting newspaper cuttings on two serial killers: Arthur Shawcross, who had murdered eleven prostitutes in the Rochester, New York, area, and the Green River Killer, who was believed to be responsible for the murders of forty-nine women in the Seattle area.

Perhaps it was a life of rejection; perhaps some warped desire to be avenged on the mother he believed was a prostitute; perhaps it was simply because prostitutes were accessible victims. For whatever reason, in the summer of 1989, Rifkin, then thirty, embarked on a new career— a career in which he was at last, for a time, to enjoy some success.

Rifkin had already had one run-in with the police. He had been curb-crawling in Hempstead looking for a prostitute when he was picked up by two patrolmen. He had enough money with him to make bail and eventually paid a $250 fine. The experience made him wary of showing his face in Hempstead again and thereafter he confined his hunt for prostitutes to other Long Island communities and to Manhattan.

Inspired by Arthur Shawcross, Rifkin began murdering prostitutes in the summer of 1989. He was surprised at how easy it was. His first murders made no headlines. No one seemed to miss his victims. Either by accident or cunning, he varied his modus operandi, so that the police would not be alerted to any pattern, and he disposed of the bodies in several jurisdictions, so police were never aware that a serial killer was on the loose.

Rifkin chose his fifth victim at the end of the summer of 1991. It was Labor Day weekend, and Mary Ellen DeLuca, a dark-haired, olive-skinned twenty-two-year-old girl with brown eyes, had spent most of the weekend on the beaches of the Hamptons with friends. On Labor Day she returned to her hometown, Valley Stream, Long Island. She went out for the evening to visit her favorite hangouts in the Island Park area. Her girlfriends dropped her at her home and assumed she had gone inside. But she had not.

Mary Ellen DeLuca had fought drug addiction since she was a teenager. She had dropped out of school. She would disappear for days at a time into crack houses in Queens where she would exchange sex for drugs if she did not have enough money. Several times she appeared to have kicked the habit, and then she relapsed. Early in 1991, relatives discovered she was working as a prostitute to get money for drugs and virtually kidnapped her off the street. They drove her to a detox clinic, where she stayed for two weeks. For six months after that she was clean. That Labor Day weekend, she was to have her last relapse.

Instead of going into her home when her friends left her, she went in search of drugs. Joel Rifkin, meanwhile, was searching for a victim. The pickup truck pulled over next to her, and she got in. A few minutes later, as they were having sex, Rifkin closed his hands around her neck and began to tighten his grip.

Probably because he knew this victim lived on Long Island, Rifkin decided not to drive her out to a burial site in the Hamptons. Instead, he stripped her body of most of her clothes, leaving her wearing only a bra, and headed into New York City, then across the George Washington Bridge and north to West Point. There, he buried the body beneath some grass cuttings on a field used as a public dump.

A few weeks later, Rifkin chose another Long Island victim. She was twenty-eight-year-old Lorraine Orvieto. Lorraine was an intelligent, educated woman whose life had been derailed and never put back on track. She graduated from high school a year early and worked her way through college by running a housekeeping service; after she graduated from C.W. Post, she worked as an accountant in a Manhattan firm. Everything appeared to be going well for her. She would spend weekends at a summer share in Quogue in the Hamptons with several other young professional women; she had a boyfriend she loved and a career that held lots of promise.

However, as tax season approached, the hours at work became long and arduous. When she could no longer stand the pressure, she quit and tried to start her housekeeping business again, unsuccessfully. She became depressed, and when therapy and antidepressant drugs failed, she turned to harder drugs. Eventually, she became a prostitute in Bellport, Long Island, to pay for her cocaine habit. Sometimes she worked weekend parties in East Hampton and Bridgehampton, where she knew there were plenty of narcotics. Most of the time she worked the streets. That's where she ran into Joel Rifkin.

Rifkin had begun scouting his burial spots in advance of his murders. He had several more picked out in the Hamptons and in upstate New York, but he knew from his reading about other murderers that only variety in his methods would keep police from realizing a serial killer was operating. For the first time, Rifkin felt smart, successful, and sexually powerful. He was outwitting the police, avenging himself on women who had always looked down on him, and achieving a warped sexual gratification from his crimes.

Shortly before murdering victim number six, Lorraine Orvieto, he had purchased four fifty-gallon steel drums. He took her body to a hut where he kept his landscaping equipment, stripped off her clothes, and stuffed her inside one of the drums, which he dumped into a creek on Coney Island.

Over the next few months Rifkin filled the other three drums. One victim was a thirty-nine-year-old prostitute who had worked the streets for years. Maryann Holloman lived in an East Village flophouse and worked Lower East Side streets for drug money. Like Orvieto's, her naked body was stuffed in an oil drum and dumped off a Coney Island pier. The two women who were disposed of in the other two oil drums have never been identified. One was cast into Newtown Creek in Greenpoint, Brooklyn. There were only skeletal remains when she was eventually discovered. The other has never been found. The oil drum containing her body was dumped in the Atlantic.

His next murder was committed in the spring of 1992: Iris Sanchez, a twenty-five-year-old drug-addicted prostitute and mother of an eight-year-old daughter. Rifkin picked her up in Queens, strangled her to death during sex, then left her body under a mattress at a trashdump site near Kennedy airport. The urge to kill returned just a month later. He picked up Anna Lopez, a mother of three whose youngest child was born addicted to crack, had sex with her, strangled her, and drove upstate to Putnam County to dump the body in some woods.

His next victim was dumped a few miles away in Westchester County. Catherine Williams was dark-haired, pretty and vivacious. A talented dancer and athlete, she had made the cheerleading squad at her high school in Charlotte, North Carolina. She had been homecoming queen and married a town football star. After her marriage ended, she moved to New York to pursue a dream of becoming an actress. There her life fell apart. She could not find work acting and eventually settled for a job in an advertising agency, but she was living a double life. She experimented with drugs and soon found she was hooked. At night after work, when she couldn't afford to buy drugs on the street, she would go to bars in Greenwich Village or SoHo and find men who had drugs to share in exchange for sex. Friends who were doing the same would go out to the Hamptons with her on weekends to find parties where drugs were available. She didn't need a summer rental; she was pretty and always found men who gave her a place to stay in return for sex. Her drug use escalated, and she graduated to crack cocaine.

She turned to prostitution, first with an escort agency working New York City hotels and later, after drugs had taken a toll on her looks and the agency fired her, on the streets. On the night she climbed into Joel Rifkin's pickup truck on Houston Street in Lower Manhattan, she was living full-time in an East Village crack house.

By the time Rifkin had dumped the former cheerleader's naked body in Westchester, the bodies of his other victims were turning up. However, because they were in several jurisdictions and because there were few obvious links between them, police remained unaware they were the work of a single killer. Some had been discovered but not identified. Several victims had been assumed to be linked to hundreds of drug-related murders in the New York area every year. Only the discovery of the bodies in the steel drums attracted any attention and were obviously linked. Still, there were few clues to help lead investigators to the killer.

In November 1992, Joel Rifkin, now thirty-three, again drove his pickup truck to New York in search of a victim. Jenny Soto, twenty-three, an attractive, petite brunette, had been returning with her sister Jessie to their home in Park Slope, Brooklyn. They had been at Jenny Soto's boyfriend's apartment in Bushwick, but to get home they had to take the subway to Manhattan and change trains. Jenny Soto unexpectedly announced she was going to stay in Manhattan for a while and sent her sister back to Park Slope alone.

Like so many of his other victims, Jenny Soto had had drug problems, but she appeared to have put them behind her. She had worked as a prostitute and become involved with an addict who ended up in prison, but she had had a lucky break. She fell in love with a decent young man who still had dreams and ambitions, and he included Jenny in them. No one knows why, without warning, Jenny Soto decided to return to her life of drugs and prostitution, but just an hour or two after leaving her sister at the subway station, Jenny Soto climbed into Joel Rifkin's pickup to have sex with him.

When the end came for her, she fought harder than the others. Moments after having sex, Rifkin's hands tightened around her throat. She resisted with all her strength. She kicked and scratched. She drew blood. For a moment it seemed she might overcome her attacker. She broke his stranglehold, but Rifkin managed to grab her head and shoulders and jerk them from side to side. He broke her neck, and her body grew limp. Unnerved by the tremendous fight, he drove her north into the Bronx, stripped her body, and pushed her down a hill; she landed on the bank of the Harlem River.

Rifkin's reign was about to come to an end. Late in June 1993, Rifkin took his mother's car and drove into Manhattan. He began cruising his usual haunts in the East Village and Lower East Side. On Canal Street he pulled over and talked to a pretty twenty-two-year-old with dark red hair. She was a slightly built woman. After his life-and-death struggle with Jenny Soto he was taking no chances.

She told him her name was Tiffany. Tiffany Bresciani had come to New York from her home town of Metairie, Louisiana, full of romantic dreams of living a bohemian life and becoming a writer. She became an addict and, like so many of Rifkin's other victims, turned to prostitution from time to time to support her drug use.

Rifkin drove her to an empty lot near the Manhattan Bridge and had sex with her. When his hands tightened around her neck, she struggled to save herself, but she was no match for him. He drove the body back to Long Island and pulled over at a secluded spot near his home. He dragged her body out of the rear seat and placed it in the trunk of his mother's car, drove home, and parked in the garage of his mother's house. He lifted the body out of the trunk and left it in a wheelbarrow.

Several days later he got up while the rest of the household was asleep. He stripped Tiffany Bresciani's body, wrapped it in a tarpaulin, tied ropes around the middle and ends, and placed it in his pickup truck. At around three A.M., he set out to dispose of his latest victim. He had chosen a spot near Long Island's Republic Airport. It was only a hundred yards or so from a state police barracks, so Rifkin had decided that if he saw too many state troopers' vehicles about he would drive on to the Hamptons. He had been keeping track of news reports from Southampton following the discovery a few weeks before. Authorities appeared to have made little progress identifying her, and he felt it would be safe to place another body there. He had a spot picked out near Water Mill.

For once, it was Rifkin who was in the wrong place at the wrong time. As Rifkin sped down the Southern State Parkway, two troopers in a patrol car noticed that the pickup had no rear license plate. Deborah Spaargaren and Sean Ruane, eager young troopers in the middle of their overnight shift, decided to stop the driver. They positioned their patrol car close behind the pickup and flashed on their red-and-blue light bar. Rifkin picked up speed.

The two troopers tried again, this time with sirens. Rifkin drove on. Ruane lifted his loudspeaker mike and barked at Rifkin to pull over. Still, he drove on. The two troopers suspected that the driver of the pickup had more to be concerned about than a traffic violation. He did not appear to be driving drunk. They called for backup, and soon three more state police vehicles and patrol cars from the Nassau County police were also in pursuit.

Rifkin gunned the accelerator and turned off the Southern State Parkway, running a stop sign. For the next several miles he tried to lose his pursuers, making swift rights and sharp lefts in residential neighborhoods. He could not shake them. Finally, Rifkin took one turn too wide and skidded sideways into a light pole. He was unhurt, but the pursuit was over.

In moments he was surrounded. Ruane and Spaargaren shone flashlights into the cab. Rifkin seemed impassive, but the two troopers and the other officers at the scene could smell a familiar odor of decomposing flesh.

Rifkin was handcuffed, placed in the rear of the troopers' patrol car, and read his Miranda rights. Ruane, meanwhile, warily lifted a corner of the tarpaulin. The odor became stronger. He lifted more of the material and shone his flashlight inside. When he returned to the patrol car, he asked Rifkin: "Who is she?"

"She's a prostitute," Rifkin said. "I had sex with her. Then I killed her."

By the time Rifkin was taken to headquarters, one of Nassau County's top prosecutors, Fred Klein, had been alerted, and two detectives, Tom Capers and Steve Louder, were waiting. Rifkin matter-of-factly told them every detail of Tiffany Bresciani's murder from the meeting on Canal Street, to his abortive attempt to dispose of the body. Both detectives were amazed by his calm and indifference. He was not excited or disturbed either by his crime or by his arrest. They decided to press further.

"Is there anything more you want to tell us?" Capers asked.

There was a pause, and Rifkin said in a low voice: "Yes."

"Joel, were there others?"

"Yes," he said. "There were some others."

In the same straightforward tone, Rifkin poured out every detail he could remember of his career as a serial killer. The detectives could barely keep up with their notes.

He could remember some names and dates clearly. Others were

vague. Jenny Soto's violent struggles had stayed in his mind, but in some instances he could only remember physical features. He told the detectives about the steel drums and their grisly contents. He could not remember Leah Evens's name, but he recalled having sex with her, and how she died easily at his hands, and his long drive into the sunrise to the Hamptons to bury her.

Soon detectives were at Joel Rifkin's home combing through his belongings. They found what was virtually a museum of his crimes. He had kept many of the clothes and personal belongings of his victims—shoes, bras, pocketbooks, driver's licenses, and credit cards.

Eleven bodies had been found at the time of Rifkin's arrest. Five had been identified. Each investigation had reached a dead end. The discovery of Tiffany Bresciani made twelve. In addition, Rifkin told investigators of the body of Iris Sanchez, lying under a mattress at a dump near JFK Airport, and Lauren Marquez, still undiscovered in her shallow grave in the Hamptons. An NYPD helicopter flew low over the site and found the mattress exactly where Rifkin said it would be. Eerily, the downdraft from the chopper blades blew the mattress to one side, revealing the body beneath.

Rifkin couldn't remember Lauren Marquez's name but he remembered the clothes she wore and her final minutes. She was buried exactly where he said she would be found, and within days police had matched her remains with the dental records of the missing prostitute.

In all, Rifkin had left eighteen bodies in ten jurisdictions around New York. Although most of crimes were committed in New York City, prosecutors opted for separate trials in Brooklyn, Queens, Nassau, and Suffolk. Rifkin had been one of the bloodiest serial killers; more disturbingly, he had been the stealthiest. Had two state troopers not followed up on a minor traffic violation, his crimes could have continued for months—even years—unnoticed. The grieving relatives of the victims claimed that this was because his victims were prostitutes and drug addicts, whose murders the police did not take seriously. It is hard to argue with that complaint. But the authorities did take his prosecution seriously.

Partly because no district attorney wants to give up jurisdiction over a high-profile case and partly to avoid the chance of errors that could cause a retrial, prosecutors opted for a series of trials instead of one megatrial. Rifkin admitted his crimes as matter-of-factly as he had confessed to police the night he was captured with the body of Tiffany Bresciani. He gave various explanations for the murders—ranging from psychosis stemming from his adoption to his anger and shame that his mother was a prostitute (she was not) to his belief he had been given AIDS by a prostitute (he had not).

Attempts to create an insanity defense were unsuccessful and in a series of trials over two years he was given consecutive sentences of twenty-five years to life —ensuring that Joel Rifkin, thirty-six when he was sentenced for the final time, would spend the rest of his life behind bars.

CHAPTER 14

Bad Blood

IT HAD BEEN AN UNBEARABLY hot day and a sticky, muggy night, but now, at four A.M., the Hamptons air was cool at last, a welcome break from a scorching heat wave that had been oppressing New York City and the whole length of Long Island for what seemed like weeks. An attractive, twenty-year-old Southampton College student was driving home from the Beach Bar in Hampton Bays. In the mirror, as she cruised north on the William Floyd Parkway, she could see another car, a white two-door Pontiac Grand Am.

The car began flashing its headlights and passed her, then slowed, signaling her to stop. As the driver stepped from the car he pulled something from his pocket and held it up. It appeared to be a gold police badge. The man accused the young woman of driving drunk and told her to follow him. He was going to give her a Breathalyzer test. She followed slowly and a little nervously behind the Grand Am, making a mental note of the license plate. When they stopped, she asked to see that gold badge again.

This time, the man pulled from his pocket not a badge but a knife. He forced her into his car and ordered her to turn her head down and away from him. She complied, and he drove on to a wooded area. There the man made her strip, forced her down on all fours so she was looking away from him, then savagely raped her.

After the attack, he took a bottle of water and washed her body.

When she asked why, he told her he was washing away possible DNA evidence. When he finished his cleanup, he let her put on her denim vest. As she clasped the remainder of her clothes, he drove her to an exit on the Long Island Expressway and let her go.

A highly publicized and vicious rape at the height of the summer season by someone posing as a police officer was bound to get special attention from the authorities. Even so, no one connected with the case in the first crucial hours of the investigation could have guessed that this was to become one of the most notorious sex crimes in Hamptons history, not for the nature of the attack, although that was disturbing enough, but because of the identity of the attacker.

It quickly became clear that the rapist had been stalking possible victims. He had been well prepared: he had a badge and a weapon, a water bottle, and a well-conceived plan. He knew the area. He had chosen the place to stop his victim, the place to abduct her, the place to rape her, and the place to drop her again with some care. A young woman who had been in the same bar in Hampton Bays as the victim came forward to say that she had been followed home by a man in a small white car that same night. Police began to fear that a serial rapist might be at work.

They were not about to risk ruining the 1996 summer season by announcing their fears. There had been serial rapists in the East End before, and they had spread panic among the summer residents. Thousands of women spend Monday to Friday in the Hamptons with their children while their husbands are in New York at work; thousands of single women come out to the Hamptons every weekend. It is a potential hunting ground for a sexual predator.

In the early eighties, a man dubbed "the Hamptons Rapist" claimed several victims, stalking them for days, then breaking into their empty homes to wait for them to return. In each case, he apologized profusely to his distraught victims before leaving. In one case he terrorized two teenaged girls in their house for over four hours. The sale of shotguns and pistols rocketed as women in the Hamptons armed themselves. He was never caught.

Another serial rapist whose activities terrified women in the area was Scott Carroll, known as the South Shore Rapist. He attacked women in Nassau County, Suffolk County, and Staten Island, raping several of them in the course of burglaries. In each case, he wore rubber gloves, forced the victim to cover her head with a pillow case and assaulted her at knife point. The youngest victim was fourteen.

In 1986, Carroll broke into the home of *Godfather* author Mario Puzo at four A.M. As Puzo slept, his companion, Carol Gino, got out of bed to investigate a noise in an adjoining room. She looked into the study and saw a man wearing a ski mask, a brown sweater, and black shoes.

"My girlfriend was staying with me," Puzo recalled. "She was by the bathroom and she screamed. I jumped out of bed. She told me someone was in the study. I held the door shut and told her to go down to the kitchen and get a weapon. She came back with a knife."

They burst into the study but the intruder fled through sliding glass doors and jumped from a balcony. He took several items of Louis Vuitton luggage with him and six thousand dollars in cash. Later a police dog tracked the path the intruder had taken and found some of the luggage. Other matching items, which Scott Carroll had given to his girlfriend, were found at Carroll's home. When Carroll was placed in a lineup for the rape victims, they were not able to identify his face, but they were able to identify his voice.

Puzo's testimony and the voice identification helped get Carroll sentenced to several hundred years in prison on fifty-four counts of robbery, rape, burglary, and assault. Carroll's attorney, Eric Naiburg, who also represented the Long Island Lolita, Amy Fisher, had only one question for Puzo at the trial. Referring to the legendary scene in *The Godfather*, he asked Puzo if finding an intruder in his home late at night was as scary as finding a horse's head in your bed. Puzo didn't answer.

Detective Robert Titolo of the Suffolk County Fourth Squad, one of seventy-five detectives who worked on the rape of the Southampton College student, was hoping that if this was another serial rape case, she was the first victim. Only 20 percent of sex crimes are reported, so detectives were afraid she might have been only the first to come forward.

She had been able to give some highly detailed information. The knife he had used was a steak knife with a blue handle and a serrated edge. The water bottle had a red nozzle with grooves. The gold police badge had no eagle. But other information was only sketchy. She said the attacker had strawberry blond hair with a ponytail and was under thirty. By far the most important single piece of information was a description of the car and a partial license plate: G551.

Police began methodically checking license plates for the letters and digits the victim could recall, to see how many matched white Grand Ams. One was registered to Kelley Norman, a woman in Montauk who was living with a commercial fisherman whose name was well known to every Suffolk County detective and prosecutor: Kerry Kotler.

When Kotler's name surfaced in relation to the rape of the college student, a cheer went up in the offices of Suffolk County District Attorney James M. Catterson Jr. For Catterson and the other prosecutors, this was like Marcia Clark getting a second crack at O. J. Simpson. The reason: Kerry Kotler had already embarrassed and humiliated the district attorney and was involved in a multimillion-dollar civil suit against Suffolk County—one he seemed certain to win.

In 1981, Kerry Kotler was twenty-three years old and wild. His idea of a good time was to take a car or motorcycle for a joyride and outrun police cruisers. He wasn't always successful. He racked up hundreds of speeding tickets and other violations in a life of petty crime. He was also something of a Don Juan, cutting a sexual swathe through the neighborhood girls. One woman accused him of raping her after a date, but she withdrew the charges. The parents of a sixteen-year-old girlfriend had him prosecuted for statutory rape.

It was that conviction that put his mug shot in the files of sex criminals in Suffolk County. In 1981, when a young and traumatized Farmingdale housewife looked through those files for a clue to the identity of the man who had raped her a few hours earlier, she picked out Kerry Kotler's picture.

It had been a particularly nightmarish assault because it was the second time she had been raped, apparently by the same man. Three years earlier, in 1978, a man wearing a ski mask had forced himself into her house as she returned home from a store. The rapist was never caught, and his parting warning that he would be back for more still rang in her ears years later.

In 1981, a man, not wearing a ski mask this time, forced his way into her home and announced: "You remember me. I'm back for another visit. We're going to do it all over again." He proceeded to subject her to another savage assault. This time, the victim told police, while he was raping her she consciously memorized every line and crevice of his face, even the timbre of his voice. This time, she promised herself as he violated her, she would know him again; this time he would be caught.

Six days after the rape, Kerry Kotler was arrested. Police had a solid identification by the victim and what was in those days strong forensic evidence. Tissue-matching techniques were in their infancy, but a semen stain showed that Kotler's blood type matched that of the rapist. Kotler, who had run away from home at fifteen and was barely literate, permitted the police to search his home without a warrant and agreed to answer questions without a lawyer. He took a lie detector test. He was confident because he had what seemed to him to be an air-tight alibi.

Kotler had spent a lot of his time in traffic court, and on the day of the rape he was scheduled to appear again. He spent a good deal of the morning and early afternoon on the telephone to friends trying to raise twenty-five hundred dollars to pay outstanding fines and stay out of prison. Phone records showed that between 12:01 P.M. and 1:12 P.M. Kotler was almost constantly on the phone. He called his probation officer three times, his attorney twice, and two courts where he had pending cases. His probation officer and a court official called him back. There were several other calls to friends who also returned calls. At 2:34 P.M. he completed a transaction at a bank and at 2:55 P.M. he appeared in court.

The rape victim had originally told police the attack had taken place at 1 P.M., and the phone records showed he could not have carried out the rape if she was right about the time. After the phone records came to light, the time of the attack changed to about 1:30 P.M., when there was a narrow window during which Kotler could have committed the rape.

Other alibi witnesses, who were friends of Kotler's and therefore among the community's least upstanding citizens, say they were threatened and harassed. Another friend says he was actually pressured to give false evidence against Kotler: to say he had seen him with a ski mask, thereby implicating him in the first rape. One friend who did give evidence for Kotler was an admitted drug dealer and can hardly have made a good impression on the jurors.

In addition, important information was kept from the jury. Minutes after the rape, there had been a second assault a short distance away. That woman fought off the attack and gave a description similar to that given by the rape victim. Originally the two attacks were assumed to be perpetrated by the same man, and as there were only six sex attacks in the area that whole year, it does seem likely that two committed in such close proximity a few minutes apart would be connected.

However, if both attacks were committed by the same man, that man could not have been Kerry Kotler. By the time the second attack took place he was on the telephone with a court officer. The details of the second attack were deleted from police documents handed over to the defense.

The jury rejected Kotler's alibi and found him guilty of rape. He was sentenced to twenty-five years in prison. From behind bars, Kotler tried to find exculpatory evidence. Items stolen from the rape victim had never been found. He combed the Yellow Pages for the names of pawnshops and jewelry stores and sent them descriptions of the items, hoping that some would turn up and would lead to the real rapist. It was a futile effort.

More than three thousand miles and worlds away from the daily horrors of Kotler's life in prison, a brilliant young geneticist at Leicester University in England was working on a technique that would revolutionize the entire spectrum of scientific disciplines. In 1984, Alec Jeffreys and his team of researchers discovered a means of identifying and comparing the components of DNA, the chemical that carries the genetic code, harvested from samples of blood, semen, saliva, and hair.

Two years later the technique was used for the first time in a murder case in Britain. Two teenaged girls were killed, and a seventeen-year-old boy made a false confession. A comparison of his DNA with DNA taken from the scene of the crime cleared him. Later the same technique was used to catch the real killer.

DNA testing was soon being hailed as the most dramatic breakthrough in crime detection since the development of fingerprinting in 1901. Over the next several years, it came into widespread use in Britain, Canada, and the United States, primarily as a prosecution tool. DNA testing is immensely complex. For a layperson on a jury the science, with its unfamiliar terms and the evocation of a microscopic world beyond our imagination, is impenetrably dense. Prosecutors found that an advantage at first, because defense attorneys were ill equipped to challenge DNA results.

Two New York attorneys redressed the balance by learning the complexities of the science. Barry Scheck and Peter Neufeld became as knowledgeable about the subtleties of DNA-testing techniques as they are familiar with statute law. They began to revive cases and use DNA-testing techniques to vindicate convicted criminals. They discovered the weaknesses of DNA tests as they are sometimes used by prosecutors. They found out about the sensitivity of samples to corruption during the investigative process. They realized that some of the claims for DNA tests are false. For example, claims that the odds against an accidental match are hundreds of millions to one are based on ridiculously small statistical bases and are therefore scientifically worthless. They discovered that the complexity of genetic science leaves enormous room for human error. They were ultimately to gain national celebrity as the DNA specialists on the O. J. Simpson Dream Team.

Among the less well-known cases they took up was Kerry Kotler's.

A DNA test was performed on semen found on the rape victim's underwear. It was not Kerry Kotler's. Assuming the stain was left by the rapist, and prosecutors had made that assumption from the beginning, he could not have been Kotler.

If life were a movie, the narrative would cut here to the prison gates opening and the innocent prisoner's shadow shortening as he walks slowly through them to freedom. That's not what happened.

Kotler had been in prison for nearly nine years when a DNA test proved him to be innocent, and there had been many changes in Suffolk County since he had been convicted. The most important, from Kotler's point of view, was that the Suffolk County district attorney was now a brash, ambitious, controversial, and aggressive prosecutor named James Catterson.

In 1989, Catterson had run for district attorney on a Republican Party ticket pledging a no-holds-barred war on crime, particularly drug trafficking and public corruption. He made a pledge to transform the Suffolk County DA's office into a "lean, tight, and well-drilled" crime-fighting machine that punished criminals while showing care and concern for their victims. Once in office, he took personal charge of some high-profile cases and worked quickly to reduce the backlog of trials, increasing the conviction rate to 96 percent.

He also gained a reputation as a political bully boy. He banned his 142 prosecutors from plea bargaining in severe drunk-driving cases. He drove around in a luxury BMW his office had confiscated from a drug dealer. Political opponents claimed he threatened to open investigations on officials who did not do as he wished, charges he denies.

A prominent Texas prosecutor once remarked that any prosecutor can convict a guilty man, but it takes a great prosecutor to convict an innocent man. That kind of combative attitude is common among prosecutors. When Catterson reviewed the case against Kotler and the new evidence that pointed to his innocence, he did not seek his release.

Instead, he threw up every legal obstacle, argument, and counterattack that he could think of to keep Kotler behind bars. He argued that the semen stain tested against Kotler's DNA was not the rapist's, although it was presented as the rapist's at the trial and the blood-type analysis, which had helped convict Kotler, had come from the stain. He refused to have the victim's husband's DNA tested to see if the DNA was his, arguing that Kotler had no right to investigate the victim's prior sexual activity. He argued that the DNA testing methods used to clear Kotler were inherently unreliable, even though his own office was prosecuting accused criminals using exactly the same testing techniques. He argued that the lab that performed the test did sloppy work, although other Suffolk County officials had found its procedures professional. He did all this in the face of widespread criticism from other attorneys.

It was two more years before a judge finally freed Kotler, by which time he had served eleven years in prison and numerous apparent inconsistencies in the investigation and prosecution had come to light. Catterson had not been involved in the original prosecution, but the two-year-long losing battle to keep Kotler in prison was the worst defeat of his career as DA. Kotler's release triggered other cases in which prisoners convicted before the era of DNA testing insisted that their cases be reopened and Kotler himself filed a lawsuit for $15 million against New York State.

Hence the rejoicing among Suffolk County police and prosecutors when Kerry Kotler was implicated in the rape of the Southampton College student. It seemed that the department, the DA's office, and Catterson himself were about to be vindicated after all. Although the rapist had destroyed much of the DNA evidence with the water bottle, investigators had found a semen stain on the victim's skirt. DNA tests showed it was Kotler's. This time, instead of DNA evidence vindicating Kotler, Catterson announced, it would condemn him.

Still, it was eight months before police finally charged Kotler with the rape. During that period, Kotler claims, he was kept under surveillance by police helicopters, and investigators harassed him and his friends and neighbors in the Hamptons. Kotler was freed on twenty-five housand dollars bail—money put up by his girlfriend, Kelley Norman, who believed in his innocence. He returned to his work as a fisherman in the Hamptons and waited for his trials. Ironically, the trial of his civil suit against the state overlapped his trial for the rape of the student.

In July 1997, Judge Leonard Silverman of the Court of Claims awarded Kotler $1.5 million for his eleven years behind bars. The sum covered his loss of liberty, the less than optimal health care he had received, his physical mistreatment by other prisoners, and the daily indignities of prison life. The award was limited, however, by Kotler's own "successful transition from prison to freedom," suggesting that if he had committed another crime after his release he would have been awarded more money. The victory was of little comfort to him. The

Hamptons' new millionaire was by then sitting in a courtroom in Riverhead on trial for rape again.

Defense attorney Jack Litman argued that Kotler, found guilty once before of a crime he had not committed, had been the victim of a conspiracy to frame him. The rapist had flashed a gold badge to bring the victim's car to a halt, and that suggested the rapist was indeed a police officer. He claimed a condom recovered in a police search of Kotler's garbage had provided semen that was then used to plant a stain on a cotton swab and on the victim's clothing. In support of this argument, he offered the evidence of a forensic scientist who testified that the semen stain contained a large amount of bacteria, suggesting that it had been stored for some time, then placed on the skirt.

Detective Robert Titolo testified under cross-examination by Litman that he had seen no semen stain on the skirt when he collected the evidence. Litman also gingerly challenged the victim during the trial. In her grand jury testimony she had described riding back in the attacker's car after the rape with her clothes on her lap. In the trial, after the challenge to the semen stain on the skirt, she testified she had ridden back with the skirt clutched between her legs, thus explaining the presence of a stain. Although she had been able to give only a partial description of her attacker, she had described a much younger man than Kotler, and while her recollection was clear on many details, she had failed to mention his most obvious characteristic, a mustache.

The jury of six men and six women deliberated for only three days, but it was a tense and exhausting debate inside the jury room. After two days the jurors were split six to convict, five to acquit, and one undecided. They sent a note to Judge Morton Weissman indicating they were deadlocked. He ordered them to continue deliberations, and by the next afternoon they had decided on a verdict: guilty. When the verdict was read, Kotler shouted, "Not again! I can't believe they did it to me again."

Court officers handcuffed Kotler within moments of the reading of the verdict. He winked at his mother and girlfriend on the public benches and mouthed "It will be all right" as he was led away to prison. The victim, weeping after the verdict, said they were tears of joy. Is it possible that Kotler is as innocent of the rape of the college student as he is of the rape of the young mother seventeen years ago? For the evidence against him to have been planted, a carefully contrived conspiracy would have to have been mounted.

Perhaps even the crime itself would have to have been committed with the intention of framing Kotler. Such a scenario strains the imagination. But Kotler still insists, as he did once before, that he is an innocent man wrongly accused. A final irony in the case: the $1.5 million award given for Kotler's wrongful imprisonment after the first rape case may now be claimed in a civil suit by the victim in the second.

PART FIVE

Malibu East

Introduction

DAN RATTINER, the publisher of the Hamptons weekly *Dan's Papers,* summed up the changes in the Hamptons in the nineties. "Not long ago," he said, "there was only one place in the world where English-speaking people would go to see groups of celebrities at parties or eating in restaurants, and that was in Los Angeles. Now there are two. That phenomenon has come to the Hamptons."

The list of Hollywood stars, movie moguls, and directors who live in the Hamptons has been growing since the start of the decade. Most prominent among the movie colonists is Steven Spielberg, who has made his estate overlooking Georgica Pond his primary residence. Spielberg has been joined in the Hamptons by David Geffen and Jeffrey Katzenberg, his partners in the DreamWorks production venture.

Some movie stars have had homes in the Hamptons for many years—Chevy Chase, Alan Alda, and Roy Scheider, for example. But with this new influx, what had always been essentially a resort based on social standing, wealth, and power was transformed in just a few years into a resort in which the leading figures were from the entertainment industry.

Along with stars came studio executives and a host of professionals associated with movies, such as talent agents and entertainment lawyers. The stars brought with them, unwittingly but inevitably, bigger crowds and more media attention. They also drove up real estate prices. In 1997, a record summer for the Hamptons economy, more than one million people visited the area. The largest number of inquiries to the local Chambers of Commerce about real estate, tourist spots, hotels, and restaurants came not from New Yorkers but from Californians.

The Hamptons had represented a retreat from urban life but began to take on an urban bustle of its own. East Hampton village administrator Larry Cantwell says the very premise of the Hamptons has been changed. "In the past people who bought second homes here came to be anonymous and relax and enjoy East Hampton for its natural surroundings. That has now changed because more well-known people are here not for that but to continue to promote their own status. It is part of the Hamptons cachet."

This sea change in the Hamptons can be traced to one man, Steve Ross, the creator of the Time Warner media conglomerate.

CHAPTER 15

The Wives of Steve Ross

IT WAS A FUNERAL planned and executed with all the zeal, attention to detail, and complexity of a crowd scene in an epic movie. The location was East Hampton's Guild Hall. The plainly decorated auditorium, which would normally have been used for such an event, was judged to be too severe a place for what was planned to be a celebration of a flamboyant life, so one of the Guild Hall's acclaimed art galleries was chosen. In only forty-eight hours, contractors removed the paintings and sculptures, renovated and repainted the walls, relit the entire gallery, laid carpets, and built a stage. A single, vibrant, mural-sized painting by Willem de Kooning was hung on one wall.

It was a December morning, two days before Christmas 1992. There was a bone-chilling breeze off the ocean, which carried with it a sharp, freezing rain. Most Hamptons houses had been closed for months, and only the year-round residents were there. Seemingly from nowhere, the tiny driveway outside the Guild Hall and the streets beyond began to be clogged by limousines carrying Hollywood celebrities, New York City power brokers, superrich chief executives and entrepreneurs, bankers, and socialites. They had begun flying in the previous day, many of them in a fleet of private planes and helicopters in a military-style exercise in transportation logistics.

A throng gathered despite the cold to identify the mourners as they stepped from their limos and scurried the few feet to the Guild Hall.

231

Here were filmmaker Steven Spielberg and his wife, Kate Capshaw, Barbra Streisand, Paul Simon, Dustin Hoffman, Beverly Sills, Quincy Jones, Nastassja Kinski, Chevy Chase, Martin Scorsese. But most of those who ducked beneath umbrellas and out of sight were not instantaneously recognizable. They were the faceless names behind corporations who control the movie, the publishing, the communications, the recording, the television and cable, and sports industries—and especially one corporation with a stake in all of those industries and more: Time Warner.

The man to whom all these rich and powerful and famous people came to pay their final respects was Steve Ross, the larger-than-life man who created Time Warner, the global entertainment giant, by the force of his own will. The funeral had been organized by his widow, Courtney Sale Ross, a woman also possessed of an overpowering will. It was not the kind of funeral some other members of his family had wished for. It was not the funeral his two ex-wives, CBS chairman William Paley's stepdaughter, Amanda Burden, and Carol Maslow, would have staged.

Staged is the right word. Even the rabbi was not actually a rabbi. He was a Warner public relations executive who happened to be an observant Jew and "looked the part." Ross's son, Mark, was offended by elements of the spectacle, particularly the presence of a camera crew, as if it were a wedding or a bar mitzvah.

"But it's what Steve would have wanted!" Courtney Ross told him.

"Yes, but he's not going to be there!" he shot back.

Many of the mourners owed Steve Ross, some of them big time, and they showed it in a variety of ways. Barbra Streisand had not sung live in public for years and was in fact terrified of live performance—of singing off key and forgetting the words—yet she sang "Papa, Can You Hear Me" at the funeral. For years she had been the recipient of lavish gifts, lucrative contracts, and extravagant gestures from Ross, many of them buried in Warner's overhead. When she casually mentioned that she was worried about selling her home because it needed too much renovation, Ross intervened and bought it on the spot for four hundred thousand dollars. Paul Simon sang too—"Bridge Over Troubled Water," which is what, for many of Warner's creative people, Ross had genuinely been.

Spielberg was another friend who owed Ross. Among many other deals, Steve Ross had bought the rights to an *E.T.* video game from Spielberg for twenty-three million dollars in the face of opposition from his own executives, who warned him—correctly—it would be a disaster.

"Being in his life," Spielberg told the other mourners, "was being in a world that spins faster."

When Spielberg made *Schindler's List,* his Holocaust masterpiece, he had Liam Neeson base elements of his complex character, Oskar Schindler, on Steve Ross, himself a complex man who was at once charming and ruthless, generous and avaricious, tasteless and cultured, straight as a die and shady, all at the same time. In the screening room of his East Hampton home, Spielberg showed Neeson home movies of Ross, who had lived close by, and told him that was the man he was playing. Neeson's gestures and mannerisms in the movie are all Ross.

At the end of the funeral, every individual mourner was asked to come up to the graveside and drop a single long-stemmed rose on the casket. It was a long procession, and people from various and unconnected aspects of Steve Ross's life found themselves mingling with each other—from his earliest days when he was an undertaker; from the days when he ran parking garages; in-laws from his first marriage; and the superstars and the superrich who belonged to the final chapters of his life.

At one point Barbra Streisand poked a guest she didn't recognize in the back. "Who are you?" she asked.

"I'm Carol Maslow, Steve's first wife," the guest said.

"Yeah. I thought you looked kind of familiar," Streisand said, as if Maslow barely had the right to be there.

"Really," Maslow retorted. "I thought you looked kind of familiar too."

Ross changed most of the lives and industries he touched. And he changed the Hamptons. More than any other individual, he was responsible for bringing in the Hollywood superstars who have earned the Hamptons the title of "Malibu East."

Steve Ross was born Steven Rechnitz. His father acquired a new name when, having lost a fortune in the Depression, he thought it would be easier to find work if it were not so obvious that he was a German Jew. Ross married Carol Rosenthal, the daughter of the owner of a thriving family business of funeral parlors, including a famous Manhattan parlor, Riverside. He was brought into the business, learned it from the ground up, and was soon running it. The family also owned a small and not very profitable car rental company, which was about to be closed when, helped by Ross, they went into partnership with Kinney Systems, a parking lot business.

Kinney had reputed ties to racketeers, and those twin shadows, his past profession as an undertaker and connections to shady characters, never left Ross. The deal led to a Ross-inspired merger between the two very different businesses, with Ross and the Rosenthals dominating the board. Kinney became the platform from which Ross launched an extraordinary career, leading to his takeover of Warner–Seven Arts and culminating in what was to be the crowning achievement of his career, the merger of Warner and Time, Inc.

Ross and his first wife, Carol, though wealthy, had lived relatively simply compared to his later extravagance. In the late sixties, when Ross had acquired Warner, they lived in a magnificent apartment on Fifth Avenue, and while Ross could be personally extravagant, his wife was unimpressed by overt displays of wealth. She left him in 1974, by which time there was a broad gulf between them and Ross had had several long-term affairs. Soon after that, Ross, forty-seven, became involved with twenty-six-year-old Courtney Sale, a beautiful, striking blonde and the daughter of the owner of a Texas Coca-Cola bottling franchise. She had joined Warner and been given a job in marketing and promotion that involved her in two elements of the company that especially appealed to Ross: the New York Cosmos soccer team and a safari park, Jungle Habitat.

She began to date Ross, and if her ideas and suggestions at Jungle Habitat were rejected for some reason, she would call him to back her up, which antagonized almost everyone she worked with. It was not the last time that the label of "high-handed" would be laid on Courtney Sale.

Ross and Sale had been dating for a year when Ross was introduced to a dark, angular beauty, Amanda Burden, the ex-wife of Carter Burden and the stepdaughter of William Paley. To Ross, the graceful, educated, and cultured Burden, with impeccable taste and international social connections, was the ultimate sexual and social prize. A blind date led to a passionate, whirlwind romance.

Courtney Sale returned from a business trip to learn that Ross was now living with Amanda Burden and her two children. She was outraged and reportedly followed the lovers to Acapulco. Ross and Burden were staying at Villa Eden, Warner's magnificent vacation home, used to entertain executives and celebrities. She phoned from her hotel, but he refused to speak to her.

William Paley was about as pleased with his stepdaughter's match as Courtney Sale. He regarded Ross and the brash executives he surrounded himself with, some of whom were longtime business cronies, as beneath contempt. One, seeing an enormous and famous Picasso, *Boy Leading a Horse* on the wall of Paley's home in Southampton, made a joke about its being a cheap copy. Paley was not amused.

Mark Ross, the thirteen-year-old son of Steve Ross by his marriage to Carol Rosenthal, was most upset of all. On his first meeting with Burden, a dinner to introduce her and her children to the Ross children, he shoved dessert in her face.

Steve's affair with Amanda took on a fairy-tale character. She introduced him to her world, which included society functions in the Hamptons and gatherings with power brokers, diplomats, and politicians. At her urging he organized a fund-raiser for Jimmy Carter which got him on the A-list for White House functions. He introduced her to his world, which included Hollywood celebrities and recording stars.

Shopping trips required two limos—one for their purchases. Christmas with friends at Villa Eden included two private planes—one for the gifts. They rented a palatial home in East Hampton as a country retreat from their well-appointed Manhattan townhouse on Gracie Square. After living together for three years, Ross and Burden were married, but the bloom was already off the rose by their wedding day. As exciting as Ross was to be with, he had a narrow range of interests and was consumed with work. In February 1981, they moved into a palatial new Park Avenue apartment. Ross had built another floor on the roof to make it a triplex. A week later, Amanda Burden Ross moved out.

She had been gone only a few days when Ross had a friend call Courtney Sale and ask her out on his behalf. The first date of their second-time-around romance is said to have been a trip to Villa Eden. Sale had, in fact, never let go of her connection to Ross. She kept abreast of what was happening through his teenaged son, Mark. She had become close to Mark during her year of dating Ross, and she continued to see him throughout the affair and marriage with Burden.

A little under two years after he had recalled Courtney Sale to his life, Ross and Courtney were married in extravagant style at New York's Plaza Hotel. The Grand Ballroom had been decked with thousands of plants and small trees, turning it into an indoor garden. The Plaza's own brilliant chefs were pushed aside for the chef from the bride's favorite restaurant, La Côte Basque. Even the hotel's finest china was rejected in favor of several hundred place settings specially bought for the occasion.

Guests included the governor of New York. More stars crammed into the hotel for the event than anyone in the hotel could recall. It looked like the Oscars. Quincy Jones took charge of all the music, from the classical arrangements for a string quartet to the medleys of fifties pop and dance numbers for an all-female band.

Ross and Burden had lived some of the time in a beautifully located estate overlooking Georgica Pond in East Hampton, one of the pearls of the Hamptons. They had rented, but Courtney encouraged him to buy it, and she set about remodeling and redecorating. She also fought to have Ross abandon the triplex, which Burden also hated, and found a duplex, also on Park Avenue. Then she almost immediately formed plans to expand it.

They couldn't expand up, because the head of a global perfume empire was ensconced above them. They could not expand downward, because a Wall Street titan and his family lived below. When the writer William Goldman and his wife, who lived next door, separated, the Rosses bought their apartment.

Courtney Ross spent weeks traveling, mostly in Europe, some of the time with Elaine de Kooning, ex-wife of the artist Willem de Kooning. Guided by Elaine, she snapped up millions of dollars' worth of art, antiques, and architectural elements for the East Hampton house and their New York City home—from impressionist paintings to ancient Greek military hardware; from art deco furniture to Cretan sarcophagi. Courtney and Steve hired two full-time curators to take care of their expanding art collection.

If Ross had been avaricious where Burden was simply extravagant, Courtney Sale Ross took him to new heights of materialist splendor. They found a castle in Italy and bought it. It came with a surrounding peasant village and 240 open acres of land. Courtney Ross is reported to have commented that one of its attractions was its poverty. Later she said that she meant to say it was rustic.

When they traveled, they would take over entire floors of major hotels to accommodate their personal security details and vast amounts of luggage. Whole suites of the Paris Ritz were taken to be used as closets. When they chartered a yacht for a vacation cruise, they had it partially redecorated to their taste. Courtney Ross then alienated members of the crew with her manner and her insistence on being addressed only through a personal manservant.

When someone made the mistake of serving her Pepsi, she became enraged and ordered all supplies of the offending drink removed from the ship and replaced with Coke. Mom and Dad had been Coca-Cola bottlers. Yet she was equally capable of expansive gestures of generosity. She met a single mother whose daughter had been accepted at Skidmore College in Saratoga Springs—Courtney's alma mater—but could not afford the tuition. Courtney had all tuition bills sent to herself.

Courtney Ross gave birth to a daughter, Nicole, in 1983. Ross had been only intermittently available to his children from his first marriage, son Mark, and daughter Toni, and both had suffered from it, especially Mark. With Nicole he resolved to have a closer relationship.

Birthday parties for Nicole became legendary. One year thirty-four guest children and their families were flown to Disney World for a weekend of celebration. Another year, when the party had a nautical theme, tropical fish were flown in from all over the world to stock aquaria and ponds.

In the years following their marriage, Ross spent an increasing amount of his time in the Hamptons, flying into Southampton in a corporate jet from New York or Los Angeles. In doing so, he did more to change the Hamptons than anyone in recent years by encouraging some of Hollywood's biggest names to move there.

It began with Steven Spielberg. Spielberg and his then-wife Amy Irving were staying at the Ross estate on Georgica Pond when Ross announced he wanted Spielberg to buy a home nearby. They took a stroll through the neighborhood estates, an eclectic mix of New England–style mansions and avant-garde architecture, clustered around the pond. Even the handful of development plots sold for millions of dollars. Spielberg protested that his home was in Los Angeles and that in any case all the homes appeared occupied.

Ross and Spielberg knocked on the door of a home near the Ross estate. "This is Steven Spielberg," Ross told his astonished neighbor. "I just want you to know that if you are ever interested in selling your home, he is interested in buying." A few days later, the homeowner was negotiating a price with Ross, although it would be four years before Spielberg moved in. He tore down the original house and imported an enormous French barn to form the centerpiece of a new home. Later he bought another property across the pond, knocking down that house to preserve his view.

Ross encouraged other Hollywood figures, including Barbra Steisand, to make the Hamptons a base for at least some of the year. Although she has been looking for years, Streisand has never found a house in the Hamptons she wanted to buy, staying instead either at the

Ross estate or at the East Hampton house of designer Donna Karan. Tom Hanks, Martin Scorsese, Quincy Jones, and Dustin Hoffman bought houses. In Hollywood, star trends develop quickly, and soon dozens of other celebrities were calling brokers or tramping around homes. House prices, and especially seasonal rental prices, already booming in the mid-eighties, rocketed in the wake of each new marquee name.

Soon after he completed the deal that created Time Warner, Ross discovered he had prostate cancer and was dying. He spent more time in the Hamptons, often in the company of Steven Spielberg, staying out of the public eye in case any perceptible deterioration in his condition might adversely affect Time Warner stock. Immediately on learning he was seriously ill, rival executives at Time Warner began maneuvering to reduce his power and enhance theirs, positioning themselves for the day when a successor would be anointed. Ross, abetted by Courtney, did everything possible to maintain the fiction that he would recover and return to his desk, so as to limit the erosion of his position to his rivals.

Ross finally grasped at a last slim chance of survival after doctors in New York had told him that the cancer had spread and there was nothing more they could do. He went to Los Angeles for radical surgery, checking into the hospital under the name George Bailey, the principal character in his favorite movie, *It's a Wonderful Life*. The operation was declared a success, but Ross continued to weaken and died six weeks later.

Following his death, Courtney Ross inherited a vast fortune, estimated at between half a billion and a billion dollars. Ross's compensation from Warner, and later Time Warner, had been immense; it was reportedly never lower than twenty-two million and one year neared eighty million. Death benefits payable to the estate from Time Warner totaled three hundred million dollars. Courtney Ross hired Anne Radice, who had been head of the National Endowment of the Arts under George Bush, as her personal chief of staff, a job that comprised everything from organizing the Steve Ross estate to walking Courtney's King Charles spaniel, Sage.

The period of mourning was marked by the funeral and two memorial services, one in Carnegie Hall and the other at the Warner studios, plus a shareholder's meeting that became a third memorial service. Courtney then turned her full attention to life as a Hamptons chatelaine and to the development of what must rank as one of the most bizarre, most exclusive experiments in education: a school that was, to all intents and purposes, built around the needs of a single student, Nicole Ross.

The education of Nicole Ross was crucially important to her father, as it still is to her mother, in part because she will one day control a vast fortune. Part of Nicole's inheritance is a sizable chunk of Time Warner stock.

It began with a home tutor for Nicole when Courtney and Ross were spending most of their time in the Hamptons. So that Nicole wouldn't be lonely, it was arranged for the daughter of a friend, also named Nicole, to be taught with her. By the time Ross died, there were four other students, and the number gradually grew larger until there was a school—The Ross School—housed in buildings nestled among pine woods on Ross property. In 1997 it had forty-eight students, all girls, most of them the daughters of extremely wealthy year-round Hamptons residents, and there are ambitious plans to expand.

The Ross School stands out from even the most forward-thinking private schools because of its emphasis on travel and its almost unlimited resources. Students are taken on weeks-long class trips that have included India, Greece, Sardinia, Rome, Paris, Egypt, the Caribbean, and the Galápagos Islands. Each trip is meticulously recorded on video. Where most school classrooms might have pictures of Egyptian artifacts or Old Masters, Ross School classrooms have the real thing. Courtney Ross developed an advanced and global multicultural curriculum, heavily seasoned with Eastern philosophies.

"It works like this," said a former teacher. "They designed a spiral illustrating the history of civilization, like a three-dimensional timeline. Each twist of the spiral represents a new development or a new culture. Each year a class studies one turn of the spiral, and specialist subjects are linked to that core study. So let's say the class is studying ancient Greece: they'll look at geometry and ancient history and art and architecture and geography as an interrelated series of subjects rather than as unrelated subjects the way they would in a conventional school. And you bet they'll be in Greece for a few weeks."

It is an educational system based in part on Courtney Ross's own views and outlook but developed with the advice of some of the most acclaimed educational theorists. The board includes Courtney Ross, who has personally financed the school to the tune of ten million dollars, Steven Spielberg, Martin Scorsese, the distinguished Harvard academic Howard Gardner, whose projects at Harvard have been funded by Ross, George Biondo, a lawyer who served on the Montauk public school board, and a number of current and former Time Warner executives.

Students who attend the Ross School pay seventy-two hundred dollars a year in tuition but there is a sliding scale, and an attempt is made to recruit a cross-section of the Hamptons population. The students include Spielberg's children and those of Christie Brinkley and Billy Joel, but also the children of, for example, a Bridgehampton public school teacher. The pupils are said to be at least a grade and sometimes two ahead of their peers in other schools, not only in academic performance but in self-confidence and maturity.

The school is at once a towering achievement and a microcosm of its founder's fiery personality. Steve Ross had a management philosophy: hire the best and let them get on with it. That is not his widow's view. Her philosophy is "Work with like-minded people," a dictum she picked up from Dr. Jonas Salk, which can be twisted to mean "Brook no disagreement." She has a hands-on approach, firing those who do not make the grade, which can be the same as not bending to her will. "No one says no," says one former teacher.

When the school was expanding rapidly to accommodate grades five through seven, Courtney Ross hired a director, Harriet Fulbright, the widow of Senator William Fulbright, to take charge. Fulbright, who is a respected educator and who has spent most of her life in the profession, is an administrator of the Fulbright Scholarship program. She crossed swords with Courtney Ross before the school term had even begun, and although she had relocated to the Hamptons from Washington, Ross fired her—but paid her contract in full.

Teachers at the school are said to live in fear of the iron hand of Courtney Ross—especially as, like Harriet Fulbright, most have left other lives behind and moved to East Hampton. "This is a school where the students stay the course and the teachers get expelled," said one former faculty member, referring to several instances of teachers not being invited back for another term, victims of a grueling schedule and the exacting standards set by Courtney Ross. The staff puts in exhausting hours, arriving long before the pupils for compulsory yoga and sometimes attending lengthy meetings with their benefactor at night.

When Courtney Ross returned from one class trip to Rome she was in a towering rage because, in her view, the pupils were ill prepared. She reportedly reduced the teacher she held responsible to tears in front of the other members of the faculty. One teacher discovered she was fired only when she was not invited to the end-of-term staff meeting. Another was handed a note by Courtney Ross's chauffeur. She can be equally brusque with parents. Once she was faced with a revolt by parents over the schedule for class trips. She sent parents a letter saying that if they were dissatisfied their children might be happier at another school. The revolt was quelled.

At the same time, while a high proportion of teachers has not been invited back, Courtney Ross points out that every member of the staff given the chance to return takes the opportunity. One who didn't return was Iris Love. Love is an internationally respected archaeologist and one of the heirs to the Guggenheim fortune. She had been a friend of Steve Ross for years before his death and had joined the Ross family on their extensive travels. She was hired to give a series of lectures at the Ross School.

Despite the long friendship, Love and Courtney Ross clashed over Ross's treatment of the teachers. Love also developed a close friendship with Ann Radice, the Ross chief of staff. Love and Radice took the same vacation time, although they say they were not actually traveling together. When they returned, both were fired. Courtney Ross says, through her attorney, Bert Fields, that the dismissals were not triggered by Radice's friendship with Love.

Courtney Ross has an option to buy 130 acres near the estate to expand the school—enough land to found four or five good-sized colleges—and she will invest tens of millions of dollars more in what she says is her future life's work. She plans to increase the size of the student body dramatically. The school expanded from a middle school to include high school grades in September 1997 and became coeducational. In the future there will also be a "Wellness Center" combining Eastern and Western notions of emotional and physical health. There will be what Ross describes as an "Elders Center" on the school grounds where elders and children will learn from each other. Together the school and the two centers will form the Ross Institute. The school will become less exclusive, at least in some ways. A recent Rome trip was recorded on a Web site, "Forum Romanus," for other schools to access. There are plans to create a communications center and to go online, making the Ross Institute's philosophy and educational resources available to inner-city schools.

CHAPTER 16

The Hamptons World
of the Super-Rich

ON THE OUTSIDE, it is just an enormous white tent the size of a circus big top, which has been erected over the tennis courts, pool, and tennis house of a sprawling Hamptons estate. On the inside, it is a bizarre and ostentatious diorama, a Disney imagineer's conception of a monument to late-twentieth-century excess. It is the mother of all parties, marking the fiftieth birthday of one of Wall Street's most powerful financiers at his estate in Quogue.

But it is more than that. At a moment of gloom and fear on Wall Street, this is a billionaire's personal display of confidence, exuberance, and bravado. Vast Oriental carpets have been thrown over the grass courts. The tables are draped with heavy gold-fringed brocade cloths you only see in seventeenth-century oil paintings, still lifes where the artist is trying to show his patron how clever he is at painting folds and creases.

The centerpieces of these tables are open treasure caskets, like the chests pirates bury in children's stories. Each of these little treasure caskets overflows with strings of pearls. In the swimming pool two identical twins of startling voluptuousness and heartbreaking beauty, their legs and lower abdomens encased in fish costumes, pose as mermaids. Exotic birds call from huge antique cages, and flower arrangements six feet tall, the kind you only see being delivered in Fred Astaire movies, are scattered strategically between the tables.

All the senses are assaulted. The air is heavily scented with five hundred burning citronella candles and torches in terra cotta pots. Air-conditioning pumps this scent out of the tent so that the citronella hangs over the estate like an aromatic beacon. The ears are pounding from the live music of a talented show band that has the tuxedoed and décolletaged guests gyrating enthusiastically. The sense of taste is overwhelmed by kilos of beluga caviar and gallons of Louis Roederer Cristal being consumed at every table.

But the greatest assault is on the eyes. A vast structure designed to mimic the interior of a Flemish palace, with beamed ceilings and stuccoed walls, burning sconces, and ornate burnished chandeliers has been erected within the tent. There are professional dancers in seventeenth-century costumes. There are tableaux vivants—an entertainment and an affectation that virtually disappeared from parties in the Gilded Age—in which live actors form living, breathing pictures. In this case they are re-creating no less than ten larger-than-life Dutch Masters.

The most eye-catching is a naked woman who is re-creating Rembrandt's *Danaë*. According to gossip columnist James Revson, as the evening wears on several guests, aroused by the splendor and decadence of the occasion, will leap over the velvet ropes separating the tableaux vivants from the bon vivants to paw Danaë.

The guest of honor strides through the party, his face a portrait of joy and satisfaction that it would take a Rembrandt to capture. He is financier Saul Steinberg, the helmsman of a ten-billion-dollar insurance and real estate empire and a man whose friends and business associates are not easily impressed, least of all by money. They almost all are wealthy. But tonight, and Steinberg can see it in their child-bright faces and hear it in the oohs and aaahs that have punctuated the proceedings throughout the humid August evening, they are impressed to the core. Those guests are a cross-section of the eighties power elite, a hit list of the decade's movers and shakers and makers and, in one or two cases, eventual losers.

Commerce Secretary Robert Mosbacher and his then-wife Georgette, the social cyclone, in one of her legendary low-cut dresses; literary agent Mort Janklow; American Express chief James Robinson and his wife Linda; *New Yorker* editor Tina Brown—then editor of *Vanity Fair*—and her husband Harold Evans, at the time the editor of the *London*

Sunday Times; Time Warner czar Steve Ross and his wife Courtney; Liz Smith, the legendary syndicated gossip columnist; Richard Snyder, the then-president of Simon & Schuster; the emperor of leveraged buyout, Henry Kravis, and his then-wife Carolyn Roehm; Texas Air chairman Frank Lorenzo and his wife Sharon; ABC's Barbara Walters; the designer Arnold Scaasi; Katherine Graham's daughter, the writer Lally Weymouth; Vartan Gregorian, then president of Brown University; Abe Rosenthal, the former *New York Times* executive editor, and *Vogue* beauty editor Shirley Lord; U.S. Senator Al D'Amato, Blaine Trump, Donald and Ivana Trump; Revlon's Ron Perelman and his then-second-wife Claudia Cohen; Ellin Saltzman, fashion director of Saks Fifth Avenue; and a whole tribe of Tisches—Larry, Billie, Bob, Joan, and Jonathan—to whom the Steinbergs have forged a spectacular marital alliance...and some 250 others.

An enormous, five-tiered cake finely decorated with gold and silver leaves is rolled out on a platform. It is flanked by two children dressed as cherubs from a Renaissance frieze.

Gayfryd Steinberg, Saul's wife and the woman who has conceived and created, planned and organized and directed this spectacle over eight months, and, it is said, paid for it from her own accounts, makes the toast. "My mother always says, don't tell people you love them—show them! This is my way of saying I love you!"

Saul, holding the attention of three hundred of America's richest and most powerful men and women, announces: "Recession? Anybody who is talking about a recession, forget about it!" and there are cheers. "The party? Awesome—but now that I think about it, it's appropriate. Maybe a little understated." There is laughter. Turning to Gayfryd, Saul Steinberg ponders for the right words, then says: "Honey—if this moment were a stock, I'd short it!" More laughter.

The party was Gayfryd Steinberg's brief shining moment at the summit of nouvelle society, the end of her climb and also the beginning of her fall. The absence of restraint, the byzantine extravagance, of Saul Steinberg's fiftieth birthday party on August 5, 1989, made more than just the gossip pages.

Almost before the clean-up had ended, before the smell of citronella had dissipated and the Hamptons air was still again, the Steinbergs had become virtual pariahs. Newspapers and news magazines excoriated them for spending what was widely estimated to be at least one million dollars and possibly two and a half million on a single party—ten thousand dollars a head. At a time when the most lavish party givers at least had the good sense to mask their extravagance by turning their affairs into benefits, truly private parties were unusual.

"Wouldn't it have been better," one of the guests was reported to have remarked during the festivities, "to just give us each a hot dog—and ten thousand dollars?"

The *Washington Post* devoted two features to the party's excesses and the era of eighties decadence it allegedly symbolized. The *New York Times* editorialized on its moments of risible bad taste. Liz Smith defended it. She and others pointed out, with justification, that money spent on the infamous birthday party was but a fraction of the Steinbergs' largesse in other, more sober areas; the Steinbergs give many more millions to a variety of worthy charities than even Gayfryd could possibly spend on a party.

Gayfryd, the daughter of a Canadian telephone company clerk, dropped out of college at age twenty to marry a metallurgist. The marriage lasted just six years. One month after their divorce, Gayfryd, then living in New Orleans, married an oil tycoon, Norman Johnson. She was still married to Johnson when she first met Steinberg at a party given by an art dealer, Richard Feigen. By the time they met again, this time at a party at Steinberg's house in the Hamptons, things had changed a little in Gayfryd's life. Her husband had pleaded guilty to evading seven million dollars in taxes and was serving fourteen months in prison.

Gayfryd, described in *People* magazine as "never one to spend her nights playing solitaire," had already asked Norman Johnson for a divorce. She and Steinberg were married in 1983. Her social climb was marked by extravagant and creative generosity. She became an organizer and fund-raiser for PEN, the writers' organization. She joined the board of New York University's Institute of Fine Arts and sponsored classes for underprivileged students in Harlem. *Vanity Fair,* not noted for its generosity of spirit, remarked that Gayfryd was "the most likely to succeed" of all the eighties new-money socialites. *U.S. News & World Report* dubbed her "the Queen of Nouvelle Society."

But that single Hamptons party for Saul was to turn her image from that of Mother Teresa to that of Marie Antoinette. An extravagant wedding she organized for her stepdaughter, Laura, and billionaire Jonathan Tisch at New York's Metropolitan Museum a year earlier, in which the flowers alone were said to have cost a million dollars, did not help. So stung were the Steinbergs by the press criticism of that party, Gayfryd considered letting Saul's birthday pass without the million-dollar bash. "But," she confided to friends, "I thought, why should Saul be penalized? So I went ahead." They were unprepared for the tidal wave of venom that followed. Columnists compared Steinberg unfavorably with the most vulgar Gilded Age robber barons, pointing out that the robber barons created, invested, built, founded, while financiers like Steinberg were little more than corporate predators.

The criticisms of the Steinbergs blew like a chill winter wind through the Hamptons. Realizing that their presence at the party could be taken as an endorsement of the vulgar display, some guests began to distance themselves, several even denying they were ever there—in the face of clear evidence to the contrary. Some began to bad-mouth Gayfryd in private while defending her in public. Others, like Carolyn Roehm, wife of billionaire Henry Kravis, defended her in public with words that appeared to some to be double-edged. Yes, she said, it was okay for Gayfryd to throw such an extravagant party. No, she wouldn't dream of doing so herself.

Within a few months, Gayfryd's fellow Hamptonite Ken Auletta, a writer close to the opposite end of the philosophical and economic scale, had exacted some kind of vengeance. He attacked the Steinbergs' work with PEN as a search for legitimacy on the backs of writers (actually it was more like a search for funds by an impoverished and disorganized writers' group), and the Steinbergs resigned in a huff.

Some Hamptons socialites were suddenly afraid to invite the Steinbergs to functions in case their very presence gave a flavor of extravagance and excess to the event. They never gave a similar party again, but they did not live down the reputation they won for themselves with the Hamptons' million-dollar party. Even when they threw a bat mitzvah in 1997 for their daughter—a modest affair by their standards—gossip columnists raised the old specters.

Extravagance in the Hamptons comes in many forms and need not express itself so promiscuously as it did at the Steinbergs' party. For example, consider the success of two small businesses in the Hamptons, Dial-a-Dinner and A La Car. Both bring takeout food to Hamptons residents—not from Chinese restaurants and pizzerias, but from five-star restaurants. Dial-a-Dinner was founded by David Blum when he was a seventeen-year-old pizza delivery boy, and specializes in delivering meals to the Hamptons from Manhattan. The deliveries are usually by car, but sometimes customers will have their meals flown in. George Hamilton had a meal from his favorite New York restaurant, Arcadia, flown to the East Hampton airport and put in a waiting limo to be taken to his Hamptons retreat.

Imelda Marcos, wife of the late Filipino president Ferdinand Marcos, who stayed in the Hamptons for a brief time in the mid-eighties, had caviar from the famed Manhattan restaurant Petrossian flown out to her in Southampton at a cost of thirty-five hundred dollars. Billy Joel, Alec Baldwin, Ron Perelman, and Calvin Klein are reportedly regular customers. But most clients are, in the words of the owner, "regular folks" who wouldn't dream of letting their weekend go by without steaks from the Palm or poached salmon from Le Cirque.

The rival service, A La Car, does not deliver from Manhattan but does deal with the top Hamptons restaurants, bringing seafood stew from Sapore di Mare or delicacies from the wood-burning oven at Nick and Toni's. Many clients call from the traffic jams on the Long Island Expressway so that dinner is waiting for them when they reach their destination.

Another form of extravagance focuses on the garden. Lavish gardens have become de rigueur in the Hamptons, with landscapers working virtually around the clock in the weeks prior to the start of the summer season to get newly planted trees looking as if they have been there since the first settlers. Crimson king maples and golden honey locusts, which cost tens of thousands of dollars apiece, have become status symbols. It's not even enough just to have the trees growing in your instant Eden. You have to become a "tree collector." For the Hamptons money elite of the nineties, a fine collection of rare trees has become the equivalent of what having a younger and more beautiful second wife was in the eighties: another part of having it all.

Martha Stewart says she has seen rich men swoon at the sight of a healthy specimen. "It's pretty funny hearing so many wealthy guys bragging about the size of their weeping copper beeches and yews," says Stewart. "I've noticed that when they glimpse a rare tree and a pretty girl at the same time, they often look a lot more excited about the tree."

Youth in trees, unlike in ideal trophy wives, is not highly prized. Size, rarity, and the difficulty of transplantation add to the social cachet of some trees, but in the end it comes down to expense. Some trees now gracing Hamptons estates have been driven from the Pacific Northwest in refrigerated tractor-trailers, and some have been planted with the aid of military size Sikorsky helicopters to obviate the necessity of rutting the lawns with wheel tracks. Some trees even come with a provenance, proof of their lineage. One Hamptons nursery sold purple beeches that had been installed at the 1968 World's Fair in Chicago. Louis Meisel, a SoHo art dealer, boasts three of the first Purple Fountain weeping copper beeches introduced into America on his estate in Sagaponac.

"Everybody has copper beeches," Meisel says. "But they don't weep. Mine weep." He and his wife Susan have a collection of two hundred rare or exotic trees on the estate. Warner Le Roy, owner of the Tavern on the Green and the Russian Tea Room, has six hundred rare trees on sixty-four acres in Amagansett.

"They don't just buy from nurseries and dealers," says a Connecticut nursery owner with numerous clients in the Hamptons. "Some of these guys will be on a business trip or vacation or they'll be driving back to New York and see a tree they like, pull over, and try to make a deal. They don't want to wait for trees to grow. They don't have the time. They close on a house in March and they need a two-hundred-year-old English country garden by the end of April. And if you can't do it for them, they'll find someone who can."

The almost desperate effort to establish an instant Eden is one of the main sources of conflict in the Hamptons—the others being divorce and, of course, marriage. The bloodiest conflicts are not among spouses, however, but between neighbors and usually center on territorial disputes. Take, for example, the long-running feud between Martha Stewart and New York developer Harry Macklowe.

Stewart first emerged in East Hampton in 1988 in the midst of a bitter divorce from her publisher husband Andy, a partner in the publishing company Stewart, Tabori & Chang. The Stewarts' daughter, Alexis, who was then at Barnard, had spent numerous weekends in the Hamptons and suggested her mother move out there. Stewart is a decisive woman. She set up appointments to see ten houses in one day and hated the first nine. The tenth was a Victorian pile built in 1878— one of the first summer homes on exclusive Lily Pond Lane in East Hampton. She paid $1.6 million for it and immediately sank another million into the house for renovations.

Just owning the house raised Martha Stewart's social and public profile several notches. Her new neighbors included *New York Daily News* publisher Mort Zuckerman and heiress Frances Anne Dougherty. Soon she was the owner of a second Hamptons house, this one a Star Trek contemporary on Georgica Pond, in an enclave that includes Steven Spielberg, Calvin Klein, and Ron Perelman.

Martha was quickly embroiled in a series of feuds and legal actions with zoning officials and at least one of her neighbors. Most were typical of the kind of disputes that make headlines in the Hamptons purely because of the celebrities involved.

In one, Martha Stewart asked permission to build a swimming pool eight feet from a neighbor's home on Lily Pond Lane instead of the regulation twenty-five feet. Denied. When she built her pool elsewhere on her property, she sheltered it behind a nine-foot fence, three feet higher than she was entitled to build without permission. The board called it a fence. Martha called it a trellis. Case dismissed.

Martha's dispute with Harry Macklowe, a neighbor on Georgica Close Road, was different and ultimately involved the district attorney. It began simply enough: Martha cleared some trees and undergrowth on what she believed was her property, some wetlands adjoining Macklowe's estate. Macklowe, notorious for having torn down a New York City building without a permit in the dead of night, claimed the land was his and installed plantings, lights, and a fence. Stewart, still claiming the land was hers, sued to have Macklowe forced to remove his installations. The dispute was little more than an occasional footnote in the New York gossip columns for months, although both sides fought the issue as if it were a challenge to the Constitution.

In May 1997, the dispute suddenly escalated. Martha Stewart had been having dinner at the Palm restaurant with several friends, including a British designer, John Ward Pawson, and his assistant, Enzo Manola, whom Martha had picked up from the Hampton Jitney from New York earlier that evening. After dinner, which cost eight hundred dollars, Martha Stewart, Pawson, and Manola drove to the Georgica Pond house, as Pawson later told police, "to observe the beautiful moonlight."

"Martha drove us in her car, a large dark-colored truck," Pawson said. "When we arrived at the house the three of us walked down to the water. When we got there Martha observed that a fence had been erected by her neighbor, Harry Macklowe. Martha became upset and seemed depressed. We heard people working on the other side of the fence. We walked back to the road and Enzo and I walked over to Mr. Macklowe's driveway, stopping before the gate."

Martha Stewart got into her vehicle, drove into her neighbor's driveway, and confronted the workers, all but one of whom ignored her. The one who didn't was Matthew Munnich, a twenty-three-year-old trainee foreman with an Amagansett landscaping company. Pawson says that there was a short exchange between Stewart and Munnich during which he heard Munnich say, "Are you calling me a liar?" Pawson and

Manola got into Stewart's vehicle. They reversed out of the driveway and drove on to Lily Pond Lane and Stewart's other house.

Stewart has a notoriously volatile temperament and is said to have torn some of her own hair out during an argument with her husband. Munnich told police that as she drove out of the driveway, Stewart pinned him against an electronic security box. "I was trapped against the box, the side view mirror on the driver's side, and the driver's door," he said. "I started to yell, 'You're fucking crushing me! Stop the car!' She looked right at me and kept backing up." He was not seriously injured but claimed to be badly bruised.

Munnich filed an assault complaint, and it was investigated by the village police. Police Chief Glen Stonemetz believed it was an open-and-shut case and drew up charges of reckless endangerment and attempted assault against Martha Stewart.

It is usual procedure for the village police to pass the file up to the Suffolk County district attorney's office for review. According to Stonemetz, what happened next was anything but usual. Instead of being reviewed by one of scores of prosecutors, it found its way to the desk of the district attorney, James Catterson, with one of his senior investigators assigned to the case. It took more than two months for Catterson to conclude there was no case for Martha Stewart to answer.

Catterson said, "Justice and common sense dictate that the confrontation between Ms. Stewart and Munnich, as objectionable as it may appear, does not warrant arrest and criminal prosecution. Not every event that adversely affects a person's life deserves to be litigated in criminal court. Celebrity status cannot be considered a relevant factor in deciding whether or not to prosecute in a particular case."

Stonemetz was outraged by the decision. The police chief insisted that the incident merited no more than a misdemeanor charge, but certainly no less. And there was a widespread belief that Catterson and not Stonemetz had considered Stewart's status as a celebrity in deciding the issue. The *East Hampton Star* backed Stonemetz in an editorial, saying: "An incident such as this never would have reached the district attorney's desk if it weren't for the fact that Ms. Stewart is a celebrity."

Disputes like the one between Macklowe and Stewart rarely escalate beyond preliminary litigation, as both sides are usually too busy making money elsewhere to concentrate the time and effort that such feuding demands. However, the dispute between developer Barry Trupin and his Southampton neighbors in the early eighties became an epic struggle and left the Hamptons with a structure that was, for a time, one of its most recognizable landmarks.

Barry Trupin and his wife Rene bought a sprawling beachfront mansion called Dragon's Head with the aspiration of creating one of the most spectacular, extravagant, and, in the eyes of his neighbors, tasteless homes in America. Trupin, who describes himself as a poor boy from Brooklyn, made three hundred million dollars by arranging tax shelters and buying and selling real estate. Among his corporations was one he called Rothschild Reserve International, although he had absolutely nothing to do with the famous Rothschild family.

In 1979, Barry and Rene Trupin drove out to the Hamptons from Manhattan in their 1932 Rolls-Royce with their hearts set on a beachfront estate. In those days it was still possible—just possible—to pick one up for under a million. They found the biggest house in Southampton's neighborhood of big houses, a decaying Georgian-style home called Dragon's Head that Henry Francis du Pont had built in 1923.

At first the Trupins did little but make the house livable. Then, in 1981, Trupin embarked on an ambitious project to create something between a Gothic fantasy and a French château by building wings, towers, and turrets on top of the original house. In order to have somewhere to live during the building work, they bought another mansion, Roy Radin's notorious Ocean Castle, a short distance away along the beach.

Trupin hired John Olsen, a contractor experienced in the rapid construction of hotels, and several local subcontractors to do the work. Among them was Roy Wines, who, as well as being a contractor, was also the mayor of Southampton. Trupin neglected, however, to apply for any of the usual permits. The first time anyone other than the workmen knew anything was afoot at Dragon's Head was when the steel framework of Château Trupin began to rise above the eyeline, including the framework for two six-story castle turrets.

The Trupins set off on a buying spree in Europe, picking up, among many other antiques, a pair of neoclassical marble mantelpieces that had graced the Rothschilds' townhouse in London's Piccadilly for $1.5 million, a suit of armor made for Henry II for $3.2 million, a Victorian piano for $1 million, and tons of Carrara marble. They bought glass mermaids and antique stuffed Kodiak and polar bears, a jade fireplace from a Scottish castle, and dozens of griffins, gargoyles, and old beams.

It was all stored in the du Pont mansion's football-field-size living room, so that it resembled the final scene of *Citizen Kane*.

The plans for Dragon's Head began to leak out. Social Southampton discovered that Trupin wanted a three-story waterfall, as well as an indoor saltwater pond designed to look like part of Australia's Great Barrier Reef and stocked with exotic fish—live sharks, according to legend. The Trupins had in fact inquired about stocking it with dolphins but found that doing so was illegal and that they would have to make do with angelfish, parrot fish, and groupers. There were also plans for a complete English public house to be transported and rebuilt inside the mansion, and there was to be something called "Muhammed's Alley," an Arabian fantasy room where guests would recline on Turkish pillows.

Socialites in Southampton were aghast at Trupin's plans. To them Barry Trupin, with his gold chains and crisp new banknotes, and Rene, in her leather mini-skirts, ankle boots, and too-blond hair, represented everything they despised, "the trickle-down set"—the newly rich who were flaunting their wealth by buying property in the Hamptons. It was the Trupins and others like them, Old Guard Southampton believed, who were responsible for the frivolous new boutiques that had sprung up on Jobs Lane and the new condos and other developments that were ruining the East End.

"To these Old Guard people," said one local who developed a grudging admiration for Barry and Rene, "the Trupins were too loud and too rich, and they used the new-money tag to hang them. But you know, old money here is what somebody's grandfather made in a pig-packing plant in 1938. That was new money once too."

A neighbor, Charlotte Harris, a former girlfriend of John F. Kennedy, began a campaign to have the work on Trupin's mansion halted because the height limit for buildings was being exceeded and because Trupin had failed to apply for the required permits. The village zoning board, headed by a local physician, Dr. E. Korman, entered the fray. Dr. Korman was nicknamed "Dr. No" for her summary refusals of plans for tennis courts and other improvements to people's homes. *New York Magazine, W, Newsday,* and the *Washington Post* all appeared to side with Harris, agreeing that the forty-four-thousand-square-foot Trupin mansion was, in *Newsday's* words, "the Height of Hideosity."

Trupin complained that opposition to his beachfront Shangri-La was based as much on anti-Semitism as on environmental and zoning concerns. Determined to keep the turret that now rose above the beach like Cinderella's Castle at Disney World, Trupin built up the height of the surrounding land, burying part of the mansion, and—technically, anyway—lowering the relative height of the turrets. Even after that project was completed, the zoning board found forty places where the height of the mansion exceeded regulations.

Trupin had his supporters, especially among the contractors and tradesmen who were profiting from the millions of dollars in work that Trupin and other arrivistes were bringing to the Hamptons. But after a legal battle that lasted four years, and threatened at one point to bankrupt Southampton, Trupin abandoned the building he had once hoped would be his château. For years it remained a monument to eighties excess and a Southampton landmark—or eyesore.

Dragon's Head was taken over by raccoons and squirrels and looked like a derelict Transylvanian palace until it was bought for $2.3 million, nine million less than the asking price, by silver-haired developer Francesco Galesi. Galesi also had problems with the zoning board, and in 1995 the house—and with it the offending turret—was badly damaged by fire. By then, Trupin had much more serious problems to think about. Early in 1997, with much of his fortune gone, he was indicted for tax evasion.

Not all new money gets the *Not Welcome* sign. Ron Perelman has become the Hamptons' First Citizen on his estate on Georgica Pond, and he has held on to his social status and his wealth through three marriages and divorces. Perelman is the grandson of a Lithuanian immigrant, Morris Perelman, who built a successful paper products company in Philadelphia. Ron Perelman served an apprenticeship in business and finance under his father, Ray, who built the paper products company into a conglomerate, Belmont Industries, in the fifties.

Ron would sit in on board meetings at age eleven and discuss the pros and cons of this or that acquisition with his father. In 1965, when he was twenty-two-years old, Ron married wife number one, eighteen-year-old Faith Golding, whom he had met on a vacation cruise. She was one of America's richest heiresses, certainly the nation's richest teenager, whose family owned the Sterling National Bank and large tracts of property in Manhattan and the Bronx. For the next twelve years, Ron Perelman continued to work for his father, building an empire in which he had no financial interest, other than the prospect of a substantial inheritance. Perelman was eager to control his own destiny, and in 1978, when his father refused even to contemplate retirement, Perelman struck out on his own in New York. He bought an unprofitable chain of jewelry stores and sold off its assets at a fifteen-million-dollar profit. He went on to make a series of spectacular acquisitions, some financed by junk bonds, including the Hollywood film processing company Technicolor and the cosmetics giant Revlon. Perelman was different from the deal-hungry corporate raiders of the eighties who were devouring companies and using their assets to pay off debt run up in the takeover. Perelman stayed with his acquisitions and specialized in turning around companies that had lost their way.

He was less successful at steering his marriage out of trouble, however. His divorce from Faith became complex because she claimed he had financed his key purchase of a licorice extract company, MacAndrews & Forbes, which became his primary holding company, with her money. Perelman was represented by Roy Cohn, the celebrated deal maker and attorney, but even he had trouble with the complexities of the financial arrangements between the spouses. After a protracted dispute, which got so petty at one point that they argued over a fraction of a percentage point on the interest on money Perelman owed her, Faith settled for eight million dollars, which was both a fraction of the money she brought into the marriage—a hundred million by one estimate— and a pittance compared to what his subsequent wives would get.

Perelman met wife number two in January 1984 in Le Cirque, the legendary Manhattan power restaurant, where Perelman routinely has lunch. He was at his favorite table sucking on a foot-long cigar, his rear end parked on a cushion to increase his apparent height (he is only five-foot-six).

His eye caught that of brash financier Dennis Stein, who was then engaged to Elizabeth Taylor. Stein was having lunch with a prominent gossip columnist, Claudia Cohen, and introduced her to Perelman. It's disputed whether Claudia Cohen asked for the introduction or Perelman. Either way, they were instantaneously attracted to each other.

"Claudia had an air of glamour and a sense of fun that Ron's life lacked," says a business associate of Perelman's. "She knew everyone and she was an entree to elements of New York life that even Ron's money couldn't purchase. And while he's no Richard Gere, his five billion dollars has to have made it workable."

Cohen and Perelman were married in 1985 and staged a reception for four hundred at the Palladium, at the time New York's chicest disco, at which the Pointer Sisters performed for ten minutes for eighty-thousand dollars. The Perelmans became the most prominent power couple in New York and the Hamptons, but the idyll did not last long. After two years, they separated amicably, a parting made all the more friendly by an eighty-million-dollar settlement.

After his split with Cohen, Perelman began looking for a Hamptons estate to match his social and financial status. His personal fortune was estimated at the end of the eighties at between four and six billion dollars. In 1993, Perelman stunned the Hamptons social set just as the summer season was about to begin. The Creeks, the vast bohemian playground on Georgica Pond owned by art dealer and artist Alfonso Ossorio, had been for sale since his death in 1990. Barbra Streisand was among those who had looked at the mansion but she had balked at the asking price: twenty-five million.

As the house sat unsold, developers had eyed the sixty-acre property, which, under the zoning regulations, had room for twelve homes. Perelman saw the house on a Sunday and on Monday there were already thirty contractors on site, replacing bathroom fittings and light fixtures. He had closed the deal for a reported twelve million dollars. The house is a bizarre, black stucco mansion with some remarkable features, including a terrace designed to be in the shade at precisely four P.M. throughout the summer—just in time for afternoon tea. It has two master bedroom suites, each with three large rooms, and a theater that seats four hundred.

The grounds are dotted with Ossorio's sculptures and millions of dollars' worth of rare trees, some imported from Japan at enormous expense. Ossorio, who bought the estate in 1952 for thirty-five thousand, had the house stuccoed in black so that the sculptures and the trees would stand out against it, like diamonds on black velvet.

During the next two months, over a hundred workmen replaced doors, floors, walls, and wiring, completing work that by one estimate would normally have taken close to two years. All the house lacked was a mistress, and Perelman soon discovered her in the shape of wife number three, Patricia Duff, a stunning forty-year-old blond fund-raiser for the Democratic Party. Duff was prominent in gathering donations to Gary Hart's ill-fated 1988 campaign.

She was one of the key political links between the Washington and the Hollywood establishments and had been married to the head of TriStar, Mike Medavoy. She was introduced to Perelman by Melanie Griffith and Don Johnson, and the two hit it off. The Creeks became the location for some lavish fund-raising. Duff and Perelman were married on December 12, 1994 after a volatile on-again, off-again affair.

Duff presented Perelman with a daughter, Caleigh, the following day. As a powerful, beautiful, and very rich woman, she was the subject of a good deal of nasty gossip. Hollywood wives pointed to the coincidence of the breakup of her marriage to Medavoy and the decline of his career, claiming that Duff had abandoned ship, or rather, in the cynical parlance of Bel-Air beauties, "traded up." A profile of Duff in Esquire magazine suggested that she was close to President Bill Clinton and that Hillary Clinton "went on point" whenever Duff was in the room. Perelman was offended by *Esquire's* description of Duff and immediately pulled all of Revlon's advertising. Gossip columnists received mysterious faxes, said to be from a highly placed politician who is obsessed with her, outlining her romantic curriculum vitae.

The marriage between Patricia Duff and Ron Perelman lasted until the Democratic convention in Chicago in August 1996. For reasons that remain unexplained but have had gossips' imaginations running wild, Perelman had insisted that Duff stay away from a specific Convention gathering at the restaurant owned by basketball star Michael Jordan. When he arrived in Chicago and discovered his wife had in fact been to the party, he immediately flew back to New York in his private jet, leaving Duff and Caleigh to return on a commercial flight. At a meeting at the Creeks some time later to discuss a divorce settlement, Perelman is reported to have frisked his wife and discovered that she was wearing a wire. Protracted divorce proceedings were begun at the end of 1996, and Duff was expected to emerge from the marriage fifty million dollars richer.

Duff and Perelman never became the Hamptons power couple that Calvin and Kelly Klein, Perelman's neighbors on Georgica Pond, did. Calvin Klein became part of the Hamptons' landed gentry primarily at the urging of his beautiful young wife Kelly, one of his former design assistants.

They were married in September 1986, when Kelly was twenty-nine and Klein forty-three, in a civil ceremony in Rome. They kept separate New York apartments, and this fueled much ill-directed speculation about the true nature of their relationship.

Klein had many gay friends and, according to his biography *Obsession,* by Steven Gaines and Sharon Churcher, had had a number of homosexual affairs. He had country homes in Key West, Florida, and on Fire Island, resorts that attracted rich gay men. Kelly Klein set about changing the direction of Klein's social life. She urged him to sell his Fire Island and Key West homes and started looking for an estate for them in the Hamptons. Kelly Klein is a dedicated horsewoman and had ridden in numerous equestrian events in the Hamptons for years, including the world-famous Hamptons Classic.

The Kleins wanted a showplace, and there were none suitable among the few beachfront homes available, so they rented for several summers, commuting to the East Hampton airport in Klein's private Gulfstream jet, fitted out in walnut and with deep leather armchairs to look like a study in an English country home.

Because they were Calvin and Kelly Klein, they found rents doubled at their approach. They ultimately bought the former home of Pan Am pioneer Juan Trippe and turned it into the showcase they desired at a cost of ten million dollars. Trippe, who lived on a forty-acre parcel that includes part of a narrow spit of land between Georgica Pond and the Atlantic Ocean, is said to have buried cars on his beach to resist erosion. Every now and then, the fender of a rusting Cadillac will appear out of the sand.

The remodeling of the house, which caused violent disagreements with their architect, Thierry Despont, was completed in time for the home's hundredth anniversary, in 1991. It had been a long and tortuous project, with Klein insisting that everything be rendered in a three-dimensional architect's model. W magazine reported that the Kleins and Despont were "ready to strangle each other" by the time it was completed.

The redesigned house included a vast living room; Kelly Klein insisted it was too large in proportion to the rest of the house, but Calvin Klein and Despont insisted it was not. A year into the project, a neighbor had asked if the structure was going to be a swimming pool or a discotheque. Calvin Klein then agreed with his wife that the living room was disproportionately large and had it torn out in a day.

When Klein wanted floors made of planks of just the right age and patina, he had New England scoured for three-hundred-year-old wood. A farmhouse in Vermont was located, purchased, and torn down. The planks were numbered and photographed, then individually refinished, and Calvin Klein personally supervised the installation of each one.

Other than the dark wood floors and the toilet seats that have been dyed to match them, the entire house is decorated in white. The master bedroom is seven rooms converted into one enormous suite dominated by a huge four-poster that Klein bought from Andy Warhol.

When the house was finished, the Kleins threw a house-warming-party attended by Christie Brinkley, who was then still with Billy Joel, publisher Jann Wenner, who was then still with his wife Jane, Ron Perelman, Diana Ross, and Barry Diller.

The marriage was often seen as a happy compromise between Kelly's world and Calvin's, but at other times it seemed an uneasy truce. Friends have described a Thanksgiving Day dinner Kelly Klein made at which all the guests were rich gay friends of Calvin's and Kelly Klein felt like the hired help. Certainly, the marriage resurrected his image and made him part of the social gentry, but it was not an *amour blanc* as some have charged.

Indeed, Calvin Klein made numerous extravagant and romantic gestures to Kelly. He bought her jewelry that had once belonged to the duchess of Windsor, and he located an aged horse that Kelly had once been forced to sell as a child and bought him back for her.

In August 1996, however, the Kleins threw a party at the East Hampton estate for an old friend, Ed Klein, to launch his book, an account of the love story of Jack and Jackie Kennedy. The following day, to everyone's surprise, they announced that their own love story and marriage were over. An announcement said that they were still best friends and would work out the details of a settlement. They remained separated but not divorced in the fall of 1997.

The divorce is said to have been one of the most amicable in Hamptons history, second only to that of Christie Brinkley and her second husband Billy Joel, which was so friendly that people said they should get married. Billy Joel was even an honored guest at Christie Brinkley's fourth wedding to Hamptons architect Peter Cook.

Calvin Klein's second marriage breakup was in sharp contrast to his first divorce. In 1964, Klein had married his childhood sweetheart, Jayne Centre, from his old neighborhood in the Bronx. They had a daughter, Marci, together, but the marriage became unstable as Klein became more successful and fell in with a predominantly gay circle of friends. She felt abandoned and unable to keep up.

In 1973, Calvin and Jayne Klein rented a cottage near the beach in Amagansett. Klein would stay in New York to work for most of the week, leaving Jayne Klein in the Hamptons. According to Klein's biographers, Jayne Klein had a summer affair with a virile local fireman and celebrated their romance by taking a photograph of his startlingly impressive genitalia in full manly bloom, a souvenir of stolen hours of love she understandably kept hidden. She confided details of the affair to her sister-in-law, Sherry Klein, the wife of Calvin's older brother, Barry. Sherry in turn told her husband, and Barry Klein, who had been jealous of his younger brother's success and was finally one up on him, told Calvin. Calvin Klein confronted Jayne, but she denied the affair.

Later that same summer, he arrived in Amagansett unexpectedly late at night and discovered Jayne on the beach with her lover. The dramatic breakup became a very acrimonious divorce, with one peace summit, in a New York restaurant, ending in a screaming spectacle. The divorce papers, sealed to protect their daughter, who was then a minor, contain lurid accusations from both sides.

The acceptance of prenuptial agreements has reduced the intensity of postmarital battles over money, but one prenuptial agreement made by a Hamptons power couple actually served to complicate matters. When Charles Lazarus, the creator of the immense toy chain Toys R Us, married Helen Singer Kaplan, a prominent sex therapist specializing in treating premature ejaculation, there was an agreement that a divorce would trigger a payment of twenty million dollars, a bargain given Lazarus's likely net worth of several hundred million.

Kaplan and Lazarus lived happily enough in a Victorian mansion on a sprawling estate in Quogue, one of three lavish homes. The others were a winter retreat on Lyford Key in the Bahamas and a cavernous apartment on Fifth Avenue. Avid art collectors, they filled all three homes with Rembrandts, Picassos, and Toulouse-Lautrecs. Kaplan had seen many marriages break up and knew that the children of first marriages are often neglected—or worse, swindled—by surviving second spouses.

Helen Singer Kaplan apparently did not trust Lazarus to look out for the welfare of her three adult children, Philip, Peter, and Jennifer. Or she may simply have believed that the three million dollars they stood to inherit from her estate was simply not enough to keep them in the manner to which she had become accustomed. Suffering the final stages of breast cancer in 1995, aged sixty-six, she wrote Lazarus a note from her deathbed, saying she wanted a divorce and asking for the twenty-million-dollar settlement provided for in the prenuptial.

"Dear Charles," the note began, "I exercised the agreement— Nothing personal. I do not intend for you to leave the premises. It was only for the money for the kids (and the art). Love always—Helen." She died the next day.

The move backfired. Lazarus, seventy-two, was infuriated by the request and stung by the suggestion that he would have neglected her children. He refused to pay up, claiming that the tone of Kaplan's note betrayed the fact that she had no real intention of divorcing him and that, whatever her intentions, they were rendered void by her death. His stepchildren sued and accused him of mistreating their mother, claiming he had pushed her down the stairs of their Hamptons home and injured her. The children turned down an offer of fourteen million dollars in 1997.

The issues had still not been settled years later, and according to legal experts, the questions raised by the case are so complex they may keep posses of lawyers engaged for years to come. Ironically, while Helen Singer Kaplan clearly intended her children to be financially secure after her death, her actions have achieved precisely the opposite. The costs of continuing to fight with their stepfather are steadily draining her estate.

"I knew Helen," says Steven Cody, a Hamptons neighbor. "She just was paranoid about her children being left with next to nothing. The problem is that next to nothing to her was a fortune to almost anyone else. That may be part of the distortion of living among all these super-rich people out here. There's wealth and there's beauty here, and for all her artistic tastes, like a lot of the others here, sometimes all Helen could see was the wealth."

EPILOGUE

Quo Vadis Hamptonites?

JUST AS IT has become glamorous to summer in the Hamptons, it has become fashionable to lament their popularity. The Hamptons doom merchants complain that the summer crowds have become too big, too boisterous, and too shallow; that it's now almost impossible to travel by car, let alone to park; that the rentals are too high and the beaches either too crowded or too exclusive; that the trendy bars are too loud, the locals' bars too unwelcoming; that the restaurants want a week's notice for a reservation, if they'll take a reservation; that East Hampton's Main Street is like Madison Avenue with a pond at one end and a windmill at the other. Each year, somewhere around Labor Day, someone predicts that the love affair between the Hamptons and the rich and famous is over and that some new destination is becoming more fashionable.

But Hamptons continues to enjoy an unprecedented boom. At the end of the 1997 summer season, a twelve-acre property on Further Lane in East Hampton, with two relatively modest beach cottages with admittedly vast decks, fetched fourteen million dollars, a Hamptons record. Anastassious Fondaras sold the properties to a Wall Street banker, Chris Browne, a partner in the investment firm of Tweedy, Browne.

The sale had all the large Hamptons property owners running for their calculators to see how much that made their own property worth. "If the Fondaras place is worth fourteen million, the really magnificent homes on Georgica Pond have to be up to five times that," said one

261

realtor. "It is becoming ridiculous. There just aren't enough people with that kind of money." Soon afterward, however, Larry Gagosian, the art dealer, was offered twelve million for his East Hampton spread.

"It's a boom on top of a boom on top of a boom," says a Wall Street banker who owns two Hamptons homes, one to use and one to rent out each summer. "Wall Street goes up and down. But this is like a market that just goes up—and up." It's not just real estate. The money from a development boom trickles down fast. "Nobody buys a million-plus home and then starts getting tight with a dollar," says Steve McKee, a Hamptons realtor. "Local merchants of all kinds, from carpenters to caterers, benefit every time someone with real money moves in." There is a price to pay, however. Each year the crowds get heavier.

The people paying the highest price—literally and figuratively—and at the same time reaping enormous windfalls are native Hamptonites whose families have lived there for generations. Not only have they seen the area change beyond recognition in their lifetimes, they are being forced by circumstances to quit land their forbears held, in some cases, from as long ago as the seventeenth century. Once the Hamptons were vast tracts of farmland punctuated by summer homes. Now it seems the ratios have been reversed. Only a handful of working farms still remain in the heart of the Hamptons between the villages of Water Mill and East Hampton.

The most successful, owned by the Halsey family, is a hundred-acre spread that has been farmed by members of the Halsey clan since 1640. The Halseys' farm is between the Montauk Highway and the ocean and might be worth fifteen million dollars or more to a developer. But the Halseys, unlike many of their former neighbors, have so far resisted the temptation to break the twelve-generations-old chain of agricultural tradition. Instead, they sell vegetables from a roadside stand. They specialize in gourmet produce like Romanian wax peppers, haricots verts, and Osaka purple mustard, which their forebears, who grew almost exclusively potatoes, never heard of, let alone ate.

Their roadside vegetable stand was given cachet in the Hamptons by the effusive recommendations of gourmand Craig Claiborne. As a result, celebrities like Peter Jennings, John Travolta, Laurence Fishburne and Sarah Jessica Parker, as well as thousands of well-to-do weekenders, flock to the stand on Montauk Highway throughout the spring and summer.

As real estate prices continue to rise, however, more locals are selling whatever land they might have and heading not for greener but perhaps for sunnier pastures. Florida is the favored destination for natives who have sold the family plot to developers. Bill Banks, sixty-two, whose family once farmed sixty-five acres near East Hampton, sold his holdings in small lots in the mid-eighties at the height of a building boom. He retained his house and a few acres for himself, paid back taxes, and still walked away with more than four million dollars. The deal not only made Banks rich, it also turned him into a summer resident in an area where his family had lived since the Revolutionary War.

The Banks family now winters in Florida and summers in the Hamptons. The irony isn't lost on him or his Hamptons neighbors. "For years the summer people irritated me. Now I am one," he says. "The difference is that when I come here I am coming home. I really didn't have a choice. Eventually I would have lost the farm, and for all I knew I wouldn't have gotten as good a price in the future. In fact, it turned out I would have done better to wait a few more years."

It is not just greed but survival that is behind many of the sellouts. When farmers die and their children inherit their farm, the land is assessed for taxes at its highest potential value, not its value at its current use. As a result, land that may have been potato fields for generations is assessed as if bulldozers and construction crews are about to move in. Often land has to be sold to pay crippling inheritance taxes. This has accelerated the already headlong dash to develop Hamptons land to meet the exploding demand for homes.

There is, however, a growing land preservation movement. One of its heroines is Julie Zaykowski. Julie Zaykowski's family has owned seventy-seven acres of the Hamptons since 1951. In 1992, her land was reassessed by the Town of Southampton, and her tax bill rose by 1,300 percent, leaving her with a six-figure bill. Most people would have been tempted to sell at least a large portion of their property to developers. Instead, she struck a deal under which sixty of the seventy-seven acres are permanently preserved as undeveloped land, saving her ninety thousand dollars in taxes.

Despite the dire predictions, it seems unlikely that the Hamptons will become overdeveloped or fall out of favor with a moneyed class that already has so much invested in its future. Jerry Della Femina, the advertising guru and Hamptons restaurateur, doubts that anywhere else will eventually rival the Hamptons.

"In other, less well known resorts, there aren't enough places for the Beautiful People to be seen," he says. "Only the most self-confident of the Beautiful People, therefore, can be seen there. The Hamptons are for the Beautiful People who need to be seen by other Beautiful People for the reassurance that they really are...Beautiful people."

Sources

PROLOGUE

Information for the prologue comes from *Newsday, New York Daily News, New York Post, New York Times, New York Magazine, Time Out, Cosmopolitan, Washington Post, East Hampton Star, Long Island People and Places* by Bernie Bookbinder, *History of the Town of Southhampton* by James T. Adams, *History of Two Great Counties* by Paul Bailey, *East Hampton, A History and Guide* by Jason Epstein and Elizabeth Barlow, *Chronicles of the Town of East Hampton* by David Gardiner, *The Hamptons Book* by Suzi Forbes Chase, *The Hamptons Survival Guide* by Philip A. Keith, as well as the personal observations of the author and numerous interviews with Hamptons weekenders.

CHAPTER ONE

No one writing about Jackson Pollock can avoid a debt to Steven Naifeh and Gregory White-Smith, whose *Jackson Pollock, An American Saga* is a brilliantly researched and monumental biography. The author has also consulted *Jackson Pollock* by B. H. Friedman, *Out of This Century* by Peggy Guggenheim, *To A Violent Grave* by Jeffrey Potter, and the *East Hampton Star, New York Times, Time, Life,* East Hampton police files relating to Pollock's death, and interviews with former associates in Springs and East Hampton.

CHAPTER TWO

Material for Monroe and Miller's sojourn in the Hamptons was drawn from *Goddess,* by Anthony Summers, *Marilyn Monroe, A Biography* by Donald Spoto, *Marilyn Monroe Her Own Story* by George C. Carpozi Jr., *Marilyn, The Ultimate Look at the Legend* by James Haspiel, *Legend: The Life and Death of Marilyn Monroe* by Fred Lawrence Guiles, *Marilyn An Untold Story* by Norman Rosten,

265

Timebends by Arthur Miller, *The Story of the Misfits* by James Goode, *Movie Stars, Real People and Me* by Joshua Logan, and personal interviews with Michael Byrne in 1986 and 1989.

CHAPTER THREE

The True Adventures of John Steinbeck by Jackson J. Benson, an invaluable guide to every aspect of Steinbeck's life, *Newsday, New York Times, Los Angeles Times, East Hampton Star,* an unpublished memoir of Steinbeck by Shirley Fisher, interviews with several former neighbors and associates in Sag Harbor.

CHAPTER FOUR

Truman Capote by Gerald Clarke, *Conversations with Capote* by Lawrence Grobel, *Vanity Fair, Esquire, New York Daily News, New York Post, Architectural Digest, Answered Prayers* by Truman Capote, my own interviews with friends and associates conducted at the time of his death in 1984.

CHAPTER FIVE

I covered the Andrew Crispo saga for the *New York Post* and interviewed people in Crispo's circle. Much of the material for this chapter was gathered then. I have also consulted *Bag of Toys* by David France, *Murder Along the Way* by Ken Gribetz, *New York Times, New York Daily News, Newsday, New York Magazine, The Guardian, and Architectural Digest.*

CHAPTER SIX

A Woman Named Jackie by C. David Heymann, *Jacqueline Bouvier An Intimate Portrait, Dynasty and Disaster, The Bouviers from Waterloo to the Kennedys and Beyond,* all by John H. Davis. *To Jack With Love—Black Jack Bouvier, A Remembrance* by Kathleen Bouvier, *The Kennedy Women* by Laurence Leamer, *Jackie Oh!* by Kitty Kelley, *The Hidden Side of Jackie Kennedy* by George C. Carpozi Jr., and articles in *New York Times, Washington Post, Newsday, East Hampton Star, London Daily Mail,* and the now defunct *New York Daily Mirror* and *Journal American* newspapers, as well as court documents relating to the Bouviers' divorce.

CHAPTER SEVEN

In Her Sister's Shadow by Diana Dubois is a rich, well researched and fascinating account of Lee Radziwill's life. In addition to that and some of the sources for Chapter Six cited above, I made use of information from *Holy Terror* by Bob Colacello, *The Warhol Diaries, King Edward VIII* by Philip Ziegler, *Laughter From A Cloud* by Laura Marlborough, *Capote* by Gerald Clarke, *Decorating for Celebrities* ed. by Paige Rense, and articles in the *New York Times, New York Daily News, New York Post, Washington Post, London Daily Mail, Ladies Home Journal,* and *McCall's,* as well as several interviews with friends and associates of Lee Radziwill.

CHAPTER EIGHT

Bad Company by Steve Wick, articles in *New York Times, Newsday, Los Angeles Times, Esquire, Hollywood Reporter,* court documents relating to the trial of Laney Greenberger et al., and my own reporting for the *New York Post* on the Melonie Haller affair and murder of Roy Radin, including interviews with some of Radin's business associates and Suffolk County Police investigators.

CHAPTER NINE

Seven Days, Cosmopolitan, New York Daily News, Associated Press, United Press International, interviews with police officers in Eugene, Oregon and Suffolk County, and interviews with members of Dr. Wood's family.

CHAPTER TEN

This chapter is based in large part on documents released under the Freedom of Information Act relating to the investigation, trial, and execution of those involved. *Hitler's U-Boat War* by Clay Blair was also consulted, along with articles in *Newsday.*

CHAPTER ELEVEN

Blood Legacy by Judith Reitman is a complete account of this fascinating and disturbing case. In addition to that source, the *New York Times, Newsday, Daily News, Chattanooga Times,* court records relating to the prosecution of Arlene Caris, and her own account of the killing given in a petition to the Governor of New York were consulted. A number of interviews with Suffolk County Police investigators were conducted.

CHAPTER TWELVE

The Pikul case has been covered in depth in *Marrying The Hangman* by Sheila Weller and *Deadly Masquerade* by Richard Pienciak. In addition to those sources, interviews were conducted with the Pikul's friends, neighbors and associates and articles in *New York, Newsday, New York Daily News,* and *New York Post* were consulted, as well as court documents relating to the prosecution of Joe Pikul and the custody case.

CHAPTER THIRTEEN

Garden of Graves by Maria Eftimiades gives a detailed account of the murders committed by Joel Rifkin. *New York Daily News, New York Post, Newsday, and New York Times* covered the case in some detail. Investigators from Suffolk County and members of some of his victims' families were among those interviewed.

CHAPTER FOURTEEN

The Kotler case was covered extensively in *Newsday* and *East Hampton Star.* This chapter is based on reporting in those newspapers and court documents relating to Kotler's trials.

CHAPTER FIFTEEN

Master of the Game by Connie Bruck is the definitive biography of Steve Ross and it was an invaluable resource. I have also used information from *Steven Spielberg* by Joseph McBride, and from articles in *East Hampton Star, Vanity Fair, Wall Street Journal, New York Times, Business Week, Forbes, American Lawyer, Hollywood Reporter, Variety,* and *New York Magazine.*

CHAPTER SIXTEEN

Obsession by Steven Gaines and Sharon Churcher, *Steven Spielberg* by Joseph McBride, *Just Desserts* by Jerry Oppenheimer, *Who's Here* by Dan Rattray, and articles in *Newsday, New York Daily News, New York Times, Washington Post, Wall Street Journal, New York Magazine, The Guardian, The Independent, East Hampton Star,* and personal interviews with numerous residents.

Index